KAREN BROWN'S

Swiss

Country Inns & Itineraries

KAREN BROWN TITLES

California Country Inns & Itineraries

English Country Bed & Breakfasts

English, Welsh & Scottish Country Hotels & Itineraries

French Country Bed & Breakfasts

French Country Inns & Itineraries

German Country Inns & Itineraries

Irish Country Inns & Itineraries

Italian Country Bed & Breakfasts

Italian Country Inns & Itineraries

Spanish Country Inns & Itineraries

Swiss Country Inns & Itineraries

KAREN BROWN'S

Swiss
Country Inns & Itineraries

Written by

CLARE BROWN and KAREN BROWN

Sketches by Barbara Tapp

Cover Painting by Jann Pollard

Travel Press

Karen Brown's Country Inn Series

Travel Press editors: Iris Sandilands, Karen Brown, Clare Brown, Susanne Lau Alloway
Technical support: William H. Brown III; Aide-de-camp: William H. Brown
Illustrations: Barbara Tapp; Cover painting: Jann Pollard
Maps: Susanne Lau Alloway—Greenleaf Design & Graphics

Distributed USA & Canada: The Globe Pequot Press, tel: (203)395-0440, fax: (203) 395-0312
Box 833, Old Saybrook, CT 06475

Distributed Europe: Springfield Books Ltd., tel: (01484) 864 955, fax: (01484) 865 443
Norman Road., Denby Dale, Huddersfield HD8 8TH, W. Yorkshire, England,
A catalog record for this book is available from the British Library

Distributed Australia: Little Hills Press Pty. Ltd., tel: (02) 437-6995, fax: (02) 438-5762
1st Floor, Regent House, 37-43 Alexander St, Crows Nest NSW 2065, Australia

Distributed New Zealand: Tandem Press Ltd., tel: (0064) 9 480-1452, fax: (0064) 9 480 1455
P.O. Box 34-272, Birkenhead, Auckland 10, New Zealand

Library of Congress Cataloging-in-Publication Data

Brown, Clare.
    Karen Brown's Swiss country inns & itineraries / written by Clare
Brown & Karen Brown ; sketches by Barbara Tapp ; cover painting by Jann Pollard
             p. cm. -- (Karen Brown's country inn series)
  Includes index.
  ISBN 0-930328-27-2 : $16.95
  1. Hotels--Switzerland--Guidebooks. 2. Switzerland--Guidebooks.
I. Brown, Karen. II. Title. III. Title: Swiss country inns &
itineraries. IV. Series.
TX907.5.S9B76 1994
647.9449401--dc20
                                        94-16476
                                          CIP

In memory of

Michael

You will always be in our hearts

Contents

Introduction

Switzerland is a country of incredible beauty: rugged mountain peaks enhanced by delicate wispy clouds, velvety green meadows tucked high on mountain ledges, dramatic rivers rushing through narrow gorges, tiny blue lakes sparkling like jewels in their mountain pockets, postcard-worthy villages made up of toy-like chalets. The country is almost too perfect to be real. For centuries Switzerland has inspired poets and artists who have advertised her glories on paper and canvas. Her reputation has attracted visitors from all over the world. The tremendous growth in the popularity as a tourist destination stems from the 19th Century when the ever-hearty British, challenged by tales of unconquerable mountain peaks, found their way to alpine villages in search of adventure. These sportsmen returned to England, spreading the word of the glories of Switzerland. One of these was Edward Whymper, a young English gentleman, who on July 14, 1865, at the young age of 20, came to Zermatt and conquered the summit of the Matterhorn. Whymper's enthusiasm is captured in his words of praise for the beauty of Switzerland:

"However magnificent dreams of the imagination may be,
They always remain inferior to reality."

A LITTLE BIT ABOUT THE SWISS

The Swiss call their country Helvetia. All federal documents bear the seal of the Confederation Helvetia, CH, or Swiss Confederation. The well-known Swiss red and white flag dates back to the 13th Century. In 1863 the International Red Cross, to honor its Swiss founder, adopted the Swiss flag as its banner, only reversing the colors. Swiss independence dates to the days of William Tell when the magistrates from three cantons, then under Hapsburg rule, met to courageously and successfully oppose the hand of the ruling landholders. It was in 1291, on a meadow near Lake Lucerne, at the Rutli, that the magistrates set the seal to the new Confederation Helvetia. Those original three cantons, Uri, Schwyz and Unterwalden, have expanded over the centuries into 25 (22 if you do not consider the semi-cantons of Appenzell, Basel and Unterwalden). Each of the 25 cantons jealously guards its autonomy and separate identity. The canton of Bern is the capital of Switzerland and serves as the seat of the federal government. However, the Swiss have historically shunned centralization of power, and so, rather than have too many federal branches in one city, they maintain the supreme court at Lausanne.

Although Switzerland is a small country (barely 200 miles wide and 100 miles north to south) it has a compulsory military service, determined to protect its hard won independence, national character and peace. Every young Swiss man must enlist at the age of 20 and complete 17 weeks of basic training. Then, until the age of 50 or 55 he is responsible for participating in a few weeks of annual "refresher" courses. This military force is always ready to defend the country and can be coordinated into action at a moment's notice. Often we encountered such training groups who were "stationed" at our hotel. They would practice maneuvers by day to return to the hotel in the afternoon and often spend their leisure hours washing their Mercedes. The most humorous example of their presence, however, was at night when we would retire and find heavy combat boots lining the hall, left out to be polished. Where else but in Switzerland?

Introduction

Contrary to the reputation of the Swiss people as being somewhat aloof, we found them to be exceedingly cordial and hospitable. Not a back-slapping brand of friendliness, but a friendliness wrapped in reserve and dignity—no less real though quite "proper." Perhaps the Swiss dedication to hard work, their total commitment to providing excellence of service, and their respect for privacy have been misinterpreted as "coldness."

CREDIT CARDS

Many small inns, and even some large deluxe hotels, do not accept credit cards. To help you decide how much cash or travelers' checks to take with you, we have indicated in the back of the book under each hotel description the hotels that do accept "plastic payment." The following abbreviations are used: AX-American Express, EC-EuroCard, VS-Visa, MC-Master Charge, or simply-all major.

DINING OPTIONS

Many of the places to stay featured in this guide have a restaurant (sometimes just for the use of guests) and offer the option of demi-pension, which means that breakfast and dinner are included in the price of the room. We recommend that you accept this meal plan whenever it is available. Naturally, the nightly rate is higher, but almost without exception, it is a very good value. When making a reservation ask if you can have demi-pension and the price. (Remember that usually demi-pension is quoted per person, so be sure you understand whether the rate is for one or two persons.) Each hotel has its own policy: some will only provide demi-pension with a minimum of a three-night stay, others offer the option from the first night—especially if requested in advance.

The type of menu on demi-pension varies. Most hotels offer a set menu each night, but a few (usually the more deluxe hotels) offer a choice for the entrée. There is sometimes a separate dining room for house guests who are staying on the demi-pension plan. Usually you have the same table each night which is an advantage: you can get to know your neighbors. Another advantage—if you don't finish your bottle of wine, it will be saved and appear at your table the next night. Note: There are a few hotels in our guide that *only* offer demi-pension, in that case, we have so indicated under the hotel's description. Although most hotels quote demi-pension on a per person basis, for consistency purposes, we quote the per night cost for two persons sharing a double room.

DRIVING

The roads, like everything else in Switzerland, are efficiently marked. Once you get used to the excellent color-coded sign system, directions are easy to follow. Green signs depict freeways. Blue signs mark regular roads. White signs depict the smaller roads. Yellow signs mark walking paths or roads closed to vehicle traffic. Most of the roads are excellent, but some of the smaller roads in remote areas, i.e., narrow, twisting mountain passes are not recommended for the faint of heart. It is also notable that certain passes close during the winter months. While driving in Switzerland to inquire about Swiss road conditions a hot line may be reached by dialing 163.

CAR RENTALS: The major car rental companies are represented throughout Switzerland and cars can frequently be picked up in one major city and left in another without a drop-off charge.

DRIVER'S LICENSE: A valid driver's license from your own country is sufficient when driving within Switzerland.

DRUNK DRIVING: The penalties for driving while under the influence of alcohol are very severe. Do not drink and drive.

GASOLINE (PETROL): The price of gasoline within Switzerland is very high so be sure to budget for this when making your plans. If you find yourself short of cash, many of the service stations (such as BP, ESSO, and Shell) will accept payment by a major credit card. Some of the service stations have an efficient system whereby you put coins into an appropriate slot and can pump your own gas—day or night. Some service stations are even more automated and you can purchase gas by inserting your credit card directly into the indicated slot. The service stations off the major freeways frequently close for a few hours in the middle of the day.

MOTORWAYS: Switzerland does not collect tolls on their freeways. Instead, motorists must buy a permit (that is put on the windshield) in order to use the freeways. If you rent a car, the rental company will have done this for you. If arriving from another country, you can buy a permit called *Vignette* at the border.

ROAD CONDITIONS: Highways link Switzerland's major cities and are kept in remarkably good condition. No sooner are the snows melting in the spring sun than maintenance crews begin repairing damage done by winter weather. Many villages are tucked away in remote valleys linked to civilization by narrow little roads, but even these are well tended by the efficient Swiss and are usually in good condition.

ROAD SIGNS: If you are driving, prepare yourself before leaving home by learning the international road signs so that you can obey all the rules and avoid the hazard and embarrassment of heading the wrong way down a small street or parking in a forbidden zone. There are several basic sign shapes. The triangular signs warn that there is danger ahead. The circular signs indicate compulsory rules and information. The square signs give information concerning telephones, parking, camping, etc.

SEAT BELTS: Seat belts are mandatory when driving within Switzerland. It is also the law that babies and small children must ride in proper car seats.

SPEED LIMITS: There are speed limits throughout Switzerland: freeways: maximum speed 120 km per hour; highways: maximum speed 80 km per hour; towns and built-up areas: maximum speed 50 km per hour.

ELECTRICAL CURRENT

You will need a transformer plus an adapter if you plan to take an American-made electrical appliance with you to Switzerland. The voltage is 220 AC current. It is best to check with the manager of the hotel before plugging anything into the outlets.

FESTIVALS

Proud of their local traditions and cultures, the Swiss observe many festivals and events that serve as reminders of the past. They range from centuries-old ceremonies commemorating national victories to popular pageants and processions. Colorful costumes, often unique to a particular canton, are frequently worn on Sundays and festive occasions. Music and theater, are a great accompaniment to Swiss life. From the theater and symphony in the larger cities to the local band or yodeling society in the villages, the Swiss host numerous festivals throughout the year incorporating music. Festivals and traditions inspired by the seasons are also plentiful and fun to experience. To name a few: in early summer in the Engadine, farmers in traditional costumes, parade their cattle adorned with heavy old cow bells via the villages to higher summer pastures. In the fall, gaiety prevails with the grape harvest in the numerous wine regions. In summer, special sports contests take place, such as Alpine wrestling, tugs-of-war, or *hornet*, a team game in which a vulcanite disc is "swatted" with a wooden racket. Political meetings are also staged as a traditional event. In spring, there are open-air cantonal meetings, *Landsgemeinden*, held by citizens in the cantons of Appenzell, Glarus and Unterwalden. In the town square of each canton, elections take place and issues are debated and voted upon by uplifted hand. Switzerland has a wealth of offerings in terms of tradition and festivals. The Swiss National Tourist Office is an excellent source for information and they publish an annual calendar of events at the beginning of each year.

FLY LUGGAGE

In a total commitment to ease the way for the traveler, the Swiss have devised an ingenious, outstandingly convenient method for the handling of your luggage. From over 100 train or postal bus stations throughout Switzerland you can check your luggage via the Geneva or Zürich airport all the way to your own home town airport. (Of course, you will need to follow the customs procedures of luggage inspection at your gateway city.) The Swiss call this "Fly Luggage." All you need is a plane ticket with a confirmed reservation for a scheduled flight from Zürich or Geneva. The cost is nominal and is per piece of luggage, (approximately $15 each piece). If you have a railway ticket to the Zürich or Geneva airport, you pay even less. Please allow sufficient time and do investigate check-in time requirements at local train stations for checking your luggage.

FOOD and WINE

Switzerland is bordered by Germany, Austria, Italy and France. Culinary specialties from each of these countries have been absorbed into the Swiss kitchens where talented chefs interpret these various foods into gourmet delights.

Many guide books imply that Swiss cooking is mediocre—that it has no character or style of its own. We feel that this is totally unfair. The high degree of training stressed in the Swiss hotel schools contributes to the consistently fine food and service that is found, not only in the elegant city restaurants, but also in tiny restaurants in remote hamlets. Usually every entree is cooked to order. Rarely will you see a steam table. And for a grand finale to your meal, Swiss pastries and desserts are world famous.

You will find throughout your travels in Switzerland delicious fruits and vegetables from the garden, a marvelous selection of fresh fish from the rivers and lakes, outstanding veal dishes, and wicked desserts followed by an assortment of local cheeses.

To satisfy the morning appetite, the breakfast repast is usually a continental offering of rolls, bread, butter, jelly, cheese, and Muesli, served with a beverage of coffee or tea. At larger hotels, you can often order as a supplement and for an additional charge, juices, eggs, and breakfast meats.

The following list of Swiss specialties is not comprehensive. It is merely a sampling of some of the delicacies we most enjoyed while in Switzerland. The fun of completing the list is left to your own culinary adventures.

BRATWURST: I am sure the Swiss would chuckle to see included such a mundane fare as Bratwurst in a specialty food list. However, there is nothing more delicious than the plump grilled veal Swiss hot dogs smothered in onions, topped by mustard and accompanied by fried potatoes. A cold beer makes this meal memorable.

BÜNDNERFLEISCH: In southeastern Switzerland, the Grisons area, an unusual air-dried beef or ham cut into wafer-thin slices is served as a delicacy.

CHEESES: Switzerland is famous for her cheeses. Appenzell and Gruyères are but two of the many towns that produce these mouth-watering cheeses. You will find that each area seems to produce its own variety of cheese.

CHOCOLATE: This list would not be complete without the mention of Swiss chocolate. Nestlé, Tobler, or simply "Swiss" are synonymous with the world's best chocolate. Rarely does a suitcase return home without a candy bar or two tucked into the corner.

FONDUE: The Swiss specialty of fondue has gained popularity all over the world. Melted Gruyères cheese, white wine, garlic, and kirsch are brought hot to the table in a chafing dish and diners use long forks to dip squares of bread into the delectable mixture. Fondue Bourguignonne, chunks of meat skewered on forks and broiled in oil and seasoned at will, is also popular throughout the country.

FRITURE DE PERCHETTES: Nothing could be more superb than the tiny, mild fillet of fresh perch fried in oil found on most menus during the summer in the Lake Geneva area. Be sure to try this outstanding gourmet delight.

GESCHNETZLETS: Veal is very popular in Switzerland. Perhaps the most famous and delicious method of preparation is small pieces cooked in a white wine sauce with mushrooms. This is frequently called *Veal Zürich* on the menu.

HERO JAM: This divine jam comes in many delicious fruit and berry flavors and is traditionally served with little hard rolls that break into quarters.

LECKERLI: This is a spicy, cake-like, ginger flavored cookie covered with a thin sugar icing. To be really good, the cookie must "snap" when broken.

RACLETTE: Raclette is a fun dish, a countryman's dinner and feast. A block of Bagnes cheese is split and melted over a fire. The softened cheese, scraped onto your plate, is most often served with potatoes and onions. Sometimes variations in the accompaniment are offered, such as the addition of mushrooms, tomatoes, ham, and sausage—almost as you would order variations of an omelet or quiche.

ROSCHTI OR RÖSTI: These delicious fried potatoes called are served throughout Switzerland often accompanied by sausages and roasts. The potatoes are diced and lightly browned in butter—frequently with the addition of diced onions.

WINES: To complement the meal, Switzerland produces some exceptional wines that are rarely exported—a definite loss to the rest of the world. Many of these wines are made from grapes grown in the Rhone Valley and have a light, slightly fruity taste and a tinge of effervescence. Be sure to take the opportunity to sample Swiss wines. If you want to economize, ask your waiter if he has an *offenen Wein,* an open wine is served either in a carafe or a bottle without a cork. Swiss beer is also first rate and the liquors are delicious: Marc, Kirsch, Pflümi, and Williamine are the most popular—all are potent!

GEOGRAPHY

The unique geography of Switzerland lends itself to breathtaking beauty. In the north-western section of Switzerland are the Jura Mountains. Sixty percent of the south-eastern part of the country is dominated by the Alps. In between these two mountainous areas, the verdant lowlands sweep from Lake Geneva diagonally across the country to Lake Constance. You return home with the impression of precipitous alpine peaks, deep mountain gorges, narrow mountain valleys, glaciers gleaming in the sun, beautiful mountain

valleys, glorious blue lakes, gently flowing rivers, spectacular waterfalls, soft rolling hills, picturesque villages, toy-like churches, and quaint chalets. Every turn in the road offers postcard vistas for your scrapbook of memories.

HOTELS - BASIS FOR SELECTION

Charm and old world ambiance are used as the basis for the selection of hotels in this guide. Some of our recommendations are luxuriously elegant while others are quite simple. Some are located in the center of cities while others are tucked into remote mountain villages. Our hotels vary also as to quality. Frankly, some are better than others because in a few instances we have chosen a hotel, not on its merit alone, but so that you would have a place to stay in a region or village we considered so spectacular that it *had* to have a hotel. We have indicated what each hotel has to offer and have described the setting for your consideration. We believe that if you know what to expect, you will not be disappointed. Therefore, we have tried always to be candid and honest in our appraisals. The charm of a simple countryside chalet will beckon some while a sophisticated luxurious city hotel will appeal to others. For a few lucky travelers, price is never a factor if the hotel is outstanding. For others, budget will guide their choice. Read carefully each description so that you can select the hotel that is most suited to you.

HOTELS - DATES OPEN

In the back of the book, under each hotel's description, we have indicated when the hotel is open. Some of the hotels close the end of July until the middle of August—more common, many close during the spring and again in the fall. This is especially true in mountain resorts that are open for skiing in the winter then close for rejuvenation in the spring in anticipation of the influx of summer tourists. A word of caution, however, even though many hotels quote a certain date to open or close, in reality, they often change the date a bit—perhaps because of weather and occupancy.

HOTELS - DECOR

Regardless of the category of Swiss hotel, service and quality of cuisine is generally stressed over the importance of the decor. The old world charm is usually allocated to the public and dining areas, while the bedrooms are simple and modern with light knotty-pine furniture. Rarely do you find an inn with antique decor in the bedrooms.

The most appealing room in the inn often is the *stubli*, a cozy dining room where the local villagers congregate in the evening for a drink and conversation. As a general rule, the *stubli* oozes with the charm of mellow wood paneling, rustic carved chairs and pretty country curtains. The *stubli* is frequently the oldest part of the inn.

HOTELS - RATES

In the hotel section, we have quoted rates using Swiss francs. You will need to do a little arithmetic to estimate what your holiday will cost. The 1995-96 prices quoted are those given to us by the hotels at time of publication so expect some inflation and use our rates as ballpark figures. Call your bank to verify the current exchange rate.

Even though we give room prices, it is difficult to be entirely accurate because rates are quite complex and reflect such a wide span of possibilities—there are high season rates, off season rates, in between season rates. Rates also vary by the type of room: there are deluxe suites, economy singles, family units, rooms with private bath, rooms with only a washbasin, rooms with a view, rooms without a view—the list goes on and on. Since we are limited by space, instead of showing every category, we have simplified the selection. We quote the range of high season rates for two persons sharing a double room. Included in the rates quoted are taxes, service charges and breakfast. In a few instances, breakfast and dinner are included in the price (demi-pension), when you are required to reserve the rooms with meals.

HOTELS - RESERVATIONS

We are frequently asked if reservations are necessary when traveling in Switzerland. Booking in advance definitely ties you into a structured itinerary and if you cancel it is frequently difficult to get a refund for your deposit. Also, with a pre-planned itinerary, you are not free to linger when you have fallen in love with "your" little inn. But without reservations you might not be able to get a room in some special hotel you have your heart set on. With luck you might be able to just "drop in" at some of the hotels described in this guide and secure a room, but during the tourist season many hotels fill up months in advance. Therefore, if you can plan your holiday, we do suggest making reservations for several reasons. First, hotel space in the major cities such as Zürich, Lucerne, Geneva, and Basel is usually very scarce, even in the "off season" the cities are frequently booked solid with conventions. Second, during the tourist season country inns are usually very busy with the Swiss themselves who love to escape to the mountains with their families for a hiking holiday. Third, many of the hotels in this guide are in remote areas and it would be terribly frustrating to arrive in some hamlet after hours of driving to find the only inn already filled. Here are suggestions for making reservations.

DIRECT PHONE CALL: A call to the hotel is a very satisfactory way to make a reservation. You can immediately find out if space is available and, if not, make an alternate choice. Another bonus to calling the hotel is that you can explain your particular needs and find out what the hotel can offer you—such as a family suite or a room with balcony. For each hotel we have given the telephone number including the area code. Ask your operator for specific instructions from your city, but in general, from the United States, the system is as follows: first dial 011 (the international code), then 41 (Switzerland's country code), then the city code (dropping the zero) and then the local telephone number. (Note: The zero before the city code is only dropped if calling from the United States—it must be included when dialing within Europe.) Also, check with your local operator for the best time to call—usually if you place a direct call during off-peak hours, the price is a real bargain. The best chance for finding the owner or manager who speaks English is to call when it is late afternoon in Switzerland, (Switzerland is six hours ahead of New York).

FAX: Many of the hotels in this guide have fax numbers that are included in the hotel information section. If you own a fax machine, or have access to one, this is a very efficient way to request accommodation. When faxing be specific as to your date of arrival and date of departure, type of rooms desired, number of rooms needed, and number of people in your party. Also, be sure to include your return fax number. When you fax: first dial 011 (the international code), next the country code 41, followed by the city code (dropping the zero), then the local hotel fax number. Faxing can be most satisfactory. I often fax just before going to bed to take advantage of the lower rates, and while I sleep, the business day in Switzerland begins and a hotel will often respond to my fax and send an answer before morning, our time.

LETTER: If you have ample time, a letter is an inexpensive way to request hotel space. Allow four weeks for an answer to your letter. A letter written in English is usually adequate because most Swiss hoteliers can read English even if they are not fluent. Europeans frequently reverse the month and date, so be sure to write the name of the month instead of using a number. To avoid confusion, it is best to state your date of arrival and your date of departure. Clearly tell how many persons are in your party, how many rooms you desire, and if you want a private bathroom. Ask for the rates and how much deposit is needed to secure the reservation.

TRAVEL AGENCY: A travel agent can be a great asset in "tying" together all of the threads of your holiday. A knowledgeable agent can be of tremendous assistance too in sorting through the jungle of airline fares and routing possibilities and helping you choose what suits your needs best. When a travel agent writes your transportation ticket there is usually no fee since travel consultants work as agents for airlines, shipping companies and railroads. However, most travel agents do charge a service fee when making hotel reservations due to the time involved in correspondence, deposit checks, acceptance letters, and vouchers. But the assistance given and time saved when using the services of a travel consultant can be money well spent. Choose a travel agent who is knowledgeable, easy to work with and reputable. Be frank about your budget and expectations. Ask in advance about service charges to avoid misunderstandings.

U.S. REPRESENTATIVE: Some Swiss hotels have a United States representative. In the hotel section those with a representative are noted, and one phone call can frequently secure rooms for much of your itinerary. However, please be aware that the rate quoted by a hotel representative may be higher than if you were to call the hotel yourself. In addition, some hotel representatives charge a fee. This is understandable: the hotel representative must protect against fluctuation of the Swiss franc and also cover their office overhead. Please note: we have listed the various hotel representatives as a convenience for our readers: we are in no way affiliated with any of the tour or hotel representatives and cannot be responsible for any bookings made through them.

HOTELS - TELEPHONE AND FAX NUMBERS

Please note that many telephone and fax numbers will be changing in 1995 and 1996 to accommodate the ever expanding circuit. Based on information provided by the Swiss Telecommunications Company, we contacted all the hotels scheduled for new numbers. Whenever information was available and provided, those new telephone and fax numbers have been detailed in the hotel descriptions, alongside the current numbers at the time of publication. Should you have any problems contacting a hotel by telephone or by fax, simply contact the international operator for directory assistance.

HOTELIERS

From large hotels to small inns, the dedication and personal involvement of the owners in the management of their hotels are astounding. No job ever seems too small or inconsequential to merit attention. It is not unusual to find the hoteliers supervising both the hotel and the restaurant. More often than not we would discover the owner in the kitchen, dusting flour off his apron before extending a welcoming handshake. The hoteliers, many having studied in Switzerland's own prestigious hotel and restaurant schools, take great pride in their profession, and ownership is often passed down within a family from one generation to the next.

ITINERARIES

We have included five itineraries for Switzerland, each highlighting the entire country rather than a particular region and each designed around an individual theme. *Swiss Highlights* is written for the first-time traveler to Switzerland. It is an introduction to the major cities and popular destinations. *Mountain Adventures* explores some of Switzerland's most spectacular mountain villages and settings. *Medieval Villages* traces a journey through Switzerland's most enchanting walled towns and medieval villages. Saturated with history and a romantic past, this itinerary steps into an era of knights, chivalry, castles, cobble-stoned streets, wenches, jousting, jesters, turrets, and bows and arrows. *Switzerland by Train, Boat and Bus* takes advantage of the country's fabulous transportation network and lets you most effectively soak in the splendors of Switzerland's valleys, mountains, rivers and lakes without having to attempt the roads and passes in your own car. Most of Switzerland's highlights are incorporated into this romantic itinerary. *Best on a Budget* was created for anyone young at heart and traveling on a budget, for those who seek traditional Swiss inns, and yet appreciate when the simplicity of accommodation is reflected in the price.

The five suggested itineraries in this guide crisscross back and forth across Switzerland. Because certain "key" destinations reappear in several itineraries we decided to describe them once in detail in a reference section, titled *Sightseeing Reference*, rather than elaborate on them over and over again in each itinerary. This sightseeing section begins on page 29.

These itineraries (with the exception of *Switzerland by Train, Boat and Bus*) are designed to be traveled by car. There is no better way to explore the countryside, to really understand the depths and reaches of a valley, to fully comprehend the dimensions, magnificence and power of lofty alpine peaks, and to experience the beauty and grace of lakes and rivers. Cars are easy to rent and available in most mid-sized towns and driving is on the "proper" side.

LANGUAGE

Switzerland is a country of four languages: GERMAN is spoken all over central and northern Switzerland; ITALIAN is spoken in the south; FRENCH is spoken in the west and ROMANSH is spoken by a small number of people in southeastern Switzerland. English is usually spoken in hotels and shops of tourist centers. In remote areas you might need to communicate using a dictionary and a smile.

If you enjoy diversity, in the course of a day, you will find your skills challenged with multiple languages. Quite surprisingly, you can travel a distance of just a few kilometers, from one village to the next, and find yourself in a new region and encounter a complete change in language. If you are uncertain upon arrival in a given town as to whether to use your French or German language skills, I find road and town signs an excellent clue.

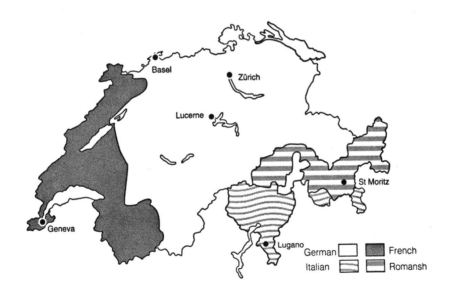

MAPS

A map at the beginning of each itinerary outlines the itinerary's route and shows suggested sightseeing and overnight stops. To assist you in determining the general region in which a town where we recommend a hotel is located, at the back of the book is a map, on page 241, outlining Switzerland's 22 general cantons. The last line of each hotel description refers to the canton in which the hotel-town is found. Following the canton map, beginning on page 243, a series of six regional maps of Switzerland pinpoint the location of each town where we recommend a hotel. In the top right hand corner on each hotel description page, the appropriate map number that you should refer to for the town location is given.

All the maps are artist's renderings and are intended to be used as guidelines. To smooth your way, it is vital that you purchase detailed road and city maps. We strongly recommend that you use the Hallwag map of Switzerland. Not only is this an excellent map with great detail, but it also has the distinct advantage of having an index so you can easily locate the towns. If your local book store does not carry Hallwag maps, they can order one for you. If you have a Rand McNally book store in your city, they are distributors for the Hallwag Maps in the United States.

RESTAURANTS

Switzerland boasts some of Europe's most outstanding restaurants. An exceptionally high degree of professionalism and excellence is maintained in even the simplest of restaurants, and the presentation and quality of food rivals any in the world. Many restaurants in Switzerland serve food piping hot from a cart—a nicety usually encountered in only the most exclusive restaurants. Then, when you have finished your entree, you are presented with a comparable second portion, brought to you on a clean warm plate with the same skillful delivery.

Many inns have two restaurants. Frequently there is a central entry hall with a somewhat formal restaurant on one side and a "pub-like," informal restaurant on the other. The latter is called the *stubli,* and if you are in the countryside this is where the farmers gather in the late afternoon for a bit of farm gossip and perhaps a card game of *jass.* Locals gather after work in the *stubli* for relaxation, and in the evening families congregate for a glass of beer, wine, or a thimbleful of kirsch.

SHOPPING

Switzerland has a tempting array of products to entice even the reluctant buyer. Shopping in Switzerland is fun: the stores are pretty and the merchandise is usually of excellent quality.

Many larger towns have stores that feature an exceptional selection of art and handicraft items, referred to as *Heimatwerk,* from the surrounding region. (While in Zürich visit the *Schweizer Heimatwerk,* a marvelous store that features crafts from all regions—you will find it near the Zum Storchen Hotel.) In Switzerland the prices are usually set, so there is no bargaining and tax is included.

Some shopping suggestions are: watches, clocks, mechanical toys, wood carvings, hand-painted pottery, cow bells (both reproduction and antique), Swiss army knives, chocolates, cheeses, kirsch, antiques, St Gallen lace, hand-embroidered items, fine cottons, children's clothing and ski wear.

SPORTS

Sports are part of the lure of Switzerland. The mountains have been tempting climbers since the middle of the 1800's when Edward Whymper crossed the Channel from England to be the first to reach the top of the famous Matterhorn. Ski areas such as Zermatt, St Moritz, Davos, Wengen, Klosters, Villars and Verbier are world famous. Mountain lakes such as Lake Geneva, Lake Lucerne, and Lake Zürich are ideal for boating, fishing and swimming. The incredible array of marked walking trails beckons hikers from far and near and the skies of the mountain valleys are often colored with the canvas of hang gliders.

SWISS NATIONAL TOURIST OFFICE

The Swiss National Tourist Office is an excellent source for information. If you have any questions not answered in this guide, or need special information concerning a particular destination within Switzerland, one of their offices will be happy to assist you.

Swiss National Tourist Office, Head Office
Bellariastrasse 38
CH-8027 Zurich, Switzerland
tel: (01) 288 11 11, fax: (01) 288 12 05

Swiss National Tourist Office
222 North Sepulveda Blvd., Suite 1570
El Segundo, California 90245
tel: (310) 335-5980; fax: (310) 335-5982

Swiss National Tourist Office
608 Fifth Avenue
New York, New York 10020
tel: (212) 757-5944; fax: (212) 262-6116

Swiss National Tourist Office
150 No. Michigan Ave., Suite 2930
Chicago, Illinois 60601
tel: (312) 630-5840; fax: (312) 630-5848

Swiss National Tourist Office
New Coventry Street
London W1V 8EE, England
tel: (0171) 734 1921; fax: (0171) 437 4577

Swiss National Tourist Office
926 The East Mall
Etibicote, Ontario H9B GKI, Canada,
tel: (416) 695-2090; fax: (416) 695-2774

TELEPHONES

CALLS TO SWITZERLAND: If you want to make a call to Switzerland from the United States, dial 011, next the country code, 41, then the city code (dropping the 0 in front of the city code), then the local telephone number.

CALLS WITHIN SWITZERLAND: If you want to call within Switzerland, there are many public telephone booths conveniently located with instructions in several languages (including English). Keep a good supply of one franc coins—these are very handy. For calling a local number, omit the city code (the numbers in the parenthesis). For calling a long distance number, dial the city code, complete with the 0, and the number.

CALLS OUTSIDE SWITZERLAND: Long distance calls from Switzerland are expensive. Use your telephone credit card such as AT&T or Sprint to make calls to the United States. Before leaving home, find out the telephone number in Switzerland that connects you directly to the United States.

TRANSPORTATION

Although cars afford the flexibility to deviate on a whim and explore enticing side roads or beckoning hilltop villages, Switzerland's transportation network is so superb that you can travel conveniently by train, boat or bus throughout the country—from the largest city to the smallest hamlet. So, if you were ever thinking of a vacation without a car, this is the place to try it. The ingenuity of the network is almost beyond belief. The schedules are so finely tuned that buses, trains, and boats all interconnect. Not only do the time schedules jibe perfectly, but usually you can walk from where the boat arrives to the train or bus station. It is like a puzzle, and great fun.

Should you be planning an extensive holiday using the Swiss public transportation system, there is an invaluable set of books, called the *Official Timetable*, that you can purchase through Europe Train Tours, 198 E. Boston Post Road, Mamaroneck, New York, 10543, tel: (914) 698-9426, fax: (914) 698-9516, or R.D. Cook Management Corporation, 75 Rolling Hills Road, Tiburon, California 94920, tel: (415) 433-1991, fax: (415) 435-0601. Within the United States, the cost of the Official Swiss Timetable is $20.00 plus shipping and handling. In England, call the Swiss National Tourist Office to see where you can purchase the *Official Timetable*. Free of charge, the Eurail-Timetable Guide is available through Rail Europe, P.O. Box 10383, Stamford, Connecticut 06904.

The "Official Timetable" (actually 3 small books) is published once a year and contains a wealth of information. It outlines every timetable within Switzerland for boats, trains and buses. There are other train guides published, but this official guide is the only one we found that shows access by public transportation to every town—no matter how tiny or how isolated. It is a superb reference.

BOATS: Switzerland is a land of lakes and rivers and to travel the country by its waterways affords an entirely new and enchanting perspective. Often a river boat or lake steamer will depart from a dock just a few feet from a hotel, enabling you to journey from one destination to another or continue inland by connecting with either a train, bus or hired car. Concerned with preserving their heritage, the Swiss have refurbished a number of beautiful and graceful lake steamers and ferries. Not only can you see Switzerland by water but also experience some nostalgia.

BUSES: Boasting more mileage than the Swiss railway itself, the Postal Bus lines originated after World War I with the primary purpose of transporting mail. In conjunction with the entire network of railway lines, every village in Switzerland is serviced by postal bus—providing Switzerland with one of the most exceptional transportation networks in the world. Depending on the demand, there are 4– to 5–person limousines, mini-buses or the ever familiar buttercup-yellow buses. In addition to the mail, the bus lines are responsible for transporting about 15 million passengers. Their dependability and excellence of service is impressive.

In Switzerland, the position of postal bus driver is very prestigious. Those chosen for the job are unmatched in driving ability. Their record is faultless; in the history of the postal bus service there has not been one fatal accident. In addition to excellent driving techniques, the drivers also play an important role in the community—usually they are well-versed on the local news and social activities and familiar with the most recent wedding, gossip, or current business venture. Bus drivers must know every millimeter of the road, and their training is exacting and stringent. Thousands apply each year for positions available to just a few. To qualify an applicant must be no older than 28, have completed his military duty, pass a rigorous physical exam and be able to speak three languages. They undergo years of specialized training before taking position behind the wheel. Their first assignment is to drive a postal truck, then a bus in the lowlands, as a finale they must negotiate a bus up a treacherous, narrow, mountain road, and then successfully complete a seemingly impossible U-turn, observed and judged by a bus load of veteran bus drivers. Justifiably, those who achieve position as postal driver have command of the roadways and other vehicles are expected to yield. It is not uncommon to see a postal busman assisting a petrified driver who has encountered difficulty on a pass or a narrow bend and who is too frightened to move. The sound of their horn, as the postal buses wind up the incredible mountain passes, warning other vehicles of their approach, may seem familiar. Indeed it is a melody from Rossini's *William Tell Overture.*

TAXIS: Unless you are independently wealthy, try to avoid taxis while in Switzerland. They are VERY expensive. Frequently you can take a bus or tram from the train station almost to the door of your hotel. If you are on a tight budget, when you make your room reservation, ask the manager or owner if there is a direct bus or tram from the station to your hotel. If so, ask the number of the bus or tram, name of the place to get off, and how many stops it is from the station. If you have a map and luggage on wheels that you can pull, another alternative is to walk.

TRAINS: Switzerland has one of the most remarkable rail systems in the world, with more than 3,400 miles of track. Just over half are operated by the Swiss Federal Railway system while the others are privately owned. However, they are all integrated and connections are scheduled to synchronize both efficiently and conveniently. Their timetable is patterned after the perfection of the Swiss clock—trains depart on the scheduled second.

The train stations, often chalet-style buildings, are spotlessly clean, and quite frequently double as a residence for the station master. You often find evidence of domesticity— flowers cascading from the upstairs window boxes and laundry hanging on the line. Station masters are handsome in their uniforms and most speak some English.

Trains interface with the major airports. If you are flying into either Zürich or Geneva, there is a beautifully geared network. From either of these airports you can board a train directly to many of the tourist destinations throughout Switzerland. The entire setup is wonderfully convenient for the traveler. As you exit the baggage claim area, there is a counter where you can check your luggage right through to your destination and climb aboard the train completely unencumbered. If you really want to spoil yourself, when the train arrives at your first night's stop, you can take a cab to your hotel, give the baggage claim ticket to the receptionist and ask him to send the porter to the station for your bags.

TRAIN TIPS: It is very important to be able to quickly find "your" train as the schedules mesh like clockwork. Once you have the system down pat, you won't panic when you see that there are only a few minutes to get from one train to the other. You will know that this has been established as enough time to make the connection. In every station a large yellow poster with black print states all the out-going trains, listed according to departure times. You need to study your own map because where you want to disembark might not appear on the sign—you might need to look at a major city beyond where you plan to get off. Along with the schedule,

the yellow sign also states the number of the track from which each train will depart. Large white signs with black print show the arrival times of trains. When you go to the departure track, there is a diagram showing the alignment of the cars so that you can stand at the proper spot for first or second class cars. This diagram is very important because on certain routes, trains split and some cars go to one city and other cars to another.

TRANSPORTATION - PASSES

Public transportation is easy and economical to use. There are passes that can be purchased outside Switzerland through travel agents. It is an absolute joy to be able to just climb aboard a train on a whim or to hop on one of many boats that ply Switzerland's many lakes. How supremely satisfying not to need to plan ahead or rush to the station or pier in time to buy a ticket. Even if you are traveling by car, you might well want to take some sightseeing excursions by train since they whisk you right to the center of the towns. From Zürich take a quick trip to Schaffhausen to see the Rhein Falls, or an excursion to Winterthur to see the superb Oskar Reinhart museum.

All of the passes are priced for either first or second class travel. If you are not on a tight budget, the first class sections of the trains are less crowded and have more comfortable seats. Swiss rail tickets and passes are available through Rail Europe: tel: 800 438-7245, 303 443-5100, fax: 800 432-1329 or 303 444-4587. Following are some of the available passes—one surely tailored with you in mind.

SWISS PASS: The Swiss Pass entitles you to unlimited trips on the entire network of the Swiss transportation system covering 9,000 miles of railroad, boat and postal bus routes, as well as streetcars and buses in 35 Swiss cities—plus, a 25% discount on excursions to most mountain tops. The pass is available for 8 or 15 days, or 1 month of consecutive travel.

SWISS FLEXI PASS: The Swiss Flexi Pass might be perfect for you if you are on a driving vacation. It has the same benefits as the Swiss Pass, but it is more flexible. You can choose any three days of travel within a 15 day period.

SWISS CARD: The Swiss Card, valid for one month, entitles you to a transfer from a Swiss airport or border point to any destination in Switzerland, and a second transfer from any destination in Switzerland to a Swiss airport or border point. It also allows unlimited trips on all other train, bus and steamer services at half fare. (This card is not quite as convenient because you need to purchase a ticket before boarding your train, bus, boat or tram.)

SWISS RAIL 'N DRIVE PASS: The Swiss Rail n' Drive Pass combines train and car travel. It allows: three days of unlimited travel by rail, boat and/or bus, plus two days of travel by rental car with unlimited mileage, basic liability insurance, tax and free drop off inside Switzerland.

SWISS TRAVEL WITH CHILDREN PLAN: Children under 16 travel free if accompanied by at least one parent with a Swiss Pass, Flexi Pass or Swiss Card. Request the family card when ordering your ticket. Note: Some of the major intercity trains have a playroom car where children can romp and play to their heart's content.

TRANSPORTATION - SPECIAL EXCURSIONS

Switzerland has packaged some marvelous public transportation excursions that make travel a real adventure. Perhaps in no other country are there so many possibilities to enjoy the country by public transportation. Some of the possibilities are listed below.

The ENGADINE EXPRESS makes a round trip journey from Zürich to Scuol, a small town deep in the Engadine Valley. Combining train and bus, the trip leaves Zürich at 7:20 in the morning and returns at 7:50 in the evening. If you want, you can stay overnight in Scuol and return to Zürich the next day.

The GLACIER EXPRESS links Zermatt and St Moritz. The incredible, seven and a half hour adventure on the quaint bright red train crosses 291 bridges, goes through 91 tunnels and chugs over the Oberalppass and the Albulapass. Lunch is served en route in a nostalgic, old-fashioned, paneled dining car. [Reservations in the U.S.A. can be made through Rail Europe: contact information on previous page; reservations in England through Swiss National Tourist Office: tel: (0171) 734 19 21.]

The PALM EXPRESS, an all day adventure combining bus and train, begins in St Moritz, loops south to Lake Lugano, and then north again into the mountains, ending the journey at Zermatt, or visa-versa. En route the landscape changes from glaciers to palm trees. For reservations contact the booking office in St Moritz: tel: (082) 3 30 72, fax: (082) 2 67 90, [new contact for St Moritz, in April 1996: tel: (081) 833 30 72, fax: (081) 833 61.21], or in Lugano: tel: (091) 21 95 20, fax: (091) 23 69 39, [new contact for Lugano in October 1995: tel: (091) 921 95 20, fax: (091) 923 69 39].

The WILLIAM TELL EXPRESS links Central Switzerland with the Swiss-Italian Lake District. You board a nostalgic paddle steamer in Lucerne and cruise to Flüelen, enjoying en route a gourmet meal in the first class restaurant. In Flüelen, a first class bus is waiting and the trip continues through the Reuss Valley, through the 15 kilometer Gotthard Tunnel and on to Bellinzona. From here, you can continue on either to Lugano or Locarno. Advance reservations are mandatory and may be made from the United

States through Rail Europe (see telephone and fax contacts on page 26), no more than two months and no less than two weeks prior to the travel date.

WEATHER

For such a tiny nation, Switzerland offers an amazing variety of climates: the brisk mountain weather is quite different from the milder temperatures encountered near Lake Geneva, or the balmy Swiss-Italian Lake District. Of course there are seasonal changes since Switzerland attracts tourists throughout the year. Because of the sudden, unpredictable weather changes, it is highly recommended to use the so called "onion principal" in clothing. Never wear one firm piece, but instead, layers of clothing, like T-shirts, sweaters and jackets, where you can take pieces off or put them on at any given time to adjust comfortably. Also, be sure to pack good comfortable walking shoes (there are a lot of cobble stone streets) and suntan lotion for your summer and winter vacations.

The seasons in Switzerland, are varied, and all lovely. Winter beckons the sports enthusiasts with excellent downhill ski slopes, beautifully marked cross country trails, skating, and curling. Winter is also for those who simply love the charm of picturebook villages wrapped in blankets of snow. Spring is my favorite time of year. Weather in late spring can be absolutely glorious—the meadows are a symphony of color with a profusion of wildflowers, and the mountains still have their winter cap of snow. Summer is the most popular season. The days are usually mild and sunny and the mountain passes are open so you can explore all the isolated mountain villages. Autumn is lovely. The first snowstorms leave the mountains wearing new bonnets of pristine snow. The trees and vineyards are mellowing in shades of red and gold and the flowers are at their peak of bloom in every windowbox. There is a hint of winter in the air, except in the Swiss-Italian Lake District where the weather is usually still balmy.

Sightseeing Reference

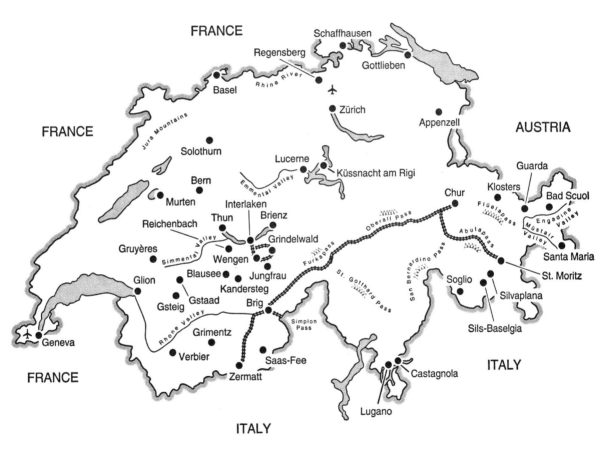

GERMANY

FRANCE

Schaffhausen

Regensberg

Gottlieben

Rhine River

Basel

Zürich

FRANCE

Appenzell

AUSTRIA

Jura Mountains

Solothurn

Lucerne

Küssnacht am Rigi

Guarda

Bern

Klosters

Bad Scuol

Emmental Valley

Chur

Flüelapass

Murten

Interlaken

Brienz

Engadine

Mustair Valley

Reichenbach

Thun

Grindelwald

Oberall Pass

Abulapass

Santa Maria

Gruyères

Simmental Valley

Wengen

Furkapass

St. Moritz

Glion

Blausee

Jungfrau

San Bernardino Pass

Soglio

Silvaplana

Gsteig

Gstaad

Kandersteg

Brig

St. Gotthard Pass

Rhone Valley

Simplon Pass

Sils-Baselgia

Geneva

Grimentz

ITALY

FRANCE

Verbier

Saas-Fee

Castagnola

Zermatt

Lugano

ITALY

Sightseeing Reference

The five suggested itineraries in this guide crisscross back and forth across Switzerland describing routes tailored for individual whims and budgets. Because certain "key" towns reappear in several itineraries we decided to have an individual sightseeing section as a quick reference of what to expect along your route. The following towns, listed alphabetically, appear in the itineraries as sightseeing and overnight destinations.

APPENZELL

Appenzell is a picture book village, popular with tourists who flock to see the fanciful paintings on the facades of the buildings, a colorful variety of artwork—landscapes, folk art, flowers, abstract designs, animals and people. Appenzell is famous also for exquisite embroidery and delicious cheeses. Politically, Appenzell is well known for its demonstration of real democracy. On the last Sunday in April, the citizens, usually wearing their colorful traditional costumes, gather in the town square to elect representatives to their local canton. This is done with a show of hands.

Another appealing aspect of Appenzell is the tranquil countryside that surrounds it. This area of Switzerland is lush with rolling, gentle green fields accented with plump, happy cows lazily munching grass to the rhythm of their cow bells. Snuggled in these lovely pastures are large farmhouses adorned with masses of flowers. The family home is attached to the barn so that the animals are easily accessible during the snows of winter.

ASCONA

In days-gone-by Ascona was a sleepy fishing village, but today tourists are its main source of activity. And it is no wonder. Ascona abounds with character. The lake laps at the dock where boats are moored next to the colorful central square that is framed by Italian looking pastel colored buildings with heavy tiled roofs. Behind the front row of houses, tiny lanes spiderweb into the medieval village. From Ascona, steamers ply Lake Maggiore, one of Switzerland's most romantic lakes. When the weather is cold and dreary in the north, it is a tempting option to head to the Swiss-Italian Lake District where the sun shines most of the year and flowers bloom all winter.

BASEL

The town of Basel is well worth a visit. It is an industrial city, the second largest in Switzerland. From the outskirts, the city is not very attractive, but when you arrive at the heart of the old town, you find a delightful medieval city—a very real city functioning as a center for banking, insurance, trade and commerce. At the border of France and Germany and linked by the Rhein River with central Europe, Basel has a very important strategic location. The Rhein River acts as the gateway to the North Sea, so Basel is also a very busy port.

The splendidly preserved old town is a delight to stroll around. Here you discover, tucked away on back streets, charming squares adorned with joyful little fountains. Visit the Cathedral that dates back to the 12th Century. Also in your wanderings visit the Market Square (*Markplatz*) that is host every morning to a flower and vegetable market. The Town Hall (*Rathaus*) dates from the 16th Century and is beautifully decorated with frescos. There is an excellent Museum of Fine Arts (*Kunstmuseum*) that features works of art of the 15th and 16th Centuries. The Museum of Antique Art (*Antikenmuseum*) features sculptures and art dating from the pre-Hellenic times.

In summer there are boat tours that offer a leisurely view of the city. This method of sightseeing is especially interesting because from the river you can view many of the marvelous old buildings that line the river and also cross under some of the bridges that so colorfully span the Rhein River.

BERN

Bern is an enticingly well-preserved 16th-century walled city, perched on a plateau that is almost made into an island by a loop of the Aare River. Further enhancing the picture, the mountains rise in the background. The setting alone would make Bern worth a stop, but the town itself has lots of character and interesting sightseeing attractions.

Marktgasse, the main street of the old part of Bern, has charming medieval buildings, arcaded sidewalks, intriguing shops and whimsical fountains.

My favorite attraction in Bern is the clock tower, that until the 13th Century was the town's West Gate. This clock tower appeals to the child in all of us. Four minutes before the hour the "show" begins: as the bell peals, there is succession of figures that parade across the clock including the most popular of all—darling little bear cubs. Bern is an easy walking city. Just a stroll from the clock tower is the Nydegg Bridge. From here you have wonderful views of the town and, if you are a photographer, some great shots.

BRIENZ and BALLENBERG

Nestled on the shores of Lake Brienz, Brienz is a picturesque town overlooking the Giessbach Falls and the surrounding alpine peaks. A famous wood carving center, most of the carvings available for purchase throughout Switzerland come from this lakeside town. It is a charming town and its web of old narrow streets shadowed by dark wooden chalet style houses and shops is fun to explore.

For a breathtaking, panoramic view of the Bernese Alps and Lake Brienz, consider a journey on the Brienz Rothorn Bahn. This wonderful old steam locomotive traverses some exceptionally beautiful scenery on its ascent by rack and pinion railway to the summit (7,700 ft) of the Rothorn. The round-trip journey takes approximately three hours and departs from the lakeside town of Brienz. [There is a hotel at the summit, both commercial and functional in decor and comfort, where you can dine or overnight, the

Ballenberg Open Air Museum

Hotel Restaurant Rothorn Kulm, tel: (036) 51.12.21.] For additional information about the train and schedules, contact: Brienz Rothorn Bahn, CH-3855, tel: (036) 51.34.44 or fax: (036) 51.37.95.

Located on the outskirts of Brienz, by the Wyssensee, Ballenberg is a marvelous open-air museum. It serves as a wonderful introduction to the regional architecture and cultures of Switzerland. More than seventy historical buildings from the various cantons of Switzerland have been relocated to this park of some 80 hectares. You can tour the park on foot or, for a fee, by horse and buggy. The museum buildings, from a half-timbered Bernese chalet to a thatched farmhouse from the Aargau, are all authentically furnished and surrounded by a lush landscape of gardens, meadows and fields of grain. People dressed in costume work the museum, bringing back a vision of centuries-gone-by. You can observe crafts such as basket weaving, purchase a picnic bounty of bread from the baker, sausage or cheese from the farmer, or settle in at the village inn for a meal. Due to the vastness of the park, even if you selectively visit just a few cantons, plan on allocating at least a half day to visit Ballenberg—however, you could easily spend up to two full days here. The museum is open April 15 to October 31, from 10:00 am to 5:00 pm. The museum has two entrances: Ballenberg-Ost (East) is most convenient from Lucerne and Ballenberg-West is recommended from Bern and Interlaken. You can arrange for a guided tour by contacting the museum in advance: Swiss Open Air Museum Ballenberg, CH-3855 Brienz, Switzerland, tel: (036) 51.11.23, fax: (036) 51.18.21.

CASTAGNOLA and GANDRIA

Castagnola is a lakeside community close to Lugano. From Castagnola there is a scenic walking path connecting Castagnola with the small town of Gandria. This trail hugs the shore of Lake Lugano and makes a pleasant walk. You can stop along the way at one of the little lake-front cafes for refreshment. Castagnola is famous for the Villa Favorita which is perched on the hillside above Lake Lugano. Housing a very impressive private art collection, the Villa Favorita is an attractive, 17th-century mansion surrounded by beautifully landscaped gardens, with magnificent views of Lugano.

CHAMPEX-LAC

Champex-Lac is a small town on the shores of a high-mountain lake 75 kilometers south of Montreux. The Mont Blanc massif rises beyond the lake, reflecting in its still waters. In summer this resort is especially appealing for families: there is boating, hiking, bicycling, swimming and horseback riding.

CHUR

Chur, though not well-known as a tourist destination, is the most important city in eastern Switzerland. In addition to being a modern commercial center, the walled, medieval section of Chur is quite attractive with narrow winding streets (many open only for foot traffic), quaint cobbled alleys, charming little squares graced by fountains and colorful buildings dating back to the 15th Century. There are pretty shops and many good restaurants. Green hills form a back drop to the town while the majestic mountains can be seen in the distance. Because Chur is on the main rail route, it makes a convenient starting point for train travel.

GENEVA

Geneva is frequently thought of as a modern city—a city of banking and commerce; an international city housing the *Place des Nations*; a city of beautiful shops; a city of museums and culture; an industrial city. All this is true, but Geneva also has one of the most attractive medieval sections in Switzerland. "Old Geneva" is located on the south side of the Rhone River. Here the hills rise steeply from the shore of the lake and the streets twist and turn in a maze of fascinating little shops, fountains, flower-filled squares and charming buildings. This area is crowned by St Peter's Cathedral that dominates the old town. The Cathedral, constructed in the 12th Century, is usually open daily. Within the church is a triangular chair supposedly the one used by Calvin, and also the tomb of the Duc de Rohn who was the leader of the French Protestants during the time of Henry IV. But perhaps the most spectacular part of St Peter's Cathedral is the climb to the top of the north tower where you have a panoramic view of Geneva and beyond to the lake and the majestic backdrop of the Alps. Also in the old town, you might want to see the town hall that dates from the 16th Century. After visiting St Peter's, wander down the little twisting streets, exploring small antique shops and back alleys. You cannot get lost because it is all downhill and when you are at the bottom, you are at the lake. There is a park along the banks of the lake—notice in the park a clock made out of flowers.

On the north side of the Rhone circling around the lake is the newer section of Geneva. In this area there are lovely lake promenades punctuated with splendid flower gardens, stately hotels, small squares and fancy shops. This too, is a perfect strolling part of the city—especially in early spring when the tulips are beautiful. Within walking distance are many, many museums and interesting places to see. The *Palais des Nations* is open daily except special holidays. However, like many museums, it is closed for a few hours in the middle of the day. There are many guided tours. The palace is located in the Park de l'Ariana and was the headquarters of the League of Nations. Now it is the seat of the European branch of the United Nations. The *Petit Palais Museum* is open daily except Monday mornings and holidays. This museum is in a mansion and features French painters from the end of the Impressionist period. The Museum of Old Musical Instruments displays a wonderful collection of European musical instruments. Since you are in Switzerland, the home of the clock, you might want to visit the Watch and Clock Museum with displays of timepieces from their origin to the present day.

You really cannot help being captivated by Geneva with its sophisticated beauty and international air. As you meander through the parks and promenades, you could be anywhere in the world—you see all nationalities and hear all languages. This is a city we all seem to love and share.

GLION and THE CASTLE OF CHILLON

Glion is a small town perched in the hills high above Montreux. Because of its superb location, with a panorama of Lake Geneva and the mountains, Glion has attracted the wealthy who have built beautiful mansions nestled among the trees. You can reach Glion by car, or if arriving from Geneva by boat, by a tram connecting the dock at Territet with Glion. There is also a train from Montreux to Glion.

Glion's main attraction is the view. However, just a short distance away, located on Lake Geneva on the outskirts of the city of Montreux, is the Castle of Chillon—made famous by Lord Byron's poem. This castle is well worth a visit. It has a fantastic setting on a small rock jutting into the lake. Walking over a bridge, you enter the Castle of Chillon where you can visit the torture chamber and many rooms with medieval furnishings.

Castle of Chillon

GOTTLIEBEN

Gottlieben is located on the Rhein River just before it enters Lake Constance. These is a dear little village hugging the water's edge. The narrow streets are picturesque and fun to explore. The town is of special interest because of the Krone Hotel, picturesquely situated on the banks of the river. Gottlieben serves as an excellent base from which to explore the region by water as opposed to by road. From Gottlieben you can take ferry boats down the Rhein to Stein am Rhein and Schaffhausen or you can travel by boat on to Lake Constance.

GRIMENTZ

Grimentz is a small, old-world farming village snuggled on a plateau at the end of the D'Anniviers Valley that stretches south from the Rhone Valley. As with other charming Swiss towns, the government protects the architectural standards. This is a town of small Valais-style wooden houses darkened almost black with age, usually with a slate roof and suspended above the ground on stone pillars. My guess is that the Grimentz of old could never have been prettier than it is today when each resident seems to vie with his neighbor to grow the most outstanding flowers. The effect is sensational—brilliant blue sky, snow-capped mountains, green pastures and antique homes exploding in geraniums.

GRINDELWALD

Grindelwald captures for many the romanticized image of Switzerland. It is a charming alpine village sprawled on a lovely expanse of meadows and surrounded by magnificent towering mountains. It is a popular destination for exploring the Jungfrau Range for it is as close as you can come by car to view the spectacular giants of the Jungfrau region: the Eiger rising to 13,026 ft, the Wetterhorn to 12,143 ft and the Mettenberg to 10,184 ft. From the little station in town the train departs for the dramatic Kleine Scheidegg and on to the Jungfraujoch. For further information, please refer to the Jungfraujoch sightseeing section that follows.

GRUYÈRES

Gruyères is a beautiful little medieval village hugging the crest of a miniature mountain just north of Lake Geneva and south of Bern. This is such a unique and charming little village that it is considered a national monument and its architectural purity is protected by the Swiss government. Climb its cobbled streets to the castle that crowns it. Perhaps your visit will coincide with a day when horn blowers dressed in traditional costume sound off on the village square—it is enchanting and memorable.

Another bonus for Gruyères, as you probably guessed from the name of the town, is its location in the center of one of Switzerland's famous dairy areas—the cheeses and creams are marvelous. Stop for a famous Gruyères quiche, linger over a crock of rich fondue, or if in season, delicious fresh berries and thick cream. Cars are not allowed into the village but there are several parking lots strategically located on the road that winds up to the town.

Gruyères is a convenient town to use as a headquarters for a few days. The countryside in summer is exactly what you dream about as being truly Switzerland. The meadows are incredibly green. Contented cows with tinkling bells graze lazily in the pastures, wildflowers abound in the fields, window boxes full of bright geraniums adorn the houses, all enhanced by the backdrop of gorgeous mountains. One short excursion takes you to the small museum-factory just at the bottom of the hill as you drive down from Gruyères. In this modern factory you see how cheeses are made in the various cantons in Switzerland and also watch a movie narrated in English, explaining the process. Also, if you are a cheese enthusiast, you can make short excursions to visit some of the other little villages in the area and sample their dairy products—you might come home a little plumper, but a connoisseur of the delicious Swiss cheese.

The secret to discovering the fairy-tale enchantment of Gruyères is to spend the night here so that the town is yours in the hushed morning and the still hours of dusk. Leave midday when the tour buses deposit their eager load of tourists and return late in the day, to sit on the terrace and have a quiet drink listening to the tinkling of cow bells, watching the meadows soften in fading sunlight.

GSTAAD

In spite of the fact that Gstaad has an international reputation as a very chic ski resort catering to the wealthy jet-set, the town retains much of its old world, small-town, charming simplicity. In summer you might well be awakened by the wonderful medley of cowbells as the herds are driven out to pasture. The setting of Gstaad is magnificent, with rugged mountain peaks rising steeply on each side of the valley. In summer the hiking or mountain climbing is excellent. In winter Gstaad offers one of the most famous network of ski trails in Switzerland.

GSTEIG-GSTAAD

Just 10 kilometers beyond Gstaad is the picturesque hamlet of Gsteig that shares the same pretty mountain valley as its fancy neighbor, yet is quainter and less expensive. Being a little village, Gsteig does not offer the luxury shops nor the extensive selection of restaurants as the internationally famous Gstaad. However, for those of you who prefer an unspoiled farming village, complete with beautifully carved chalets and a marvelous little church, Gsteig might be perfect.

GUARDA, SENT and TARASP CASTLE

Guarda has a spectacular location, perched high on a mountain shelf overlooking the Engadine Valley. The main recreation here is simply being out of doors exploring the beckoning mountain paths and soaking up the sensational beauty of the mountain peaks. However, there is some "formal" sightseeing that can be included in your plans. Nearby is Tarasp Castle that crowns a tiny mountain across the valley from Guarda. In addition to being extremely picturesque, there are guided tours of the castle during the summer months. Also near Guarda, is the tiny town of Sent, which like Guarda, is famous for its many old houses, covered with intricate designs. Sent, like Guarda, has a scenic setting overlooking the valley.

INTERLAKEN

Interlaken, which translates to between the lakes, has a fabulous location. On a spit of land connecting Lake Brienz and Lake Thun Interlaken's location makes it a prime destination for those who want to take the circle train excursion to enjoy the majestic summit of the Jungfraujoch. (Please refer to Jungfraujoch sightseeing.) There are also numerous steamers that in season depart from Interlaken and ply the waters of both Lake Brienz and Lake Thun.

Interlaken has many grand Victorian-style hotels and fancy shops and restaurants. For many years Interlaken has attracted tourists from all over the world who come to enjoy the unbeatable combination of two of the most beautiful lakes in Switzerland and glorious mountain peaks.

JUNGFRAUJOCH EXCURSION

The Jungfraujoch excursion is a journey on a series of small trains, synchronized to provide you with a perfect prize—the *Jungfraujoch,* the highest train station in Europe sitting 300 ft below the summit of the Jungfrau. The most popular starting point for this outing are from any of the following train stations: Interlaken Ost, Lauterbrunnen, Grindelwald or Wengen. Although the trip can be taken in segments, or as a side trip from one of the starting points, most tourist prefer to squeeze the ultimate enjoyment from their outing by taking the complete circle trip from Interlaken.

The Jungfraujoch excursion is one of the highlights of Switzerland, and one that is mentioned in four of the following itineraries. Unless you have traveled the route, it sounds quite complicated. It is not. We explain, step by step, how this fabulous mountain adventure is maneuvered to give you the confidence to do it on your own. You can then tailor the trip to suit your special needs, beginning and ending at the town you have chosen to spend the night. The diagram below demonstrates how the pieces of this travel jigsaw puzzle fit together.

The complete circle trip begins at Interlaken Ost (Interlaken East) train station. However, you can also climb aboard at any of the stations, for example, Lauterbrunnen, Kleine Scheidegg, Wengen or Grindelwald and the fare adjusts accordingly.

Assuming Interlaken as your departure point, it is a 25-minute train ride to Lauterbrunnen. At Lauterbrunnen you change trains for the 45-minute ride up the mountain to Kleine Scheidegg (stopping en route to pick up passengers at the little town of Wengen). It is necessary to change trains again at Kleine Scheidegg for the final ascent of the Jungfraujoch excursion to the base of the Jungfrau. The last leg of your train adventure is an incredible 55 minutes in which the train creeps up the steep mountain and disappears into a 4-mile tunnel—reappearing at the Jungfraubahn, the highest rail station in Europe. It is possible to take an elevator even higher through the mountain to a vista point. From here, on a clear day, it seems you can see the whole of Switzerland. There is also an ice palace carved into the glacier, dog sled rides, shops, post offices, restaurants, etc. For this journey, be sure to take sturdy shoes for walking on the glacier, gloves, a warm sweater or jacket, sunscreen and sunglasses.

When you leave the Jungfraujoch it is necessary to retrace your journey to Kleine Scheidegg. For scenic variety, from Kleine Scheidegg, many prefer to return to Interlaken by a circle route. To do this board the train for Grindelwald where you connect with another train that takes you directly to Interlaken.

The Jungfraujoch is a very expensive excursion, but a once in a lifetime adventure, especially when the weather cooperates and blue skies color a magnificent backdrop for these majestic peaks. There are numerous daily train departures and tickets are available for purchase at hotels, camp sites, tourist offices, train stations or travel agencies.

Sightseeing Reference

Jungfraujoch Excursion

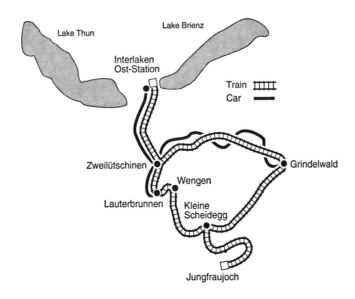

For early risers and those on a budget, there is an early morning trip that departs from Interlaken Ost at 6:35 am and arrives at the Jungfraujoch at 8:53 am, and offers a dramatic 40% discount on the cost of the passage between Kleine Scheidegg and the Jungfraujoch. The bargain excursion departs towns along the route at the following times: Lauterbrunnen–7:05 am, Wengen–7:24 am, Grindelwald–7:18 am or Kleine Scheidegg–8:02 am.

KANDERSTEG

Kandersteg is a hamlet nestled at the end of the Kandertal Valley. The road ends here so those who want to continue on across the mountain range for the short cut to the Rhone Valley must travel by train. (If you are driving, it is at Kandersteg that you need to put your car on the train for the piggy-back ride through the mountain.) But Kandersteg is far more than a train depot—this is a lovely little mountain village with a stupendous backdrop of majestic mountains, a paradise for mountain lovers.

KLEINE SCHEIDEGG

Kleine Scheidegg is the jumping off point for the final leg of the Jungfraujoch excursion (see previous description for details on this outing). Located above the timberline, the town is actually just a cluster of buildings hugging the wind swept plateau. The wide sweeping vistas of the rugged peaks of the Eiger, the Mönch and the Jungfrau are overpowering. If the day is sunny, it is great fun to sit out on the open terrace with a beer and a bratwurst while soaking in the splendor of the mountains and watching tourists set off on the tiny train that soon disappears as it tunnels into the glacier.

KLOSTERS

The town of Klosters backs up to the same mountains as Davos and actually the two ski areas interconnect like a giant spider web. Although much of Klosters is newly constructed in response to the need for tourist accommodation, the town has grown with a gracious style encompassing the Swiss chalet motif. There are many lovely shops and restaurants. The town is also very well situated for hiking in the summer or skiing in the winter. The train station is the terminus for a cable way that rises high above the village to the marvelous ski runs. Also popular in winter are tobogganing, cross country skiing, curling and ice skating. But my favorite time for Klosters is the summer when the fields are vibrant with wildflowers, while majestic mountains stand guard.

KÜSSNACHT am RIGI

Sometimes there is confusion about the location of Küssnacht am Rigi because there is a town with a very similar spelling Küsnacht—located on Lake Zürich. However, Küssnacht am Rigi is a little village on the northern tip of a small finger of Lake Lucerne. This is a charming town with some colorful medieval buildings. Since there is ferry service from Lucerne, Küssnacht am Rigi is popular for a day's excursion or an overnight stay. Küssnacht am Rigi is also associated with the folk hero, William Tell who, at a site near Küssnacht am Rigi, is said to have shot the Austrian governor with his mighty cross bow while leading his people in their battle to win freedom from Hapsburg rule.

LANGNAU im EMMENTAL

Langnau, a pretty town of well-preserved wooden houses with overhanging skirted roof lines, sits primly along the Ilfis River in the center of the lush Emmental Valley. The delicious Emmental cheese (generically referred to throughout the world as "Swiss" cheese) is produced in the valley and exported from Langnau.

LUCERNE

There is not a wealth of tourist attractions in Lucerne—the attraction is the city itself. Nor will you feel you have discovered Lucerne. Frankly, it is brimming with tourists. However, you certainly understand the attraction when you wander the charming little streets filled with colorful shops or stroll the river promenade stopping for a snack in one of the quaint cafes set out on the banks of the Reuss River. It is enjoyable to cross the multitude of bridges that cross back and forth from one side of the river to the other and meander along the shore of Lake Lucerne. Another excursion is to board one of the steamers for a lazy journey around the lake. Yes, tourists have found Lucerne, but it is so lovely, I do not think you will mind sharing it with others.

Kappellbrücke, Lucerne

Also in Lucerne is the Museum of Transport and Communications, one of Switzerland's finest museums. This display follows the development of transportation and communication up to the exploration of space. Children are especially enthralled with this wonderful museum.

Recommended for a sunny day, is an outing from Lucerne to the highest mountain peak in the area, Mount Pilatus. The most enjoyable route for this excursion is to take the lake steamer to the town of Alpnachstad and then the electric cog railway up to the top of the mountain. From the rail terminal it is only about a 10-minute walk to the peak of the mountain where there is a spectacular panorama.

Another excursion from Lucerne is to the town of Einsiedeln to see the home of the famous Black Madonna. The monastery of Einsiedeln was founded by Meinrad, a Benedictine monk, who built a small chapel for the Black Madonna (a statue of the Virgin Mary) that had been given to him by Zürich priests. Meinrad was later murdered by some men who mistakenly thought he had hidden treasures. Later the Monastery of Einsiedeln was built over Meinrad's grave and another chapel was erected to house the Black Madonna. This site has become a pilgrimage, not only for Catholics, but for tourists who are attracted to the Einsiedeln Abbey, an excellent example of Baroque architecture.

LUGANO

Lugano is an appealing medieval town hugging the northern shore of Lake Lugano. While in Lugano, there are several "musts." First, you will love exploring the old city. This is best done by walking, since many of the streets are closed to cars. Be sure to visit the Cathedral of St Lawrence (San Lorenzo) that is famous for its elegant Renaissance facade and lovely fresco decoration. Another "must" for Lugano is to take advantage of the steamers that ply the lake from its dock. You can stretch your boat ride out to an all-day excursion or squeeze it into a couple of hours. My recommendation would be to go to Morcote a charming little village rising from the shores of the lake. If possible, allow time enough in Morcote to have lunch at the Carina-Carlton Hotel's cheerful cafe that juts out over the water. If you feel industrious, you can climb up the steep back alleys which will bring you to the Church of Santa Maria del Sasso which contains some outstanding 16th-century frescos. Also in Morcote there is a delightful private park where you will find beautiful plants artistically displayed in gardens overlooking the lake. The park is only a few minutes' walk from the Hotel Carina-Carlton.

Another fun boat trip from Lugano is to Gandria, another village clinging to the lakeside filled with flowers and surrounded by vineyards. Both Gandria and Morcote are photographers' dreams.

MÜRREN

Mürren is a village perched on a tiny ledge high above the Lauterbrunnen Valley. A startlingly steep granite wall drops straight down from the town to the valley. The only access is by cable car or funicular (or, of course, by foot). Across the valley, the Jungfrau towers into the sky, incredibly close, incredibly powerful. The Jungfrau circle of towns (Grindelwald, Wengen and Kleine Scheidegg) is on the opposite side of the valley. (See the preceding description of the Jungfraujoch excursion.)

MURTEN

Murten is a sensational walled medieval village nestled on the banks of Lake Murten—only a short distance from Bern or Neuchâtel. You enter Murten through a gate in the medieval wall that completely surrounds this fairytale village with flower boxes everywhere and brightly painted fountains accenting tiny squares. The entire effect is one of festivity. Before exploring the town you might want first to climb to the ramparts and walk the walls for a bird's eye view of what you are going to see. Murten is like an outdoor museum. Strolling through the town you can study many of the 15th-century buildings and the walls that date from the 12th Century. There is a castle at the western end of town built by Peter of Savoy in the 13th Century. As you walk through the village watch for the Town Hall, the French Church, the German Church, the Bern Gate (with one of the oldest clock towers in Switzerland) and the Historical Museum that displays weapons, banners and uniforms from the Burgundian battles.

MÜSTAIR

Müstair is a simple village at the eastern end of the Müstair Valley, just before the Austrian border. This is a pretty little village of thick-walled houses dating back to the 13th Century. Very few people speak English here——the ambiance is one of an authentic old Swiss town, untouched by commercialism.

REGENSBERG

Regensberg is very, very special. Here, only a few miles north of Zürich, and about 20 minutes from the Zürich Airport, is a perfectly preserved medieval village icing the knoll laced with vineyards. In Regensberg there is one of the most exquisite little inns in Switzerland, the Rote Rose, owned by Christa Schäfer, daughter of Lotte Günthart, one of the foremost rose artists in the world. Regensberg is perfect for your arrival into Switzerland or a wonderful choice for few days to relax before heading home.

SACHSELN

Sachseln, a small town on the road from Lucerne to Interlaken, has great religious significance for Catholics who come in great numbers to pray to St Nicholas of Flüe, a peasant who, in the 15th Century, is credited with saving the confederacy. St Nicholas, the father of 10 children, was a deeply religious man who, in his 50's, felt the irresistible call to live the life of solitude (with 10 children, it is understandable). He went up into the hills behind Sachseln where he spent his life in meditation. Because of his reputation as a man of inspired wisdom, leaders came to him for advice. He is credited with the compromise in 1481 of peace between the cantons when conflict had seemed inevitable.

ST MORITZ

Known to the jet-set elite throughout the world as *the* place to be seen in the ski season, St Moritz is also popular as a summer resort. The town backs right up to the mountain so it is just a short walk to the funicular to go skiing. From its terraced position on the side of the hill, St Moritz looks down to a pretty lake that is rimmed by trees. In town, the streets are lined with chic boutiques selling exquisite merchandise. In the center of this shopping paradise is the famous Palace Hotel, very lovely, very expensive. If you want to rub elbows with the rich and famous, this is where you should be. However, in the hotel description section of this guide you find our recommendations of some very pleasant, less-expensive hotels. St Moritz has not grown with the same purity of architecture as some other ski areas such as Gstaad and Zermatt, but it is much less "concrete high-rise" than its sister ski area, Davos.

SANTA MARIA

Santa Maria is a small hamlet intersected by the road that travels through the beautiful Müstair Valley. There are many lovely old Grisons-style buildings in the town and a very attractive church. Nearby is the Swiss National Park that is an oasis for wildlife and vegetation. The park is very popular with Swiss families who come here to hike.

SCHAFFHAUSEN

Schaffhausen is a quaint medieval city that grew up along the banks of the Rhein just above the point where the river plummets to a lower level, forming the Rheinfall, one of Europe's most spectacular waterfalls. Boats cannot, of course, navigate the rushing waters, and in days-gone-by, their cargo was carried around the falls. Schaffhausen grew up to accommodate this trader traffic. Within Schaffhausen there are many characterful houses, real architectural gems—many with oriel windows adding colorful detail. There are also several fountains, old towers, and of course, a castle perched on the hill above the town. While in Schaffhausen you will want to make the very short excursion to see the Rheinfall. Sightseeing boats take you to the base of the falls.

SILS-BASELGIA and SILS-MARIA and SILVAPLANA

Approximately 10 kilometers south of the famous resort of St Moritz are the "sister" villages of Sils-Baselgia and Sils-Maria that are located on a thread of land connecting the two tiny lakes of Silvaplana and Silser.

Sightseeing Reference

The Sils area is a paradise for cross country skiing in the winter and hiking, boating, fishing, sail surfing and swimming in the summer.

Silvaplana, located about 6 kilometers south of St Moritz, is much less commercial than its next door neighbor, but is still a bustling summer and winter resort.

SOGLIO

The mountain setting of the little town of Soglio is one of the most dramatically beautiful in all of Switzerland. Mr Isler, who for many years managed the Swiss National Tourist Office in San Francisco, told us that a travel writer had seen photographs of Soglio and just couldn't believe they were real so went himself to confirm that this perfect village existed. Frankly, this is how we also found Soglio; we had seen a drawing in a travel guide and immediately we were drawn there. Soglio is perched on a ledge high above the beautiful Bregaglia Valley. The town is tiny—no more than a few narrow alley-like streets lined with wonderful old houses. The church is perfect, setting off the picture book village with its high spire soaring into the sky. The village looks across the valley to some of the most impressive mountain peaks in Switzerland. Soglio is not only a picturesque stopover, but in addition it is a wonderful center for walking. There are beautiful paths leading out from Soglio that run along the ledge of the mountain. Chestnut trees line some of the beautiful trails and although you are high above the valley the walking is easy.

SOLOTHURN

The town of Solothurn, one of the oldest Roman settlements in Switzerland, is a completely walled medieval city built along the shore of the River Aare. A modern industrial city has grown up around Solothurn, but once you cross through the gate, like magic you are transported back hundreds of years. This pretty medieval town has remained unspoiled. You are greeted by colorfully painted fountains, charming little squares, beautifully preserved buildings, the famous St Ursen Cathedral, wrought iron signs and houses with brightly painted shutters.

STEIN am RHEIN

The walled town of Stein am Rhein, built along the banks of the Rhein River, is one of the most photogenic towns in Switzerland. After entering the main gates of the little town, you find yourself in a fairytale town with each building almost totally covered with fanciful paintings. The town is very small so it will not take long to explore, but it is certainly worth a visit. If you are taking a ferry along the river, Stein am Rhein makes a super stopover for lunch or a fun place to spend the night after the tour buses depart.

VERBIER

Verbier has a spectacular setting on a high mountain plateau overlooking the valley to the glorious Mont Blanc mountain range. Although the village of Verbier has the air of a newly created modern mountain town, there are still many of the older wooden chalets around to remind you that before the skiers came, it was a simple Valais village.

WENGEN

Part of the charm of Wengen is that it can be reached only by train. You leave your car in the parking lot at the Lauterbrunnen station and take the train for the spectacular 20-minute ride up the mountain. As the train pulls up the steep incline you catch glimpses through the lacy trees of the magnificent valley below. When you reach Wengen you will be entranced: it has one of the most glorious sites in the world—high on a mountain plateau overlooking the breathtaking Lauterbrunnen Valley: a valley enclosed with walls of granite that are laced with cascading waterfalls. A backdrop for the total picture is the awe-inspiring Jungfrau massif with its three famous peaks, the Jungfrau, the Mönch and the Eiger. This is a center for outdoor enthusiasts and sportsmen. From all over the world tourists come to soak up spectacular alpine beauty. Summer is my favorite time of year in Wengen when the marvelous walking paths beckon. Along these trails there are new vistas at every turn, each more beautiful than the last. If walking is too gentle for your spirit, there are climbs you can take into the Bernese Oberland. If you are going to do some serious climbing you should hire a local guide to accompany you. In addition to being a mecca for the mountain enthusiast, Wengen also is an excellent base for the excursion to the Jungfrau. Please refer to the Jungfraujoch excursion.

ZERMATT

Cars are not allowed in Zermatt. However, this is no problem as there are car parks as you approach the town. Leave your car at Täsch, and from there it is only a few minutes' train ride on to Zermatt. As you arrive at the station you will notice many horse drawn carriages awaiting your train. In winter, these become horse-drawn sleighs. In the past few years (unfortunately) little electric golf-type carts have been gradually replacing many of the horse drawn carriages. Zermatt is not the sleepy little mountain village of yesterday. It is difficult to uncover the remnants of the "Old Zermatt"—the weathered wooden chalets weighted beneath heavy slate roofs, but they are still there hidden on little side alleys and dotted in the mountain meadows.

As you wander around Zermatt you are bombarded with the effects of the growth of tourism: shopping arcades stretching out behind old store fronts, hotels expanding, new condominiums springing up in the meadows, tourists packing the streets. I know this sounds awful, but it isn't. Zermatt is still one of our favorite places in Switzerland, for some things never change. The Matterhorn, rising in majestic splendor as a backdrop to the village, is still one of the most dramatic sights in the world. And, as you leave the center of Zermatt, within a few minutes you are again in the "Zermatt of Old" with gigantic mountain peaks piercing the sky. It is so beautiful that it is frustrating—each path is beckoning "try me." You want to go in every direction at once.

The Matterhorn, Zermatt

The great influx of tourists definitely has advantages too: fun little shops filled with tempting wares line the streets; cozy restaurants make each meal decision a dilemma; new hotels have opened giving the traveler a great selection of accommodation. The pride of making Zermatt worthy of its reputation has stimulated competition among the hoteliers and shopkeepers—each appears to strive to make his flower box more gorgeous than his neighbor's, resulting in a profusion of color.

The popularity of Zermatt has also merited a fascinating network of trails lacing the mountains used in summer for walking and in winter for skiing. A small train runs up to the Gornergrat Station that is located on a rocky ridge overlooking the town of Zermatt and beyond to the Matterhorn. There are also cable cars and chairlifts rising like a spider web around Zermatt. There is an incredible choice for the tourist—when hiking, it is possible to either choose beautifully marked trails drifting out from the village core, or take one of the chair lifts or trams or train up the mountain, from which point you can walk all or part way down. The number of tourists also justifies numerous small cafes scattered along the trails. It is truly a "gentleman's" way to hike when you can stop along the route at a little cafe for a glass of wine or cup of coffee.

Zermatt is truly the Switzerland of our childhood books and a trip to Switzerland is never quite complete without a visit to see the Matterhorn. Note: If the Matterhorn lures you, but the idea of too much hustle and bustle sounds daunting, you can have the best of all worlds by taking the tram up the mountain to the Riffelalp, a sunny high meadow overlooking Zermatt where there the Seiler Hotel Riffelalp looks straight across the valley at the Matterhorn.

ZUG

About mid-way between Zürich and Lucerne, facing Lake Zug, is one of Switzerland's oldest sites, the charming town of Zug. The medieval section that remains hugs the water's edge where the boats come in to dock. From the lake the streets web back through the colorful old gabled houses with over-hanging balconies that date back to the Middle Ages. However, excavations have shown that Zug is actually much older—it dates as far back as the Neolithic era.

ZÜRICH

In Zürich there is much to see and do. On a warm day we suggest taking an excursion on one of the steamers that ply the lovely Lake Zürich. There is a schedule posted at each of the piers stating where the boats go and when they depart. During the summer there is frequent service and a wide selection to suit your mood and your time frame.

Zürich is also a great city for just meandering through the medieval section with its maze of tiny twisting streets, colorful squares, charming little shops and tempting cafes. It is fun to walk down the promenade by the Limmat River to the lake front and cross over the Quailbrücke (bridge) to return by the opposite bank. When weary, cross back over one of the bridges that span the river to complete your circle.

For those of you who like museums, the Swiss National Museum has a display depicting Swiss civilization from prehistoric times to modern day. Zürich's Fine Arts Museum is well worth a visit. Of special interest here are some of the paintings of Ferdinand Hodler, one of the finest Swiss artists of the early 20th Century. Also on display are some of the paintings of a favorite Swiss artist, Anker, whose delightful paintings capture the warmth of family and home with simplicity and humor.

For cathedral buffs is the impressive Grossmünster whose construction dates back to the 11th Century. This very impressive cathedral dominates Zürich with its two-domed towers. It was built on a site originally occupied by a church built by Charlemagne.

Sightseeing Reference

Switzerland by Train, Boat & Bus

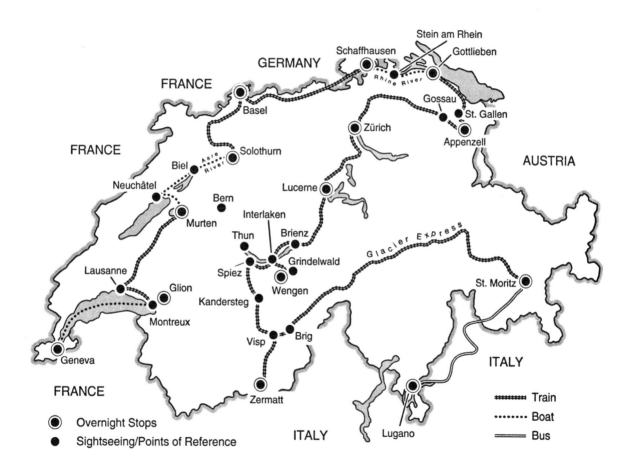

Switzerland by Train, Boat & Bus

Of all the itineraries in the guide, this is my favorite. It offers a variety of ways to travel from major cities to tiny hamlets via high mountain passes, lush valleys, lakes and rivers—all without the use of a car. This is a long itinerary. Except for a few of you with the luxury of boundless time to spend, it should not be attempted in one trip. It would take too long—unless you rush from town to town, which you must not do. Therefore, read through the suggested routing carefully and choose the segment that appeals most to you. Then go slowly. Savor each destination. Take time to enjoy the journey from place to place. Your transportation becomes a major part of your holiday. Travel at a leisurely pace. Relax and enjoy the incomparable beauty of Switzerland by train, boat and bus.

The potential of this itinerary was realized while staying in Gottlieben, a town on the River Rhein. Noticing the ferry in front of the Hotel Krone departing to Schaffhausen, I wished I could just pick up my suitcase, climb on board and disembark a few hours later in front of another of my favorite hotels, the Rheinhotel Fischerzunft in Schaffhausen. How much more enjoyable to savor the lovely Rhein, passing along the way pretty little towns such as Stein am Rhein, rather than passing large trucks on a busy highway. The idea for this itinerary welled stronger a few days later when in Solothurn, I was surprised to notice a boat connection to Murten, one of my favorite walled towns in Europe. How delightful, I thought, to journey through the countryside via canals and lakes instead of by car. So I returned home eager to see if the various travel segments by land and water could be coordinated. Knowing how remarkably efficient the Swiss transportation network is, I should never have doubted the feasibility of this itinerary. However, you will need to plan carefully as some of the ferries only operate from late spring to early autumn.

There are a few prerequisites to this style of travel. First, it is absolutely a must that you travel very lightly. If you feel you can't pack everything you need into one small suitcase, forget this itinerary. Cumbersome bags will be an aggravation, frustration and burden when trying to make quick connections between trains or boats, and certainly diminish some of the joy of travel. Second, it is *very* important that you buy one of the Swiss rail passes that are described in the introduction. I cannot overly stress the marvelous, carefree, total holiday feeling that comes from just hopping on and off trains, boats and buses without any hassle of buying tickets. (There are a few instances such as the Glacier Express where reservations must be pre-booked, but these are rare.) Third, buy the *Official Timetable*. This guide, published one a year, contains a wealth of information. It outlines every timetable within Switzerland for boats, trains, buses and even funiculars and cable cars. There are other train guides you can purchase, such as

"Cooks" guide, but this official guide is the only one we found that shows access by public transportation to every place in Switzerland—no matter how tiny or how isolated. It is unbelievably thorough. Once you get accustomed to using it, it will become your bible. You can purchase the *Official Timetable* through agencies whose address and phone contacts are given on page 22 of the introduction. If you prefer to wait until you arrive in Switzerland, the Official Timetable can also be purchased at the train stations.

IMPORTANT NOTE: In this itinerary, suggested times are given for the trains, boats and buses. These schedules are to be used as a guideline only. You must check each of the schedules locally to verify times of arrival and departure. Some trains, boats and buses operate only on certain days of the week or during certain seasons of the year. Also, departure times can change. I debated whether or not to include the times and schedules, but decided that it was important to provide you with an approximate guideline so that you could basically see how the itinerary works and how it accommodates your own travel plans. However, it is terribly important to verify the schedules.

ORIGINATING CITY   GENEVA

Geneva, the first city on this itinerary, is a delightful starting point for a Swiss vacation. Geneva is a lovely blend of the old and new—the medieval portion of the city rising on the hillside on the left bank of the Rhone and the newer city stretching out with peaceful promenades on the right bank of the river. As you stroll the lake front of this international city you will hear languages from all over the world and see costumes of many nations. In the spring Geneva becomes a small Holland with glorious tulips blooming in every little park. The shopping in Geneva is wonderful—antique shops tempt the purse in the old section and the most sophisticated shoppers can find their haven in the beautiful shops and arcades in the newer section.

DESTINATION I   GLION

The journey from Geneva to Glion is as much a sightseeing excursion as a means of transportation. This is a glorious outing taking you from the western end of Lake Geneva to the eastern tip, stopping briefly in Vevey and Montreux before arriving at Territet.

    10:30 am depart Geneva (Jardin Anglais pier) by boat
    3:37 pm arrive Territet

Upon arrival in **Territet**, go straight ahead from the pier, following signs for the funicular that climbs up the hill to Glion. (It is about a two-minute walk from where the boat docks.) The funicular runs every fifteen minutes on the quarter hour, so you will not have long to wait. After a steep, short journey through the forest, you "land" at the Glion station and can see the Hotel Victoria, a French-like chateau with mansard roof, on a knoll above and to the right of the station. It is a quick walk to the hotel. (If you have luggage, you can call the hotel and a porter will whisk down to assist you.)

Glion, a suburb of Montreux located high above the city, has spectacular views which is probably why there are so many elegant villas tucked in the trees overlooking the lake. One of these, the **Hotel Victoria**, is set in its own beautiful gardens with a sweeping panorama of Lake Geneva. Staying there you will feel like royalty. Almost all of the guest rooms have been recently renovated and are beautifully decorated, each with its own personality.

Castle of Chillon, Lake Geneva

But no matter how lovely the furnishings, nothing can compete with the magnificence of the view—for a memorable stay, request a room with a balcony overlooking Lake Geneva, the city of Montreux and the distant Castle of Chillon off its shore. You might never want to wander from the front of the hotel with its lovely shade trees, velvety lawn and perfectly tended beds of flowers. Here you can sit quietly on one of the strategically placed chairs and soak in the beauty of Lake Geneva whose deep blue waters are enhanced by the magnificence of the majestic mountains that frame her southern shoreline.

DESTINATION II   MURTEN

Leaving Glion, your next destination is Murten. It is necessary to change trains several times, but the total travel time is short and the journey is beautiful.

    9:43 am depart Glion by train
    9:55 am arrive Montreux

    10:07 am depart Montreux by train
    10:29 am arrive Lausanne

    11:14 am depart Lausanne by train
    12:21 pm arrive Payerne

    12:40 pm depart Payerne by train
     1:01 pm arrive Murten

In **Murten**, we have three favorite hotels, **Le Vieux Manoir au Lac**, a charming country manor located about a half a mile south of town on the lake at **Meyriez**, the **Hotel Schiff** also located on the water's edge but just outside the gates of the walled city, or in the heart of town, **Hotel Weisses Kreuz**. Whichever you select will make a good base for exploring the quaint town of Murten. As you enter through the thick walls you are magically transported back through the years to find yourself in one of the most romantic medieval villages in Switzerland. Murten is like a living museum—as you meander through the little streets there are marvelous examples of medieval buildings, clock towers, ramparts, brightly painted fountains and quaint little squares.

DESTINATION III   SOLOTHURN

Today's trip from Murten to Solothurn is similar to a treasure hunt as you weave your way by boat through the scenic lakes, canals and rivers of the lovely Swiss countryside.

Your adventure begins in the tiny walled village of Murten from where you take the ferry to Biel to board the boat for the final leg of your journey on the Aare River to the walled city of Solothurn.

I stressed on the previous itineraries that time schedules *must* be carefully checked. Of all the destinations, this one is the most important because the boats basically operate only in the summer and *not on Mondays*. However, if the boats do not operate to suit your time frame, it is always possible to make the journey from Murten to Solothurn by train. Another possibility, if you want to see the town of Neuchâtel, you can make this a luncheon stop en route to Biel if you leave Murten on an earlier boat.

    11:30 am depart Murten by boat
    12:55 pm arrive Neuchâtel

    2:10 pm depart Neuchâtel by boat
    4:35 pm arrive Biel/Bienne

    4:45 pm depart Biel/Bienne by boat
    7:10 pm arrive Solothurn

Although it is not far from **Solothurn's** boat depot to your hotel, it will be a bit far to walk with luggage. If you ask in advance and advise them what time your boat is arriving, the Hotel Krone will send a taxi to the pier. Or, when you dock, you can call for a cab. How very appropriate when in the ancient town of Solothurn to stay in an old inn that perpetuates the mood of antiquity. The location of the **Hotel Krone** is perfect and so easy to find—facing a little square opposite the impressive **St Ursen Cathedral**.

Solothurn is much larger than Murten, but also a marvelously preserved, completely walled medieval city located on the Aare River. So "perfect" that it was awarded the coveted Henry Louis-Wakker prize for excellence in renovation. It is fascinating to walk through this ancient town so full of the colorful atmosphere of bygone years.

DESTINATION IV   BASEL

Your train journey today is short.

    10:15 am   depart Solothurn by train
    10:45 am   arrive Moutier

    10:49 am   depart Moutier by train
    11:37 am   arrive Basel

There is such a famous hotel in **Basel** that it would be a shame to stay anywhere else. The **Hotel Drei Konige** is one of the oldest inns in Switzerland, dating from 1026. The hotel is also very historical, having been the site of the famous meeting among three kings (Conrad II, Henry III, and Rudolf II) who drew up the treaty for the transference of territories that are now western Switzerland and southern France. This historical meeting led to the name of the hotel *Drei Konige* that means Three Kings.

The location of the Hotel Drei Konige on the **Rhein River** is terrific—not only can you enjoy watching the ever-changing drama of the river traffic passing by the hotel, but you are also only steps from the center of Basel. Although Basel is a large city, its heart is still a fun-filled medieval town of tiny squares, gay fountains, marvelously preserved old buildings, beautiful cathedrals, bridges and many interesting museums.

DESTINATION V   SCHAFFHAUSEN

It is a simple and quick train ride from Basel to Schaffhausen:

    2:16 pm   depart Basel, Badischer Bahnhof by train
    3:27 pm   arrive Schaffhausen

Munot Fortress at Schaffhausen on the Rhein

Schaffhausen, on the banks of the Rhein, is one of Switzerland's best preserved medieval towns with its many river jetties overshadowed by the circular keep of **Munot Fortress**. Schaffhausen is a maze of alleys with clock towers, statues and painted houses. Its name originates from the "ship houses" where cargo was stored when ships had to be unloaded for their goods to be carried past the falls and rapids. We recommend a hotel in Schaffhausen that is so delightful that the hotel would almost be worthy of a visit even if the town itself were not an attraction. The **Rheinhotel Fischerzunft** has an absolutely perfect location directly on the promenade on the banks of the Rhein.

Just west of Schaffhausen is the famous **Rheinfall** (Rhine Falls) that made it necessary for merchants to unload their river cargo and carry it around the falls before continuing their journey upstream. (The town of Schaffhausen grew up to service this river commerce.) The falls are just a short drive from town. Whether you arrange for a car rental or taxi, be sure to go—this waterfall is the most dramatic in Europe. You can view the falls from the shore or you can take a tour on a little boat that maneuvers right up under the giant cascade of water.

DESTINATION VI   GOTTLIEBEN

This journey along the Rhein is wonderful. It combines a splendid boat ride through quaint river villages with the practical aspect of traveling between two delightful hotels. You can select a direct ferry that takes about four hours or you can get off the ferry in the charming village of **Stein am Rhein** to have lunch before boarding the ferry again for the completion of your journey to Gottlieben.

    9:15 am depart Schaffhausen by boat
    11:10 am arrive Stein am Rhein

A luncheon stop is suggested in the picturesque medieval walled village of Stein am Rhein. Settle under an umbrella at one of the riverside restaurants, or park on a bench with a refreshing *apfelsaft, bratwurst und brot* and enjoy the continual passage of boats that ply the river. Stein am Rhein is a charming town to explore on foot. Its streets wind up from the river to the heart of the old town. *Hauptstrasse* and the Town Hall Square are extremely picturesque with their flower-decked fountains and oriel windowed houses.

    3:40 pm depart Stein am Rhein by boat
    5:40 pm arrive Gottlieben

When you arrive at **Gottlieben** your hotel is conveniently located just a few steps from the pier. The **Hotel Krone** offers comfortable accommodation, a lovely indoor restaurant and a cafe on the banks of the river for dining outside when the days are warm.

DESTINATION VII   APPENZELL

It is necessary to take a ferry plus several trains between Gottlieben and Appenzell. It sounds complicated, but the Swiss in their predictable fashion have tailored the connections to work as if a jigsaw puzzle—the connections fit together perfectly.

11:40 am depart Gottlieben by boat
12:15 pm arrive Kreuzlingen

12:57 pm depart Kreuzlingen by train
1:23 pm arrive Romanshorn

1:32 pm depart Romanshorn by train
1:57 pm arrive St Gallen

2:45 pm depart St Gallen by train
3:34 pm arrive Appenzell

In Appenzell, the decoratively painted **Hotel Säntis** and the **Hotel Appenzell** are located on a small square in the center of town. The village of Appenzell, a popular tourist destination because of its colorfully painted houses, is situated in a beautiful dairy farm area of Switzerland with soft rolling green hills dotted with farmhouses that are a combination of home and barn.

Hotel Appenzell, Appenzell

You can take a train from Appenzell to Zürich by making a connection in Gosseau, but if the day is pleasant, it is more fun to combine your journey into a sightseeing excursion. This trip will include the great beauty of the verdant Appenzell rolling green hills, the charm of the medieval village of Rapperswil, and the fun of arriving in the city of Zürich by steamer.

    10:01 am depart Appenzell by train
    10:35 am arrive Herisau

    10:53 am depart Herisau by train
    11:39 am arrive Rapperswil

You can make a direct ferry connection from Herisau to Zürich, but a suggestion would be to lunch in the medieval town of **Rapperswil**. If time allows, visit the museum in the 13th-century massive **Rapperswil Castle** perched on a knoll just above the center of the town. This museum contains, among other artifacts, a fascinating collection of Polish treasures brought to Switzerland for protection during World War II.

    1:45 pm depart Rapperswil by boat
    3:40 pm arrive Zürich

When you arrive in **Zürich**, it is about a ten-minute taxi ride to the **Hotel Tiefenau**, a cozy hotel tucked in a small side street just a few minutes' walk from the heart of Zürich. The owners, Erica and Beat Blumer, are perfect hosts and the ambiance of their hotel is that of a private home. So, if you want to be away from the bustle of the center of Zürich and avoid the slick commercialism of some of Zürich's famous hotels, the Hotel Tiefenau makes an excellent choice—but you need to book far in advance for this little charmer.

Although very popular with travelers from around the world, Zürich does not have the feeling of a tourist center. Instead, as you walk the streets you feel the bustle of a "real" city. Of course there are tourists, but shopping next to you in the little boutique will be the local housewife, hurrying down the promenade are businessmen on their way to work, and a couple from Zürich will probably be sitting next to you at a sidewalk cafe. Nevertheless, there is a carnival atmosphere to Zürich; a gaiety to the city. From both sides of the river the old section of Zürich radiates out on little twisting streets like a cobweb. Along the lake front are parks and gardens. From the piers there is a fascinating variety of boat excursions to little villages around the lake. Being a large city, there is an excellent selection of museums to explore.

DESTINATION IX   LUCERNE

Lucerne

A constant "commuter" service exists between Zürich and **Lucerne** taking approximately an hour. The trains usually leave a few minutes before each hour. When you arrive in Lucerne it is only a few minutes' taxi ride to one of our favorite Swiss hotels, the

Wilden Mann. The location of the Wilden Mann Hotel is fabulous—on Bahnhofstrasse, in the middle of the old section of Lucerne within easy walking distance of all points of interest. The hotel embodies all that is best about Swiss hotels—the owner present to oversee every detail of management, excellent service from the staff, attractively decorated bedrooms, fine antiques liberally used in the public rooms, and a charming restaurant and intimate *stubli*.

Lucerne is a wonderful town for lingering: just strolling through the quaint streets and enjoying a snack in one of the small cafes overlooking the river can easily fill an afternoon. There are always many tourists—Lucerne's enchantment is no secret. Everyone seems happy. There is a holiday air to the city.

DESTINATION X   WENGEN

A frequent direct train service runs from Lucerne to Interlaken, usually about every two hours. From there it is a beautiful short ride to Wengen.

> 1:24 pm depart Lucerne by train
> 3:16 pm arrive Interlaken Ost station
>
> 3:32 pm depart Interlaken Ost station by train
> 3:54 pm arrive Lauterbrunnen
>
> 4:10 pm depart Lauterbrunnen by train
> 4:24 pm arrive Wengen

I wish for you a clear day for this segment of your journey, truly one of spectacular beauty. First the train heads south from Lucerne, winding through gentle green valleys dotted with pretty farmhouses—a scene of rural beauty. From Interlaken, the train heads south to **Lauterbrunnen** where you change to a smaller train that chugs up a steep incline to **Wengen**, an idyllic small town clinging to a shelf perched high above the

Hotel Regina, Wengen

Lauterbrunnen Valley. Without a doubt, this is one of the most breathtaking settings in the world. As an added joy, there are no cars allowed in town—no pollution, no noise.

Our favorites places to stay in Wengen are the **Alpenrose**, the town's first hotel, and the **Hotel Regina**, an imposing Victorian building perched on a knoll overlooking the town. Neither the Alpenrose nor the Regina are pretentious, but each offers the warmth of family-owned establishments, and has memorable views of the three spectacular mountains: the Eiger, the Mönch and the Jungfrau.

Wengen is a perfect starting point for the unforgettable **Jungfraujoch Excursion**—one you must not miss. This circular train trip, that winds its way through the meadows and then twists its way to the base of the Jungfrau, is one of the most dramatic rides in Switzerland.

From Wengen, it is easy to return to Interlaken, where just steps from the Ost station, you can climb aboard one of the ferry boats that makes its way along the river and on to Lake Brienz. A trip on this ferry with lunch at one of the small villages is highly recommended.

The **Open Air Museum Of Ballenberg** is an interesting sightseeing excursion from Wengen. Visiting Ballenberg is a wonderful way to learn about the various architectural styles and the crafts of Switzerland. This development reminds me of Rockefeller's preservation of the town of Williamsburg, reconstructing the style of living, and crafts of the American heritage. Ballenberg is located in an enormous park-like setting in a meadow above Lake Brienz. Houses, grouped according to region, have been brought to the park to show the most important forms of housing and settlement. Old ways of living and working and crafts are demonstrated and the interiors of the houses offer a glimpse into yesterday with their antique furnishings. To reach Ballenberg from Interlaken take the boat or train to Brienz, and from there take the bus to the park.

DESTINATION XI   ZERMATT

Your journey today will take you through some of the most spectacular mountain vistas in the world. This is an ideal trip by train since the section from **Spiez** to **Brig** takes the "short cut" through the **Lotschberg Tunnel** that is restricted to train traffic. The final leg of your journey must be by train, cars are not allowed into Zermatt.

    8:59 am depart Wengen by train
    9:15 am arrive Lauterbrunnen

    9:35 am depart Lauterbrunnen by train
    9:57 am arrive Interlaken Ost

    10:39 am depart Interlaken Ost by train
    10:59 am arrive Spiez

    11:54 am depart Spiez by train
    12:59 am arrive Brig

    1:23 pm depart Brig by train
    3:45 pm arrive Zermatt

There are no cars in **Zermatt**. However, when you arrive at the station you will see waiting in the adjacent square, electric carts, or horses and buggies, sent from most of the hotels, waiting to pick up their guests. Zermatt has a rich selection of places to stay. In the heart of town, we recommend several hotels—each has its own personality, each is quite delightful in its own way. Look in the hotel section to see which place seems to suit you best. If you want to be "eye to eye" with the Matterhorn, one of our favorite places to stay is the **Hotel Riffelalp**, located on a mountain shelf high above Zermatt. If this is your choice, you will have one more leg to your journey. To reach Riffelalp it is necessary to take a 20 minute cog-wheel tram from Zermatt to Riffelalp Station.

The picturesque town of Zermatt has grown from the once tiny farm community to a booming tourist destination. Condominiums dot the hillsides and new hotels are constantly under construction. However, there are strict building codes, and fortunately the quaint nature of the town survives, watched over by the towering, oh-so-dramatic Matterhorn. Best of all, Zermatt offers unparalleled walking and hiking possibilities. I'm sure you could stay a month exploring new paths each day.

DESTINATION XII   ST MORITZ

Your trip between Zermatt and St Moritz is truly a dream come true for any train buff. It used to be that you had to hip-hop across Switzerland changing trains at various stations to travel between these two famous mountain towns, but a few years ago an enterprising Swiss entrepreneur connected the two towns by a private railroad, the enchanting **Glacier Express**. You board the little red train in the morning in Zermatt and pull into St Moritz station eight hours later. It is necessary to make reservations in advance for the Glacier Express. You can do so in the United States through Rail Europe (tel: 800 438-7245 or 303 443-5100, fax: 800 432-1329 or 303 444-4587). The Glacier Express chugs over some of the highest alpine passes in Switzerland, crosses meadows, tunnels through mountains, traverses glaciers and weaves through canyons, all while you relax at your picture window. There is even more to the adventure if you plan ahead and make a luncheon reservation at the same time you book the train. If so, you have the pleasure of dining in an old-fashioned dining car brimming with nostalgia—wood paneled walls, bronze fixtures, tables set with crisp linens and fresh flowers on the tables. The train is expensive, but the journey is a "train trip of a lifetime."

    10:10 am depart Zermatt via the Glacier Express
    5:58 pm arrive St Moritz

Upon arrival in **St Moritz**, there are many hotel possibilities. Look in the hotel section for the descriptions of our favorites: the **Hotel Eden**, the **Hotel Languard**, and the **Landgasthof Meierei**.

If you prefer a quiet location, the Landgasthof Meierei is located a bit out of town, with a pretty setting on the lake with a view back to St Moritz. The Eden and the Languard are located in the center of town, more convenient to the train station and close to the boutiques.

DESTINATION XIII   LUGANO

The Swiss offer an intriguing list of possibilities for integrated train and bus travel, giving some of the more popular routes a special name. One of these is called the **Palm Express** that makes a one day scenic journey from St Moritz to Lugano by bus, then on to Zermatt by train. For this itinerary, we have snatched the scenic bus section from St

Moritz to Lugano. Note: Reservations are mandatory for the Palm Express. You can make these through your travel agent before leaving home, or else by calling the Palm Express office in Lugano: tel: (091) 21 95 20 or fax: (091) 23 69 39 [new contact as of October 1995: tel: (091) 921 95 20, fax: (091) 923 69 39], or in St Moritz: tel: (082) 3 30 72, fax: (082) 2 67 90, [new contact as of April 1996: tel: (081) 833 30 72, fax: (081) 833 61 21].

8:10 am depart St Moritz train station by bus
12:20 pm arrive Lugano train station

The bus heads south from St Moritz passing by the pretty little Silvaplana and Silser lakes, then over the twisting **Malojapass** and drops down to the beautiful **Bregaglia Valley**. The road passes through a bit of Italy before crossing back across the border again and on to Lugano. The bus arrives at the **Lugano** train station. Across from the train station, you can take a funicular down the hill and get off just a short walk from the **Hotel Ticino**. The Hotel Ticino, that in days-long-gone-by was a convent, is located on the tiny Piazza Cioccaro in the old section of Lugano. It is not a fancy hotel, but filled with old-world character and enhanced by the graciousness of its owners, Claire and Samuel Buchmann.

Lugano is a delightful city. Although it has grown tremendously, its core still has the atmosphere of a small medieval village. From Lugano you can either continue on into Italy for further adventures, or if you want to complete your "Swiss Circle" there is frequent direct train service to Zürich taking only about three hours.

Switzerland by Train, Boat & Bus

Swiss Highlights

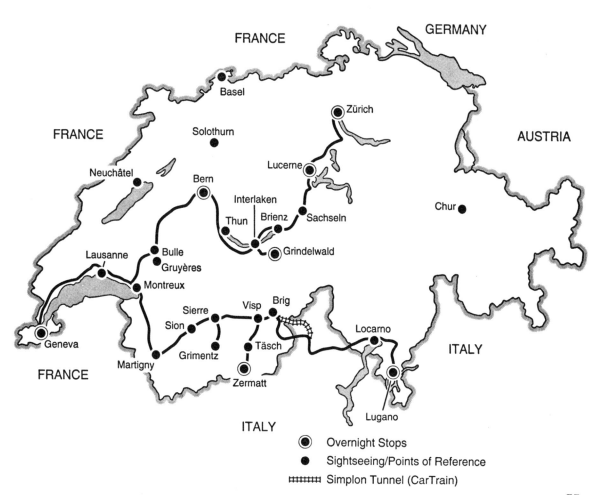

FRANCE

GERMANY

Basel

Zürich

FRANCE

Solothurn

AUSTRIA

Neuchâtel

Bern

Lucerne

Interlaken

Chur

Thun

Brienz

Sachseln

Lausanne

Bulle

Grindelwald

Gruyères

Montreux

Sierre

Visp

Brig

Sion

Grimentz

Täsch

Locarno

Geneva

Martigny

ITALY

Zermatt

FRANCE

ITALY

Lugano

⊙ Overnight Stops

● Sightseeing/Points of Reference

╫╫╫╫╫ Simplon Tunnel (CarTrain)

Swiss Highlights

Cobbled Square of Gruyères

For the traveler who wants to see the highlights of Switzerland including the picture book perfect destinations repeatedly seen on postcards and read about in books, this is an ideal itinerary. The following path leads you through some of the most scenic areas of Switzerland and introduces you to a wonderful variety of famous cities, charming villages, beautiful lakes, lush valleys and splendid mountains. The towns and destinations featured deserve the accolades of loyal tourists who return year after year to savor Switzerland's stunning scenery. If you have only a few days, you can take segments of this itinerary. As an example, you could take only the Zürich to Geneva portion. If you have already, on previous holidays, enjoyed Zürich, Lucerne and Interlaken (one of the most famous trios) you could begin this itinerary in Geneva and end it in the Swiss Italian Lake District. If your time is extremely limited, you could very easily journey from Zürich to Geneva in one day and even have time to squeeze in sightseeing along the way. This itinerary provides a framework to piece together your own custom tour of Switzerland's highlights.

ORIGINATING CITY ZÜRICH

If your arrival is by plane, the Zürich Airport is an excellent introduction to marvelous Swiss efficiency. As in all countries, you must identify and collect your luggage, but once that task is accomplished, the Swiss have managed to eliminate most of the hassle and have conscientiously made life as simple as possible for the traveler. There is no need to bother with porters or suffer the burden of economizing by dragging your bags along at your side, as there are usually an ample number of luggage carts neatly lined up ready for your free use. After loading your baggage on a cart, you do not have to go through any luggage inspection unless you have something to declare. Once through the baggage area, everything is well marked. If you need to make a hotel reservation, there is a desk set up for this purpose. If you want a car rental, this too is well marked. If you want to take the train into either Zürich or direct to many of the other towns in Switzerland, the train station (*bahnhof*) is located on the lower level. There is a train information booth just to the left as you exit customs and a counter where, for a minimal charge, you can check your baggage directly from the airport to almost any train or bus station in Switzerland. There are also many shops, a post office, and banks, all efficiently set up and identified. When I first came out of the customs area, pulling my luggage cart, I was concerned to notice the arrows for the train station pointing down the escalator. Again, no problem. The Swiss have thought of everything: there are directions on each luggage cart showing how to take it on the escalator with you. You can take your cart all the way to the train or, if renting a car, directly to your car.

Taking the train into Zürich is really the quickest and most efficient means of transportation unless you have several persons in your party, in which case a cab might prove preferable.

For your first night in Switzerland, **Zürich** offers a rich selection of places to stay. One of our favorites is the **Zum Storchen Hotel**. This is not a simple country inn, but rather a sophisticated hotel with all the amenities a large city hotel has to offer. Underneath the modern improvements of the Zum Storchen emerges the charm of one of the oldest hotels in Switzerland. The location is excellent too—in the center of Zürich directly on the banks of the Limmat River just a few minutes' walk from where it flows into Lake Zürich. But, in less expensive categories, there are other excellent choices of accommodation listed in the hotel section such as the **Hotel Tiefenau**, a charming, intimate inn, the beautifully refurbished **Hotel Florhof,** or the **Hotel Sonnenberg**, a hotel located in the suburbs with ample space for children to run and play.

DESTINATION I   LUCERNE

Even if you are planning your holiday as a driving vacation, refrain from picking up your car until you are ready to leave Lucerne. The roads are very congested between Zürich and Lucerne and there is no freeway linking them. Once you arrive in either city there is no need for a car—actually, a car becomes somewhat of a nuisance. Walking is one of the major attractions of both cities. Therefore, in this particular itinerary, I suggest you take the train from Zürich to Lucerne. There are trains constantly plying back and forth between the two, and it is a most pleasant journey—taking just about an hour.

In Lucerne, the **Wilden Mann** is a perfect inn within a city. Rarely do you find a hotel, except in the countryside, that retains such a cozy, intimate feeling. The Furler family personally oversees every aspect of this charming, antique-filled hotel located in the heart of the medieval section of Lucerne. Their dedication to perfection shows in every detail.

DESTINATION II   GRINDELWALD

En route for Grindelwald, head south from Lucerne toward **Hergswil**. Near **Stansstad** follow the highway signs south toward **Brienz**. About midway between Lucerne and Brienz you pass through the town of **Sachseln** located on **Lake Sarner**. Take a few minutes to stop in Sachseln where you find in the center of town the church that is a very important for Swiss Catholics. Within the nave are the remains of **St Nicholas of Flüe** who is not only a religious hero, but also a patriotic hero of the Swiss. St Nicholas gained fame in the 15th Century when he is credited with keeping peace within Switzerland and furthering the growth of the confederation. A peasant, he had a reputation as a fair and peace-loving man. When disagreement threatened war between the cantons, parish priests went to consult Nicholas, who negotiated a compromise and instead of battling, Solothurn and Fribourg joined the confederation in 1481.

Leaving Sachseln, you pass through the little towns of **Giswil, Daiserbuhl** and **Lungern** before going over the **Brunig Pass**. The road leads downward from the Brunig Pass to the town of **Brienz**. Brienz, beautifully situated on the lake, is a very popular resort and also one of Switzerland's centers for wood carving. On the outskirts of Brienz, located by the **Wyssensee, Ballenberg** is a marvelous open air museum that serves as a wonderful introduction to the regional architecture and cultures of Switzerland. Historic buildings that were slated for destruction, were saved, relocated and restored to their original and authentic state. A path weaves through this park of over 80 hectares, and travels a course that takes you through the various cantons of Switzerland. You can tour the park on foot or, for a fee, by horse and buggy. Due to the vastness of the park, even if one decides to selectively visit just a few cantons, plan on allocating at least a half day here.

Open Air Museum at Ballenberg

Continuing on from Brienz, the drive along the north side of **Lake Brienz** is beautiful, with lovely views as you pass through the little towns of Oberried, Niederried, and Ringgenberg before arriving at Interlaken.

Interlaken (the name means "between lakes") is situated on a neck of land joining Lake Brienz with **Lake Thun**. The location is fabulous, with two gorgeous lakes stretching out on each side of the town plus excellent views of the **Jungfrau**. Understandably, the town has been a center of tourism for years. There are many large Victorian-style hotels, appealing shops and inviting cafes lining the streets. Although Interlaken is a bit touristy, you can never dispute its spectacular location nor deny that Interlaken is a convenient stopover for the circle trip by rail to see the Jungfrau. However, our suggested alternative to staying in Interlaken is to continue just a short drive beyond

Swiss Highlights

Interlaken to Grindelwald where the mountains are right at your finger tips. Leaving Interlaken in the direction of Lauterbrunnen, you soon come to a split in the road. Turn left at this junction, following the road upward as it climbs toward the little town of Grindelwald.

Grindelwald is the closest mountain village to which you can drive when visiting the Jungfrau region. The setting of this glacier village is spectacular, with views of three giant mountain peaks, the **Eiger**, the **Mettenberg**, and the **Wetterhorn**. Grindelwald serves as a perfect gateway for the train ride up to the base of the Jungfrau and is also a haven for hikers and climbers. In Grindelwald, we recommend two lovely small hotels, the **Fiescherblick** and the **Gletschergarten**, both located at the end of the village, away from the busiest hub-bub of tourist activity. Read what we have to say about each in the hotel section. You can't go wrong with either choice—both are lovely, flower-bedecked, large, chalet-style hotels, whose origins were family homes.

Allow two nights for Grindelwald for you will need most of one day for the Jungfraujoch excursion. Allow more days if you also want to enjoy the beauty of the mountains. Grindelwald is an ideal place for either strenuous mountain climbing or leisurely walks along gentle trails.

DESTINATION III   BERN

From Grindelwald return to Interlaken and then take the highway marked to Thun. If you have allocated the whole day to sightseeing, a stop at **Thun**, located at the west end of Lake Thun, would prove the ideal spot for lunch. Thun is a picturesque medieval village with a castle crowning the hillside. The castle is now a museum and is open to the public. From its turrets you can enjoy a beautiful panorama of Thun, the lake and mountains beyond. Getting to the castle is fun because the pathway up from the village is via a covered staircase.

Leaving Thun, stay on the freeway to Bern. It is only a short drive and the faster road will afford more time for sightseeing. Another of the beautifully preserved medieval towns, **Bern** is nestled in a loop of the River Aare at a point where the river banks fall steeply to the river below. To further enhance the setting, the Alps rise in the background. The setting alone would make Bern worth a stop, but the town itself is brimming with character—truly a storybook 13th-century wonderland. The whole town seems to have a festive air—from its comical fountains to its jolly clock tower. Bern is also the only Swiss city which has been declared a world heritage landmark. Situated at the edge of the intriguing old sector of the city is the elegant **Gauer Hotel Schweizerhof**. With such an excellent location it is an ideal base from which to explore

The River Aare and the skyline of Bern

Bern on foot. From the Schweizerhof you can walk to most of the tourist attractions or wander along the arcaded sidewalks. A less expensive choice, also centrally located, is the **Hotel Belle Epoque,** a comely small hotel in art deco decor. Also well located, and very reasonably priced, is the simple, **Hotel Hospiz zur Heimat.**

DESTINATION IV   GENEVA

Leaving Bern, it is just a short drive south to the town of **Fribourg,** located on the banks of the **Sarine River.** Fribourg is a beautifully preserved medieval city with a Town Hall, Cathedral of St Nicholas, clock tower, and Church of Notre-Dame.

Gruyères is located only a few miles off the freeway running south from Fribourg. After leaving Fribourg, you soon see signs to Bulle and Gruyères. At that point, you will need to leave the freeway. After passing through the town of Bulle you will soon spot Gruyères crowning the top of a small hill. This village is actually one main street of beautifully preserved buildings, at the end of which is a castle, open to the public daily during summer. Gruyères is such a wonderful little town that it is considered a national monument. Cars cannot be driven into town, but parking is provided below the village. The town attracts so many tourists that its charm is marred somewhat by mobs of people during the tourist season. However, with such beautiful views of lush green meadows and towering mountains, Gruyères is certainly worth a detour. Another plus—this is the heart of Switzerland's dairy area: stop for a famous Gruyères quiche.

Leaving Gruyères, return again to the highway and continue south to Vevey. From Vevey, take the freeway west toward Geneva. An alternative to the freeway would be to travel the lakeside road dotted with many charming waterfront towns.

Geneva is a lovely city graced by French influence. Geneva is frequently thought of as a "new" city—a city of banking and commerce, an international city housing the Place des Nations, a sophisticated city of beautiful shops, a cultural city with many museums, an industrial city. All this is true, but Geneva also contains one of the most attractive old towns in Switzerland. On the south side of the River Rhone the hills rise steeply and twist and turn in a maze of little shops, fountains, flowers, and charming buildings. This area is crowned by **St Peter's Cathedral.**

Geneva is home to a string of majestic hotels that line the lake. Our special favorite of these queens is **Le Richemond**. Le Richemond is not immediately on the lake shore promenade, but just half a block away facing a small park. If you prefer to be in the old quarter of Geneva, **Hotel les Armures** has character and charm. Within walking distance of the water and the old quarter, is a lovely, elegant hotel, **La Cigogne**.

DESTINATION V   ZERMATT

Leaving Geneva, retrace your route along the north shore of **Lake Geneva**. The way has two choices: either a fast freeway or a much slower country road that traces the lake's shore, meandering through the quaint towns that line the lake. Mountains enclose both sides of the valley and on the lower hills, terraced to the water's edge, stretch the acres and acres of vineyards that make this region so well-known.

The vineyards and the small villages make a beautiful drive. Allow yourself enough time to follow roads that wind down to the villages on the lake and sample some of the region's wonderful wine.

At the east end of Lake Geneva, take a short detour to visit the **Castle of Chillon**. Chillon is dramatically perched on its own little peninsula jutting into the lake. After visiting the castle, return to the freeway and continue following the Rhone River as it winds its way down the flat valley. The section of the Rhone Valley between Lake Geneva and the Zermatt turnoff is pretty, but does not have the pristine beauty found so frequently in other Swiss valleys—the road passes through many industrial areas. However, there are countless side valleys and intriguing passes to explore.

Vineyards along the shore of Lake Geneva

Many of these side valleys (accessible by narrow twisting roads) are well worth a detour if you have the time. A favorite is a pass climbing up to the tiny village of Grimentz. The turnoff for Grimentz is near the city of **Sierre**. At Sierre, watch carefully for signs for the road that runs to the south of the highway and directs you on to Grimentz.

The small mountain village of **Grimentz** is an architectural gem and is protected by the Swiss government. The steep, narrow, curving access road to Grimentz is physically demanding so don't attempt this side trip in the winter. But in the summer, if the day is clear and you are not intimidated by mountain driving, Grimentz makes a rewarding detour. This very old village is filled with marvelously preserved Valais-style homes whose heavy slate roofs are weighted down by chunky rocks to protect them against the winter storms. Park your car at the entrance to the village and stroll down the tiny streets that are closed to all but foot traffic. The lanes are lined by simple wood houses whose rough-hewn, blackened-with-age exteriors contrast dramatically with masses of flowers cascading from every window. It is hard to believe that the Grimentz of old could ever have been as picturesque as it is today, for each resident seems to vie with his neighbor for the most stunning display of brilliant red geraniums. The effect captivates the senses: brilliant blue sky (with a little luck), snow-capped mountains, green pastures, characterful wooden houses and flowers, flowers, flowers. If the timing is right, after wandering through the village, stop for a cheese fondue lunch at the **Hotel de Moiry**.

After the side trip to Grimentz, return to the freeway, and continue east. As you near Visp, take the well-marked turn off south toward Zermatt. The only choice you have along the way is where the road splits: the left branch of the road leads to Saas-Fee and the right leads to Zermatt.

You cannot drive into **Zermatt** as no cars are allowed within the city limits. However, this is not a problem as there are car parks at each of the small towns neighboring Zermatt. **Täsch** is as far as you can go by car, so park here, buy your ticket at the small station, and board the train for the rest of your journey. After only a few minutes' ride you arrive at the Zermatt train station where you will notice horse drawn carriages waiting in the plaza in front of the station. In winter, these convert to horse-drawn sleighs. In the past few years, electric golf-type carts have gradually replaced some of the horses and sleighs. Most of the major hotels will send their "carriage" to meet the incoming train—each hotel has its name on the cart or carriage or the porter's cap. If for some reason you do not see "your" porter, you will find many electric taxis also available or you can call the hotel from one of the telephone booths next to the station.

Zermatt offers many places to stay. A favorite, the **Hotel Julen**, is located just beyond Zermatt's city center so you feel you are somewhat out of the bustle of the tourist rush. The hotel has an inviting old world charm, with a cozy fireplace in the reception hall, antiques artfully arranged throughout, an attractive restaurant and a cheerful little patio in the rear. If you are very lucky, you might even be able to snare one of the bedrooms from which you can watch the various moods of the majestic Matterhorn.

It is a long day's drive from Zermatt to the Swiss-Italian Lake District. The journey involves travel both by car and train. In order to coordinate schedules and allow for enough time, an early departure is suggested. First you need to return by train from Zermatt to Täsch, pick up your car and drive to the town of Brig. (This is about an hour's drive.)

If you want to include a little sightseeing prior to your journey from **Brig**, stop to visit **Stockalperschloss** which is one of the most interesting castles in Switzerland. Built in the 17th Century by a very wealthy merchant, Kaspar Jodok Stockalper Von Thurm, this castle was the largest private residence in Switzerland and is now open to the public, May to October from 9:00 am to 11:00 am, and from 2:00 pm to 5:00 pm. The castle is closed on Mondays. There are frequent guided tours that take about 45 minutes.

The portion of your journey by train begins at Brig. From here you travel over the mountains and across the border into Italy. You do not abandon your car. Try to time your arrival at about half past the hour because the train departs on the hour from Brig. When you arrive in Brig, follow the signs for the train station, where you purchase the ticket that permits you to take your car on the train from Brig through the **Simplon Tunnel**. After purchasing your ticket, drive your car onto the train. (Putting your car on the train to go over a special pass or through a tunnel is quite common in Switzerland and the sign is always the same—a train car with an automobile sitting on it.) The signs will direct you to the road leading to the left of the station that circles over the train tracks and then veers to the right and ends up at the track on the opposite side of the station. At this point, there are signs showing you which lane to get into for the train. The train will arrive about 10 minutes before the hour and the sides of the train are let down so that you can drive on. Your train is the one going to Iselle. Iselle is at the opposite end of the Simplon Tunnel and is the Italian town at which you will drive off the train. Keep your ticket because when you drive off you turn it in as proof of payment.

Ascona on Lake Maggiore

If you have any problem with claustrophobia, you might not like the train ride and can, of course, always take the option of driving the twisting Simplon Pass. But if you don't mind dark spaces, the train ride is quite a thrill—Walt Disney would have had trouble devising a more dramatic tunnel. You enter the Simplon Tunnel (at 12 miles one of the longest in the world) and ride inside your car for 20 minutes in total darkness as the train swings gently from side to side. The train ride is not only an adventure, it also cuts about an hour's driving time from your journey.

When you leave the train in **Iselle,** you continue south a short distance to the town of Crevoladossola, and then only a few minutes farther on, to Domodossola. There are signs at Crevoladossola to direct you left along a road to Locarno. This is a "short cut" to the

Swiss-Italian lakes, truly a spectacular drive following a river gorge. But frankly, it is a very narrow road and a bit treacherous, so you may want to stay on the main highway and head south toward Verbania and then follow **Lake Maggiore** north toward Locarno. Before reaching Locarno, you come to the little town of **Ascona** nestled at the northern end of the lake. This would be a good place to lunch or have a cup of coffee. There are many street cafes that overlook the lake. My favorite is the cafe in front of the **Hotel Tamaro**. After a break for a snack and perhaps a little shopping spree on one of the ancient little streets branching out behind the lake front, continue on through Locarno and from there to Bellinzona where you join the freeway heading south to Lugano.

Lugano has a complicated street plan and it is difficult to find and maneuver your way to the heart of the old section. Be sure to have a good map and patience—even though you can pinpoint on the map where you want to go, it is not easy. You might have to make several loops about the old town on one-way streets until you finally succeed in entering the old section. Take heart, it is worth the effort. The outskirts of Lugano is an unattractive large metropolis, but once you are in the heart of the city you will discover a real gem, the Lugano of old.

Tucked away in this atmospheric section of Lugano is the delightful **Hotel Ticino**. Fronting a small square, the Piazza Cioccaro, the Ticino is tiny but full of charm. The Piazza Cioccaro is closed to cars, but if you are a guest at the Ticino, you can pass the barricades and drive to the entrance of the hotel to leave your luggage. When you check in, the receptionist will tell you where you can park your car. To the right of the reception area is a small dining room—intimate and attractive. Beyond the reception desk, stairs lead to the upper floors where the bedrooms and lounges are located. A central patio is a reminder of long ago when the hotel was a convent.

Lugano is a wonderful small city in which to linger. The ambiance is more Italian than Swiss—not a surprising situation since you are almost on the Italian border. The old section of town is wonderful for browsing and the lakeside promenade a delight for lazy strolling.

Most fun of all, there is a wonderful selection of boats waiting at the pier to take you to beckoning little towns snuggled along the shores of the lake. From Lugano, you can cross into Italy where it is an easy drive on to the international airport of Milan, or you can head north again into the Alps and complete a circle back to Zürich.

The Limmat River, Zürich

Medieval Villages

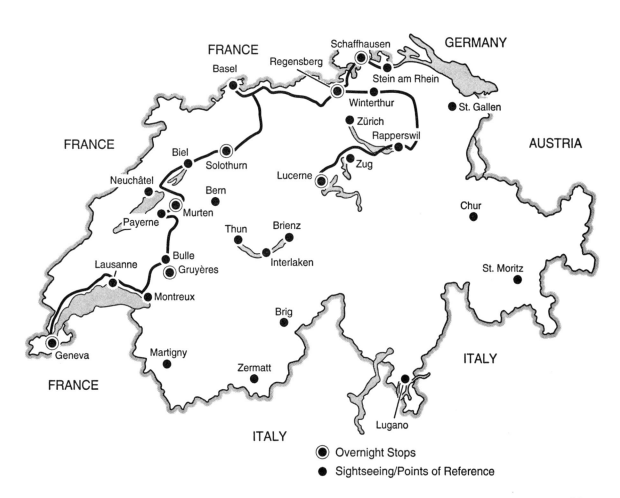

Overnight Stops
Sightseeing/Points of Reference

Medieval Villages

Murten

Switzerland has some of the most enchanting and remarkably well preserved medieval villages in Europe. Scattered across her countryside are towns whose character and atmosphere allude to a style of life that slipped by many centuries ago. Walled ramparts often enclose a maze of twisting, narrow streets, stone buildings, painted fountains, intricate clock towers, turrets and a wealth of history. Sometimes capping the crest of a hill or perched precariously on a valley's ledge, these villages captivate the imagination and are fascinating to explore.

This itinerary wanders from Lucerne to Geneva through glorious countryside and intriguing medieval towns. If you are the second-time-around traveler who has already followed the standard tourist trail between Zürich and Geneva via Lucerne and Interlaken and who would like to discover Switzerland with a different approach and emphasis, this itinerary might be perfect for you. Another possibility for this routing would be to use it in conjunction with the *Swiss Highlights* itinerary—the two dovetail perfectly to complete a circle of Switzerland. The true medieval village connoisseur among you will say that many of the walled villages have been left out. This is true. There are many others scattered throughout Switzerland, but these are some of my favorites and are spaced in such a way as to map a delightful journey.

ORIGINATING CITY   LUCERNE

Lucerne, with its magical setting, is a delightful starting point for this itinerary since it serves as a wonderful introduction to Switzerland and offers a tempting sampling of what is to come—lakes, mountains, a twisting river, wonderful bridges, colorful flowers, fountains, boats, decorative buildings and a beautifully preserved old town.

Kapellbrücke, Lucerne

Medieval Villages

Remnants of stone walls serve to trace an outline around the old town of Lucerne. Although the ramparts that once encircled the city have deteriorated with time, the old section remains a marvelously preserved example of a medieval city, an exceptionally attractive one. A river winds through the town and meanders down to the lake. Stately old buildings line the river and architecturally lovely old bridges span its width. Built in the 14th Century, the **Kapellbrücke** is one of the most famous of these bridges. With its wooden roof, walls painted with murals, and even a little chapel midway, this delightful bridge has almost become a trademark of Lucerne.

DESTINATION I   REGENSBERG

From Lucerne head north towards Zürich. You might want to deviate from the highway about 20 minutes after leaving Lucerne to stop at the town of **Zug** located at the north end of the **Zuger-See** (Lake Zug). Zug is a very old city with many buildings dating back to the 15th Century. There is a small core of the old city that is a perfectly walled enclave entered through a gateway under the clock tower. Soon after leaving Zug change directions and follow a road heading south along **Lake Zürich**. Watch for signs to Rapperswil, located on a small peninsula that juts out into Lake Zürich. **Rapperswil** has a wonderful location on the banks of the lake, many colorful squares and exceptionally preserved medieval buildings. A majestic castle, on a rise in the middle of town, contains the **Polish Museum**. During World War II many of the art treasures of Poland were smuggled out of the country and brought here for safe keeping. Many still remain and are on display at the museum.

From Rapperswil continue north for approximately 30 minutes to **Winterthur**. This is quite a large commercial city, but the central section still retains a great deal of medieval charm. The most interesting section is near the train station. Nearby, one of the main streets has been closed to all but pedestrian traffic and has a variety of shops housed in quaint medieval buildings. Only a short walk farther on is one of the most famous museums in Switzerland, the **Galerie Oskar Reinhart**, truly an exquisite small museum. It houses works by the famous European artists from the 18th to the 20th Centuries beautifully displayed in lovely natural lighting. Especially enjoyable are the paintings by Anker who captured the warmth and charm of family life in Switzerland. The museum is usually closed on Monday mornings and every day from noon to 2:00 pm.

From Winterthur head west toward Bulach— about a 20-minute drive. Upon arrival in Bulach carefully follow the signs heading west towards Dielsdorf—another 10 minutes beyond Bulach. The town of Regensberg is just on the western outskirts of Dielsdorf, perched on a nearby hilltop.

Regensberg is very, very special. Within only a few miles of Zürich is this perfectly preserved medieval village crowning a small hill. Vineyards climb up to the little town whose atmosphere beckons you back 500 years. Lodged in this romantic village is one of the most exquisite little inns in Switzerland, the **Rote Rose**.

Rote Rose, Regensberg

An excursion to circle some of the walled villages in the Regensberg area might also prove of interest. It is only about a 20-minute drive to the ancient spa town of **Baden**. As you approach Baden it looks like a rather industrial town, but venture further and head for the core of the old village. Here you will discover, hovering above the banks of the Limmat River, the charm of yesteryear. Baden has many wonderful old gaily-painted houses with steep roofs and dormer windows that step down the hillside in columns until the last row becomes the river bank itself. A covered wooden bridge forms a picturesque scene at the middle of the old section of town, and a church with a high steeple sets the backdrop to the picture. This spa town of Baden has been famous since Roman times and its waters especially popular for the treatment of arthritis.

From Baden drive on to **Aarau**, another beautifully preserved medieval town. Like Baden, as you approach the town it looks like an industrial city, as indeed it is, being famous for textiles. However, the center of the old town is delightful, with narrow twisting streets, colorful houses with steep brown roofs, frequently with fresco decorations under the eaves, and carved little bay windows jutting out over the tiny streets. Aarau is a perfect town for strolling.

Regensberg

Medieval Villages

Assuming Regensberg as your point of departure, it is a short drive on to **Schaffhausen**. Even with a leisurely departure one can plan on an arrival in time for lunch at the wonderful **Rheinhotel Fischerzunft**, aptly named because it has a superb location right on the pedestrian promenade running along the Rhein. There is interesting sightseeing in the Schaffhausen area and the Rheinhotel Fischerzunft is a delightful place to stay. If you really want a special stay, request a suite overlooking the Rhein.

The town of Schaffhausen is a well-preserved, walled, medieval city. It developed as a result of the Rhein traffic and resultant commerce. To the west of town is the **Rheinfall** (waterfall) whose cascading waters halted the flow of river traffic. Arrangements had to be made to circumvent the falls and transport the cargo by land. As a result, Schaffhausen grew to accommodate the tradesmen with housing and food. In town are a number of painted houses with quaint projecting windows called oriel windows. There are also several delightful fountains, old towers and, of course, a castle on a knoll above the city. While in Schaffhausen

Stein am Rhein

you will certainly want to make the very short excursion to see the Rheinfall. Where the water comes crashing down, there is a park and a concession where you can take a boat right out to the base of the falls.

Another excursion from Schaffhausen is a visit to the walled town of **Stein am Rhein**. Although packed with tourists during the summer season, it nevertheless looks like a fairytale village, with each building almost completely covered in colorful paintings and designs. An option would be to take the ferry from Schaffhausen to Stein am Rhein for lunch and make it a day's outing. Ferry schedules are available at the Rheinhotel Fischerzunft and also at the ticket booth on the dock, just steps from your hotel.

DESTINATION III   SOLOTHURN

To reach Solothurn from Schaffhausen, head south following the signs for Zürich, but before entering the city, turn east following the signs to Basel, a convenient stop on the way to Solothurn. **Basel**, in spite of its size, still retains a wonderful ambiance of days-long-gone-by. As you approach, the old section of town is easy to find—identified by the two towering spires of the cathedral. From the Munster Platz you can explore most of the old section on foot.

From Basel it is a short and easy drive to Solothurn. **Solothurn** might appear unattractive on the outskirts, but once you pass through the medieval wall the modern world is left behind and you enter a sector of the town that transports you back through the centuries. You should not have a problem finding the **Hotel Krone**. It is on one of the main streets and faces the plaza in front of the large **St Ursen Cathedral**. The bedrooms in the main building are spacious and nicely decorated. In the newer wing that stretches behind the hotel, the rooms are much smaller, but these are mostly for singles' use. The main dining room at the Krone is charming and always busy with not only tourists, but also the local citizens. The Krone seems to be the center for much of the social life in town with wedding receptions, business meetings and parties.

The town of Solothurn is one of the oldest Roman settlements in the Alps. With many squares, fountains and colorful buildings it is a fun town for meandering. It will not take you long to see the whole city so I would suggest some other sightseeing excursions from Solothurn. One day drive up into the **Jura Mountains** to visit the little walled town of **St Ursanne** that you enter by crossing the river and passing through the quaint gates. St Ursanne is located in a beautiful section of Switzerland famous for horse breeding. In the summer there are rolling green meadows with splendid-looking horses grazing and adorable colts frolicking in the fields.

Another excursion from Solothurn is a visit to **Bern**, a wonderful old city brimming with whimsical fountains, colorful squares, arcaded shops and perfectly preserved medieval buildings.

DESTINATION IV   MURTEN

Although it is just a short drive from Solothurn to Murten, there are a couple of walled villages along the way. Leaving Solothurn, take the highway west toward Biel. **Biel** is another picturesque medieval town, but if time is short it might be best to bypass Biel and continue directly on to the tiny town of **La Neuveville**, a pretty walled village on the banks of Biel Lake. Near La Neuveville is **St Peter's Island** where Jean-Jacques Rousseau stayed in 1765. By taking a boat from La Neuveville, it is possible to visit the island and see the house where Rousseau lived. Farther along the shore from La Neuveville is another outstanding miniature walled village, **Le Landeron**. In summer both Le Landeron and La Neuveville are sensational, with masses of flowers, picturesque buildings, brightly painted fountains, clock towers, little antique shops and outdoor cafes. But do not linger too long—your next destination is even more inviting. **Murten,** snuggled along the banks of **Lake Murten**, is a fairytale village. The best vantage point for viewing the town is from the top of the ramparts that surround it. The town deserves to be wandered lazily to fully enjoy the twisting little streets, fountains, old buildings and little squares.

If you want to surround yourself with the ambiance of days-gone-by, stay at the **Hotel Weisses Kreuz,** a superbly run small, family-owned hotel with rooms tucked into a cluster of characterful old buildings in the heart of the old town. Within walking distance from the medieval walls that encircle Murten, on the water's edge is the pleasing **Hotel Schiff.** Also snuggled on the lake, but in driving distance of town, is the deluxe, exquisitely appointed **Le Vieux Manoir au Lac.** All hotels are excellent—the choice would depend upon your preference as to location, level of luxury, and price.

DESTINATION V GRUYÈRES

Your next destination, the picturesque town of Gruyères, is just a short drive along the main highway from Murten. To extend your journey and include some sightseeing into your day, I would suggest the following detours. First, instead of returning to the main highway, drive south along **Lake Murten.** Soon after you pass the south end of the lake you come to the town of **Avenches.** It is hard to believe as you look at this sleepy little hamlet of about 2,000 that in the 1st and 2nd Centuries it was a powerful Roman city boasting a population of over 20,000. You can grasp the mood of this "lost city" of the Romans when you visit the amphitheater built to seat 10,000. In a tower over the amphitheater's entrance is a museum displaying some of the artifacts found in the excavations and an interesting pottery collection.

Another excursion en route to Gruyères would be to travel just south of Avenches to the town of **Payerne** and visit its famous 11th-century abbey. This Benedictine Abbey is supposed to have been founded by the Empress Adelheid, wife of Emperor Otto I. The church is one of the finest examples of Romanesque architecture in Switzerland with simple lines but marvelous proportions and use of golden limestone and gray sandstone.

Gruyères

Romont, a small walled, medieval town, is also on the way to Gruyères. To reach Romont it is necessary to travel the small country roads leading southeast from Payerne—about a half hour's drive. The town was built by Peter II of Savoy in the 13th Century and occupies a very picturesque site on the knoll overlooking the Glane Valley. From Romont continue southeast on the small road toward Bulle. Just beyond Bulle the small town of **Gruyères** will appear ahead of you crowning the top of a miniature mountain. To reach Gruyères you wind up the little road toward the village, but you cannot take your car into the town as it is closed to traffic. However, there are several car parks on the approach to town. The **Hostellerie des Chevaliers** is located just above the car park at the entrance to town. Guest rooms at the rear of the hotel look up to the medieval walls and have lovely views of lush green meadows backed by beautiful mountains. The chef is famous for his culinary art and guests come from far and near to dine at the restaurant of the inn. On the cobbled square of Gruyères we recommend two simple country hotels, the **Hostellerie de St Georges** and the **Hotel Fleur de Lys.**

Gruyères is such a postcard-perfect village that it attracts bus loads of visitors who crowd the small main street during the day. However, most of the tourists leave at night and the town returns to its fairytale quality. Return in the evening to the idyllic Swiss village and the town is yours to enjoy. Plan excursions during the day to avoid the bustle of the midday tourist rush. One possible outing would be to go to the small **cheese museum** just at the bottom of the hill from Gruyères. In the museum (which is also a cheese factory) demonstrations are given on how cheeses are made in the various Swiss cantons. There is also a movie, (in English), with an explanation of the process. Cheese enthusiasts might want to linger in this area and take more short excursions to visit other little villages and sample their dairy products—you might come home a little plumper, but a connoisseur of delicious Swiss cheese.

Other side trips that might be appealing would be to travel the distance to **Lake Geneva** and explore the many quaint little towns along the lake. Of course, the ever-pleasurable rides on the lake can be picked up from most of the lakeside towns. From Gruyères you can easily visit the famous **Castle of Chillon** located on a tiny peninsula jutting into the Lake Geneva just beyond **Montreux.** This castle originally belonged to the Counts of Savoy, but its great fame came from Lord Byron's famous poem *The Prisoner of Chillon.*

When it is time to leave Gruyères there are several options. It is just a short drive around Lake Geneva to **Geneva** where there are train connections to all over Europe plus international flights. Or it is an easy trip to complete your "medieval" circle and return to Lucerne via the beautiful **Simmental Valley,** stopping along the way to visit the walled town of **Thun** where you can take one of the lake steamers to Interlaken.

Mountain Adventures

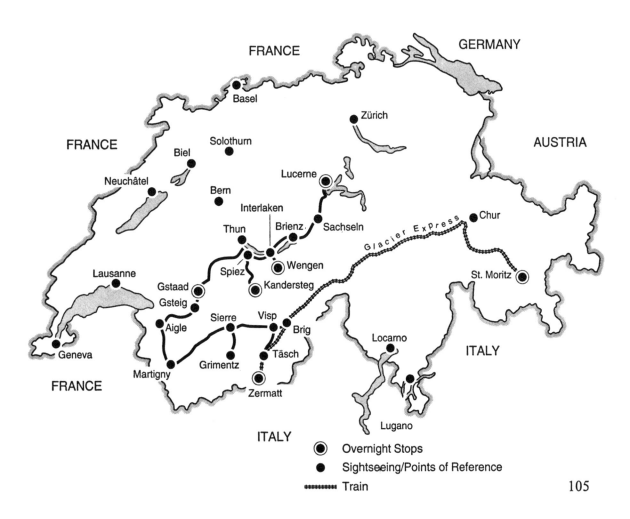

Mountain Adventures

Kandersteg

This itinerary is for the true mountain lover, for the traveler whose year will be happier for the memory of a perfect sunset over a snow-capped mountain peak, whose problems will shrink into perspective as the mind wanders back to gentle meadows graced with wildflowers, whose tensions will fade as the soul recalls the stroll up a quiet mountain path. To enjoy this itinerary, you need not be an Olympic champion, just take pleasure in being outdoors. You will be in style as long as you have one common denominator—love of the mountains. Of course, if you are a mountain climber, the beckoning of the Matterhorn will probably be overwhelming and I wish for you a perfect few days to obtain your goal. If you enjoy skiing, then the slopes of Gstaad will be irresistible. However, if you simply like to meander down quiet trails dappled with sunlight, and your idea of exertion is to stoop to pick a flower, this itinerary is also perfect for you. The mountain resorts of Switzerland teem with European hikers enjoying the mountain air and walking trails. These holiday seekers for the most part are not your image of the disciplined, trim, serious athlete. The majority of hikers are couples or families dressed in woolen sweaters, corduroy knickers, bright knee socks, sturdy walking shoes and walking sticks laughing and talking as they meander along the trails. Therefore, feel most comfortable, no matter what your ability, to join this jovial, friendly group of "mountaineers."

If time is limited, you can follow the routing from Lucerne to Zermatt and end your trip there. Return to Lucerne or Zürich or Geneva, or else head south to the Swiss-Italian Lake District. However, if you can possibly extend your holiday, try the Glacier Express—a private railroad connecting Zermatt and St Moritz. This all-day train ride over some of the most glorious mountain passes in the world is a highlight of any trip to Switzerland. Even if the visibility is zero, the journey on this little red train will still be fun. What a memorable experience to arrive at the train station in Zermatt by horse and sleigh (or horse and buggy in summer), climb onto the train, settle down in the clean bright compartment, enjoy a gourmet meal in the Victorian dining car, chat and laugh with fellow passengers, and arrive relaxed and happy in St Moritz.

So, include all of these mountain villages, or, if time is short, select the resorts that sound most suited to you. Switzerland is blessed with alpine heights, and to visit Switzerland is to enjoy her mountains. Don't go home without strolling along some of the paths and soaking up fabulous mountain vistas.

ORIGINATING CITY   LUCERNE

Because there are no international airports in the high mountain areas, this itinerary begins in one of Switzerland's most famous cities, **Lucerne**, a charming medieval town with a fairytale setting—directly on the lake with a beautiful mountain backdrop.

Although Lucerne does not have it's own airport, there is a direct train from the Zürich airport—a quick and convenient journey taking just over an hour. Spend a few days in Lucerne relaxing before heading south into the mountains. We highly recommend the **Wilden Mann Hotel**, located in the romantic old part of Lucerne, as a superb introduction to the wonders of Switzerland. Another choice for Lucerne is the newly renovated **Hotel des Balances**, located directly on the **Reuss River**. Across the square from the Hotel des Balances is the very reasonably priced, **Hotel Krone**. Another option, on the hillside overlooking the city is the dramatic, **Château Gütsch**. No matter which hotel you choose, wait until you are ready to begin your driving itinerary before picking up your car.

DESTINATION I   WENGEN

Today's destination is the town of Wengen in the region of the famous Jungfrau. The drive is easy and very beautiful. An early departure would be best, enabling you to linger along the way. Head south from Lucerne toward Hergswil. Near Stansstad follow the highway south toward Brienz. On your way you will pass through the town of **Sachseln**, located on Lake Sarner about midway between Lucerne and Brienz. This is a good stopping point if you want to include a coffee break with a little sightseeing. Sachseln is very famous, for in the center of town is a beautiful church where **St Nicholas of Flüe** is buried. From Sachseln follow the highway to Brienz and then on to Interlaken. At Interlaken follow the signs south toward Lauterbrunnen. This is a lovely short drive, but this is as far as you can go with your car. At **Lauterbrunnen** you must park, leave your car and board a train for the last leg of your journey. As usual, the Swiss are extremely efficient and have organized a number of visual aids to simplify the situation. The car park at Lauterbrunnen is well marked. Once your car is parked, follow the signs to the train station from which the trains leave frequently. The ride up from Lauterbrunnen to Wengen is just spectacular: as the train climbs from the valley you look down as from an airplane to the **Lauterbrunnen Valley**. The journey is truly magnificent, with steep

Lauterbrunnen Valley and Staubbach Falls

cliff-like mountains rising steeply from the flat valley and mighty waterfalls cascading down the sides—very reminiscent of the Yosemite Valley. It is only a 15-minute ride up to Wengen, but on a clear day, 15 glorious minutes.

Wengen's location is spectacular—high on a mountain meadow overlooking the Lauterbrunnen Valley and beyond to the awe-inspiring mountains. This is a center for outdoor enthusiasts and sportsmen. From all over the world tourists come to soak up the mountain beauty. In winter skiing is the main attraction. In the milder months walking paths stretch out in every direction for the hiker, offering a new vista at each turn, each more beautiful than the last. Leisured mountain viewing or gentle strolls are matched with the strenuous mountain climbs of the **Bernese Oberland** if you are adventuresome.

Mountain guides can be hired to give you advice and assistance. Remember always to consult a local guide if you are planning any serious climbing.

We recommend two places to stay in Wengen: the **Alpenrose** and the **Regina**. We love them both. Study our descriptions in the hotel section and decide which hotel you prefer. Please call ahead and advise the hotel of your arrival time and they will send an electric cart to the train depot, or phone the hotel when you arrive and leave your luggage at the station to be retrieved later. You can walk to either hotel. The Regina is perched on the hillside above and to the right of the train station and the Alpenrose is located on a small street down the hillside. At either hotel, splurge and request one of the best rooms with a view balcony—the reward is an unforgettable mountain panorama. Both hotels are family owned and operated. Many guests return year after year to spend their holiday surrounded by fellow guests they have met in past years.

While staying in Wengen the prime sightseeing excursion is to visit the region of the Jungfrau. This is a circle trip taken by a series of little trains to the summit of the **Jungfraujoch.** Dominated by the **Jungfrau** this is the highest train station in Europe and from its vantage point, you will marvel at the spectacular vistas of the surrounding, awe-inspiring peaks. Known the world over, this trip is probably the most famous mountain sightseeing adventure in Switzerland—one you will not want to miss.

DESTINATION II   KANDERSTEG

It will be difficult to leave the region of the Jungfrau, but when you can wrench yourself away more splendor is awaiting you. A short drive back to Interlaken brings you again to the main highway circling the south side of **Lake Thun**. When you arrive at Interlaken travel west in the direction of Spiez. Just off the main road that travels between Interlaken and Thun, **Spiez** is worth a short detour before leaving the lake and heading down the alpine valley in the direction of Kandersteg. With the alpine peaks and the lake

Spiez

as a magnificent backdrop, the village of Spiez lies on the shore of its own picturesque bay with a little marina and is crowned by its medieval castle.

From Spiez travel south on a road that winds along the path of the Kander River, through the beautiful **Kandersteg Valley.** The road and its journey ends at the mountain village of Kandersteg.

In **Kandersteg** there is a selection of places to stay that fit all budgets and personal preferences. The town is small so they are easy to find. A super deluxe, elegant, very sophisticated choice is the **Royal Hotel Bellevue**. In contrast, another possibility is tiny **Landgasthof Ruedihus**, tucked at the very end of the valley after the road passes through the center of town. Whereas the Royal Hotel Bellevue is a world class resort with all the trimmings, the Landgasthof Ruedihus is a tiny, very old inn with only a few rooms, but so loaded with antique charm that it will win your hearts immediately. A third choice is **Waldhotel Doldenhorn,** a lovely hotel backed right up against the forest at the foot of the mountains, under the same ownership as the Landgasthof Ruedihus.

Kandersteg makes an excellent base both for sightseeing and enjoying the natural wonders of the area. Hiking is especially appealing. An endless number of walks lead off every point of the compass, each more tempting than the last. At the end of the village a chair lift rises from the valley to **Lake Oeschinen** where rugged cliffs jut dramatically at the edge of the clear mountain lake. The lake lies below the terminal of the chairlift and is reached via a beautiful path through mountain meadows. On a clear day a lovely outing is to walk down the mountain rather than take the chair lift, on the return to Kandersteg. Another excursion from Kandersteg is to drive to the end of the other fork of the valley to the town of Adelboden. To do this, it is necessary to retrace the road a short distance to the town of Frütigen. At this town take the **Engstigental Valley** road branching off to the left. This is a beautiful drive terminating at **Adelboden,** an attractive, resort village with many old wooden farmhouses nestled on the hillside. Again, there is a fantastic backdrop of majestic mountain peaks. As you return to Kandersteg on the right hand side of the road are signs to the **Blausee** (Blue Lake). Park your car near the main road and walk along a wooded path through a forest of twisted, mysterious trees. You begin to wonder where in the world you are going when suddenly you come upon a tiny, gorgeous lake—a photographer's dream. The incredibly blue, clear lake is set in the forest with a jagged alpine horizon. There are usually many people here, as it is a favorite excursion of the Swiss who like to come to eat lunch on the side of the lake in a little chalet-type restaurant, with tables set out on the terrace on mild days. This is also a popular stop for families with children who enjoy taking one of the boat rides or just circling the lake on the twisting little path following the shoreline amongst the gnarled forest. The effect is rather like a scene from *Hansel and Gretel.*

Kandersteg is also well known as the point at which the road ends and only the train continues on to the Rhone Valley. For those traveling by car in this direction the car can be put "piggyback" on the train for the ride through the mountains to Brig.

DESTINATION III   GSTAAD

It is not a long journey from Kandersteg to Gstaad. Retrace the half-hour drive back toward Spiez, and almost as soon as you reach the main road running along the shore of Lake Thun there is a branch off to the west that follows the lovely **Simmental Valley**. In less than an hour you should reach the turnoff to Gstaad and then it is only another few minutes' drive into town. There are many places to stay in **Gstaad,** but our favorites are the **Hotel Olden**, a charmingly painted, chalet-style inn, and the **Post Hotel Rössli,** a former postal station of weathered wood. Both of these well-run, family owned and managed hotels are on the main street in the center of all the enticing boutiques. Ruedi

Widner, the proprietor of the Posthotel Rössli is a celebrated local mountaineer and has a reputation as an excellent ski guide. Heidi Donizetti, who owns the Hotel Olden, has an excellent voice, and on occasion entertains at dinner—a tradition dating back many years when she and her sister used to sing and yodel for the guests. It is great fun to stay right in the quaint village of Gstaad, but if you prefer to have lovely vistas, a short drive away is the intimate **Hotel Alpenrose.** Guestrooms at the Alpenrose are spacious, beautifully decorated and enjoy mountain views.

Hotel Alpenrose, Gstaad

In spite of the fact that it has an international reputation as a very chic ski resort catering to the wealthy jet set, Gstaad retains much of its old world, small town, charming simplicity. In fact, in summer you might awaken to the melody of cow bells as the herds are driven out to pasture. The setting of Gstaad is magnificent with the surrounding rugged mountain peaks. In summer the hiking or mountain climbing is excellent and in winter Gstaad offers one of the most famous network of trails for skiing.

DESTINATION IV   ZERMATT

From Gstaad, continue on the road south beyond through the small picturesque village of **Gsteig**. Gsteig is situated at the end of the valley, and from this point the road climbs sharply past Les Diablerets and on to the town of Le Sépey. At Le Sépey travel southwest toward Aigle, where you then travel south along the Rhone Valley in the direction of Martigny.

At Martigny follow the river as it winds northeast toward Sierre. If you are in the mood for adventure, when you reach Sierre, watch for the turn off to the **Val d'Anniviers** and follow the road south, following signs to Grimentz. The narrow road twists and turns up the mountain. When you come to Vissoie, turn right to **Grimentz**, a fantastic Valais village clinging to a mountain ridge. In summer, it is an especially pretty sight— exuberant displays of brilliant red geraniums that seem even more vibrant in contrast to the wood, blackened with age, of the antique chalets. Stop here to enjoy a fondue at the **Hotel de Moiry** before retracing your way back to the Rhone Valley where you continue east toward Brig. Make advance arrangements to turn your car in at **Brig**. This can be done with the major car rental companies.

DEVIATION: If you are not planning to take the Glacier Express to St Moritz, and want to keep your car, instead of continuing to Brig, turn right (south) off the highway at Visp and follow signs to Zermatt. Cars are not allowed in Zermatt. It is, therefore, necessary to park nearby in **Täsch** and board the train for the remainder of your journey to Zermatt.

For those of you who plan to continue the remainder of your journey by train, turn in your rental car at Brig, and then board the train for Zermatt. There are frequent trains that leave at 23 minutes after each hour for the ride that takes about an hour and 45 minutes. Sit down and relax—the ride through the valley is glorious, ending only when the valley comes to a halt—blocked by the mighty peaks enclosing Zermatt.

Zermatt

Advance hotel reservations are a must in **Zermatt**. Although there are many hotels, there are also many tourists competing for the prime space. We have many recommendations listed for you in the hotel section. Each has its own personality. Each is quite wonderful in its own way. If you want to really capture the magic of Zermatt, you might want to opt for the **Monte Rosa**, the first hotel in Zermatt whose history goes back to 1865 when the young English gentleman, Edward Whymper, led the expedition that finally conquered the Matterhorn.

DESTINATION V   ST MORITZ

Be sure to spend several days in Zermatt. If you enjoy walking, there are endless possibilities. Not only do trails spider-web out of the village in every direction, but trams and cable cars climb the mountains, tempting one to wander through the glorious high mountain meadows.

When it is time to depart Zermatt, a real treat lies in store—the **Glacier Express**, a privately owned train that departs Zermatt in the morning heading north to Brig, then continuing east, threading through the end of the Rhone Valley, passing through the

Furka Pass Tunnel, climbing over the **Oberalppass** and the **Albulapass**, before dropping down into St Moritz. This jolly bright-red train is the perfect way to traverse this spectacular, awe-inspiring route. Seats, however, must be reserved in advance. If you want to enjoy the fun of eating lunch in the quaint, wood-paneled, Victorian dining car, this also must be pre-arranged. You can do it at the same time you book your seat or by calling the Swiss Dining Car Company in Chur, Switzerland, tel: (081) 22 14 25, [new contact as of April 1996: tel: (081) 252 14 25]. Note: In the United States, reservations for the Glacier Express can be made through your travel agent or by calling Rail Europe, tel: 800 438-7245 or 303 443-5100, fax: 800 432-1329 or 303 444-4587. In England, check with the Swiss National Tourist Office for where to make reservations.

8:54 am depart Zermatt via the Glacier Express
4:58 pm arrive St Moritz

St Moritz is one of the most popular of the jet-set ski areas, attracting the rich and famous from around the world. The town has an outstanding setting—one side backs onto the ski slopes, the other looks down to a lovely lake. Due to the popularity of the area, many hotels have sprung up to accommodate the tourists who flock here summer and winter. St Moritz is fun. It is a great place to shop in the designer boutiques and to people watch—especially in winter when many celebrities come to stay at the luxurious Palace Hotel. If money doesn't matter, you too might want to splurge at the Palace Hotel, but our suggestions include three smaller places to stay. Right in the center of town there are two family run hotels—both excellent choices: the **Hotel Eden** and the **Hotel Languard**. If you prefer a more country ambiance, the **Meierei Landgasthof**, a bishop's farm dating back to the 1600's, might interest you. It is situated in a meadow, across the lake looking back at St Moritz.

When you are ready to complete your holiday, you can take a train back to **Zürich** or perhaps, continue by bus (the Palm Express, see page 27 for contact information) to **Lugano**.

Best on a Budget

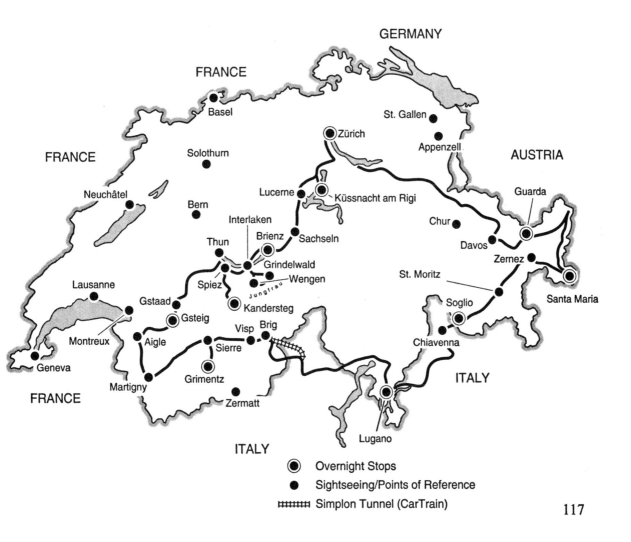

GERMANY

FRANCE

FRANCE

AUSTRIA

Basel

St. Gallen

Zürich

Solothurn

Appenzell

Neuchâtel

Guarda

Lucerne

Küssnacht am Rigi

Bern

Chur

Interlaken

Davos

Thun

Brienz

Sachseln

Zernez

Grindelwald

St. Moritz

Santa Maria

Spiez

Wengen

Jungfrau

Lausanne

Soglio

Gstaad

Kandersteg

Chiavenna

Gsteig

Visp Brig

Montreux

Aigle

Sierre

ITALY

Geneva

Grimentz

FRANCE

Martigny

Zermatt

Lugano

ITALY

◉ Overnight Stops

● Sightseeing/Points of Reference

▦▦▦▦ Simplon Tunnel (CarTrain)

117

Best on a Budget

Soglio

This itinerary was a last minute inspiration. Just as *Swiss Country Inns & Itineraries* went to press in its first edition, Barbara Tapp, our illustrator, was studying photographs we had taken of Swiss hotels with the purpose of finding material to assist her with the hotel sketches. Coming across a snapshot of **La Elvezia al Lago** that we had put in the reject file, Barbara asked why we weren't including this "beautiful little lakefront inn." We gently explained to her that the hotel was not quite of the caliber of the others in the guide—it was just too "modest." The building was attractive but not an architectural masterpiece, the rooms were very clean but quite small. Barbara then asked the price. It was extremely low. "Oh, you must include it," she said. "This is just the type of hotel my husband Richard and I would adore. Our budget would stretch so much further. We could stay a week with meals for what a few days would cost in some of the deluxe hotels for room only." Barbara asked if we had others in the inexpensive category that were not going to be included. Actually, we had been intrigued by several small inns found off the beaten path, such as the **Hotel Baren** in Gsteig and the **Hotel de Moiry** in the medieval village of Grimentz. Barbara's enthusiasm for the qualities of these "little gems" was contagious. So this itinerary is for my friend Barbara and for others, young at heart, adventurous in spirit and traveling on a budget. Prices have gone up since our first edition, but the value received in these small inns is still outstanding.

ORIGINATING CITY   ZÜRICH

Zürich makes a convenient starting point for any holiday in Switzerland. Trains from all over Europe pull into Zürich's central station and airplanes from around the world land at her conveniently located airport. If you arrive by plane, it is so easy and inexpensive to just take the train directly from the airport to the center of Zürich. And although there are some super-expensive, ultra-luxurious hotels rimming the lake, happily for the budget minded traveler, there are also some moderately priced hotels available. One of the best of these is the **Hotel Sonnenberg**, located in a prestigious residential district in the hills overlooking Zürich.

DESTINATION I   KÜSSNACHT AM RIGI

From Zürich, head south out of town in the direction of Lucerne. About 35 kilometers after leaving the city, the road merges into the N4 that you follow all the way to **Küssnacht am Rigi**, a small village located on a northern finger of **Lake Lucerne**. The **Hotel du Lac Seehof**, owned and managed by the fifth generation of the Trutmann family, has a stellar position: right on the lake, adjacent to the ferry landing. The bedrooms are pleasant—some of the more deluxe have antique decor. But if budget is on your mind, ask for one of the three guest rooms without a private bathroom. They offer good value for the money. The hotel has an inside dining room, but it is the lakeside terrace that is most entrancing—on balmy evenings it is superb to linger over a romantic dinner under the trees with the lights gently reflecting in the water.

From the pier in front of the Hotel du Lac Seehof, you can climb aboard one of the many ferries that ply Lake Lucerne. There are many charming towns you can visit by boat, but the prize, that should not be missed, is Lucerne. Plan to spend one day there as a side trip from Küssnacht, exploring the maze of little lanes in the old town, and cross back and forth along the colorful bridges that span the Reuss River which winds through the center of the town.

Note: New to this edition is another budget recommendation: the charming **Swiss Chalet** in the nearby town of **Merlischachen,** described on page 196 in the Hotel Description section.

DESTINATION II   BRIENZ

From Küssnacht am Rigi travel south of Lucerne to a spectacularly beautiful region of lakes and mountains. Two lakes, Lake Brienz and Lake Thun hinged by a speck of land, referred to as Interlaken, are surrounded by towering peaks that reach to the heights of the ever famous Jungfrau. Nestled on the shores of the lake that bears its name is the charming town of **Brienz**. A great wood carving center, most of the carvings available for purchase throughout Switzerland come from this dear, lakeside town. Brienz is also famous for its Swiss violin making school. It is a charming town and its web of old narrow streets shadowed by dark wooden chalet style houses and shops is fun to explore. On the hillside, in a residential district just above town, is a charming, reasonably priced inn, the **Chalet Hotels Schönegg & Spycher Garni**. The guest rooms in the weathered old Chalet Schönegg are especially appealing in their alpine decor and charm.

Chalet Schönegg, Brienz

With Brienz as a base there are a wealth of excursions to choose from. For a breathtaking, panoramic view of the Bernese Alps and Lake Brienz, consider a journey on the **Brienz Rothorn Bahn**. This wonderful, old, steam locomotive traverses beautiful scenery on its ascent by rack railway to the summit (7,700 ft) of the Rothorn. The round-trip journey requires approximately three hours and departs from the lakeside town of Brienz. There is also a hotel at the summit, functional in its decor and comfort, where one can dine or overnight, Hotel Rothorn Kulm.

In the vicinity of Brienz, there are a number of falls that cascade down near the heavily wooded water's edge, the most famous of which, the **Giessbach Falls**, are accessible by train from the Brienz station and a funicular.

On the outskirts of Brienz, located by the **Wyssensee, Ballenberg** is a marvelous open-air museum that should be incorporated into anyone's travels in Switzerland. Set on vast acreage of gentle landscape of lush meadow and fields planted with grain and flowers,

Style of houses representative of different cantons in Switzerland

this open air museum offers a wonderful introduction to the regional architecture and cultures of Switzerland. Historical buildings representative of the different cantons of Switzerland have been relocated to this site. One can wander the park on a path that journeys from canton to canton. People work the museum dressed in costume and stage an era of centuries gone by.

DESTINATION III   KANDERSTEG

The drive around the lake from Brienz and back into the mountain valley to the village of **Kandersteg** is beautiful. Perhaps the most spectacular portion is when you pass through the scenic area surrounding the famous resort of **Interlaken** that is strategically located on a bridge of land connecting two of Switzerland's most beautiful small lakes, **Lake Thun** and **Lake Brienz**. Follow the road that traces the southern rim of the lakes. Before reaching the town of Spiez, watch for a turnoff for a road heading south into the **Kandersteg Valley**. Beyond the town of Reichenbach, watch for a sign on the right side of the road for the **Blausee** (Blue Lake). Park your car and, on foot, follow the wooded, scenic pathway to this gem of a little lake with its curtain of rocks rising in the background. One wonders how nature can compose such magic. If you are ready for a snack, there is a charming little chalet-style restaurant nestled along the shore. The Blausee is very popular and will be crowded if the day is nice—especially with families, since this tiny lake appeals to the little ones.

From the Blausee, continue down the valley to Kandersteg. The road actually ends in this typical Swiss village. To continue further one would have to take a train over the mountains. Kandersteg enjoys a splendid setting of meadows and towering alpine peaks. People come to this gorgeous setting to hike. There are a wealth of trails for all levels of ability.

When you arrive in **Kandersteg**, continue right through the heart of this small town to its outskirts. When you have traveled about as far as the road will take you, off its right hand side you will see a picture perfect, small chalet, the **Landgasthof Ruedihus**, that not only abounds with charm, but also is an excellent value. This flower bedecked gem, is one of the oldest in the valley and has been restored to perfection, not only outside, but inside too. Antiques and pretty country fabrics are used in the decor. This charming inn has two restaurants, one upstairs, more formal in decor and gourmet in menu, the other is off the entry, cozy under wooden beams. This second restaurant, the stubli, is a gathering spot for locals as well as resident guests. The menu in the stubli has a wonderful offering of raclette and fondue. This would prove a memorable spot to sample one of Switzerland's most popular dishes, fondue or raclette.

Now world famous, fondue needs little introduction—melted Gruyères cheese, white wine, garlic, and kirsch are brought to the table in a chafing dish and diners use long forks to dip squares of bread into the delectable mixture. Raclette is a countryman's dinner. A block of Bagnes cheese is softened over a fire. The top of the block is then scraped onto your plate and traditionally served with boiled potatoes and onions. Sometimes variations in the accompaniment are offered, such as mushrooms, tomatoes, ham, and sausage.

While in Kandersteg, there are many side trips that beckon. You will certainly want to include the **Jungfraujoch Excursion**. This train ride to the base of the Jungfrau (see map and details in the Sightseeing Section) is one of Switzerland's highlights. There are other wonderful possibilities for sightseeing in the area. With Kandersteg as your base, it is a short drive into **Interlaken** where you can meander through the town enjoying the ambiance of this Victorian-style resort. Better yet, take a lake excursion either on Lake Thun or Lake Brienz. Also  highly recommended is a jaunt to see the medieval town of **Thun** with its dramatic castle perched on the hillside. A covered wooden staircase leading up to it adds to the fun of visiting the castle. If it is time to consider gifts, Thun has an interesting shopping street with a mall of shops on an upper level and an elevated sidewalk.

Best on a Budget

After your stay in the mountain village of Kandersteg, retrace your way to the main highway and continue west following the **Simmental Valley** toward Gstaad. Continue through the charming resort of Gstaad and in about 15 minutes you will come to **Gsteig** that shares the same glorious valley as Gstaad, but not the same "jet-set" prices. Yet the town of Gsteig is wonderfully quaint, although, without fancy restaurants.

Hotel Baren, Gsteig

When you reach Gsteig you cannot miss the **Hotel Baren** on the right-hand side of the street near the small church. The building's facade is such a marvelous example of the intricate carvings characteristic of the Oberland region that the hotel is protected by the government as a national treasure. The town of Gsteig is custodian of the hotel and selects the management. The dark wooden gables of the Gasthof Baren are covered in detailed designs and in summer the window boxes are filled with flowers; virtually a mass of brilliant red. The bedrooms are quite simple. For the most luxurious of the accommodation offered, be sure to ask for the only one of the seven guest rooms which has a private bath. The food has the reputation of being simple, but very good. The cozy dining room with its wooden tables and chairs and gay checkered curtains is a favorite with the locals.

Linger for a few days in Gsteig to enjoy the beauty of this tiny valley. There are many wonderful trails for hiking in the summer, and in winter there is the world-famous skiing at nearby Gstaad. This is also a lush farming region and I'll always remember the weathered old chalets whose eaves are hung heavy with treasured cow bells. One day enjoy an excursion to the town of **Gruyères**, a charming little picture-book medieval village hugging the top of a small hilltop. The town is really only one main street full of picturesque buildings. Surrounding this "toy town" are incredibly green meadows that seem to flow up to the mountains—it is a scene from *Heidi*. The town is famous for its excellent cheeses and creams as Gruyères is in one of the excellent dairy sections of Switzerland. If you go to Gruyères be sure to stop at a local restaurant for some quiche and, when in season, some berries smothered in unbelievably thick cream.

DESTINATION V   GRIMENTZ

After leaving Gsteig, your next stop is the tiny town of Grimentz. The drive from Gsteig to Grimentz is beautiful, but involves mountainous driving and the route is only recommended after the snows have melted. As you leave Gsteig, follow the road that begins almost immediately to climb up into the mountains. The road twists over the mountains, passes through the town of Les Diablerets, the ski resort of Villars and then winds down into the Rhone Valley. Upon reaching the main highway turn east, and when you reach Sierre, follow the signs for the road heading south to Grimentz.

The town of **Grimentz** nestles on a side of the mountain overlooking the valley and beyond to the high alpine peaks. The village is a masterpiece of perfection, with almost all of the buildings constructed in the traditional Valais style with dark weathered wood, slate roofs and balconies. All this is set off in summer by masses of brilliant red geraniums. The **Hotel de Moiry**, found on the edge of town, is quite simple, but for the location, an excellent value. The Grimentz area is wonderful for high mountain walking. From here it is possible to hike to neighboring villages and return by postal bus.

A wonderful, weathered old barn hung with cow bells near Gsteig

DESTINATION VI   LUGANO-CASTAGNOLA

When it is time to leave Grimentz, get an early start because you have a long day's drive. Return to the main Highway 9, turn right (east), and continue through the Rhone Valley to Brig. From Brig you have a choice of either driving over the **Simplon Pass** or taking a train through the **Simplon Tunnel**. Unless your budget is really slim, the train is by far the easiest way to cross the mountains and a fun adventure in its own right. If you choose the train remember to allow enough time to purchase tickets and get your car to the designated boarding point. Directional signs are very explicit: they show a car on top of a train. The trains leave on the hour to travel through the longest train tunnel in Europe. You stay in your car during the trip and jostle in total darkness until you emerge approximately 20 minutes later at the town of **Iselle** in Italy. Although there is a short cut to the Swiss-Italian Lake District by following the turn-off near Domodossola through the Vigezzo Valley, I would suggest you stay on the main highway since the road is much better. Continue on toward Verbania and then follow the shoreline of **Lake Maggiore** through the picturesque town of **Ascona** (an excellent luncheon stop) and then via Locarno to Bellinzona and then south via the freeway to Lugano. Just a few miles to the east of Lugano, you reach the small suburb of Castagnola.

La Elvezia al Lago, located on a foot path linking the towns of **Castagnola** and **Gandria**, is not directly accessible by car although you can take a car or taxi to a nearby parking area called San Domenico. You also have the option of taking the ferry from Lugano and getting off almost in front of the hotel (boat stop is Elvezia al Lago), but check the schedule carefully because there is not frequent service. One of our readers, who unfortunately had problems finding the hotel, kindly sent good directions if you are driving: "Leaving Lugano, take the highway toward Gandria, passing Castagnola. Turn right on Via Cordiva (signposted San Domenico). The Via Cordiva deadends in the San Domenico parking area where you will find a phone booth. From here, either call for the hotel to send their boat to pick you up at the adjacent dock or follow the footpath east to the hotel (about a 10-minute walk)." The Elvezia al Lago is perched on the water's edge, easy to spot with its jaunty blue and white awnings. This is a modest hotel, and although the guest rooms are quite small, they all have a view of the lake. Best yet, in the morning you can awaken to the music of the birds, have breakfast overlooking the lake and spend the day soaking in the gorgeous view. The owners, Mr and Mrs Lucke, will do their best to see that your stay is a happy one. Unless there is a last minute vacancy, you cannot make a reservation in advance during the busy season for less than several days.

However, this is not a problem—use this gem as a base and linger in the lake district for as long as time permits for there is truly so much to see and do.

From Castagnola take the boat into **Lugano** that still has a charming, medieval central core with excellent shops and restaurants, or to the little town of **Morcote** and dawdle over lunch at the **Carina Carlton Hotel's** little waterfront terrace.

Hotel Carina Carlton, Morcote

DESTINATION VII   SOGLIO

If your holiday time has run out then you could conveniently end your vacation in Castagnola. You are just a short drive to the international airport at Milan or a pleasant train ride back to Zürich. However, if you can squeeze in a few more days there is high adventure ahead. The southeastern region of Switzerland (the Grison) offers some of the most spectacular scenery in the world.

Leave Lugano driving east in the direction of Italy. At the town of Menaggio turn north and drive along **Lake Como**. At the north end of the lake take the highway north toward the town of Chiavenna. The Swiss border appears just a few miles past Chiavenna and soon, high on a ledge to your left, you will spot the town of **Soglio** in the distance. This little town is one of the most dramatically beautiful in all of Switzerland; picture perfect—typifying the classic image of a Swiss alpine setting. A tiny village of just a few streets, the skyline dominated by a church spire, Soglio clings to a ledge high above the **Bregaglia Valley** and looks across to jagged peaks, whose moods are affected dramatically by the time of the day. Early morning light leaves a sliver of gold on the snowy escarpment enhanced by shifting clouds caressing the mountain peaks. We highly recommend the **Pension La Soglina** which affords the opportunity to overnight in Soglio. La Soglina, newly constructed in a chalet style has the great advantage of being on the hill above town where guests are treated to a panorama of the mountains across a patchwork of tile rooftops.

Soglio is so spectacular that it deserves several days. There is not much to do in the village itself, but if time affords, linger here, relax, venture on a hike or two and soak in the splendors and beauty of the setting that, we think, is one of the most outstanding in all of Switzerland.

DESTINATION VIII   SANTA MARIA

To leave Soglio twist back down the narrow road leading to the valley below and turn onto the highway in the direction of St Moritz. Famous first as a health spa, **St Moritz** is now considered the playground of the wealthy. From St Moritz continue north following the **Engadine Valley.** You will pass through **Zuoz**, a small medieval village, along the way. Then head east from Zernez where the road travels through the heavily forested **Swiss National Park,** over the **Ofenpass** and then down into the unspoiled rural beauty of the **Müstair Valley.**

Stretched along the sweep of the Müstair Valley are a number of unspoiled hamlets including **Santa Maria** that appears at the bottom of the Ofenpass. The **Theater Hotel Chasa Capol** is located almost at the eastern end of the little town of Santa Maria.

Dating back to the 8th Century, this little inn is truly unique—in addition to a hotel it houses a theater, chapel and a remarkable wine cellar. The hotel is owned by the Schweizer family who are involved in the management and supervision of the restaurant where dining and service are special. The bedrooms are simple in their decor, and although rates are not as low as other hotels on this *budget* itinerary, they are an excellent value. The Chasa Capol is a delightful site for exploring the Müstair Valley and for taking advantage of the many miles of unspoilt trails in the nearby Swiss National Park.

DESTINATION IX   GUARDA

When it is time to leave Santa Maria, drive east for a few miles to where the Müstair Valley flows into Italy and then loops back across the Swiss border. Following this suggested route saves backtracking along the same road. After crossing the border the route heads north just a few miles beyond customs and again across another border into Austria.

Shortly after entering Austria, the road travels back into the Engadine Valley and into Switzerland. This might sound confusing, but as you can see by the itinerary map very few miles are actually involved and it is an easy trip. The other advantage to this route is that it travels near Samnaun, a town near the Austrian border, soon after reentering Switzerland. **Samnaun's** biggest attraction is its completely tax-free shopping. *Zoll Frei*, the prices are incredible and people come from all over to purchase Austrian and Swiss clothing, hiking equipment and ski gear.

The final destination for this itinerary is in the **Upper Engadine Valley**. Driving the valley from the east, you will pass the famous spa town of **Bad Scuol** and then soon after the medieval town of **Guarda** appears perched on a ledge above the valley, very similar to Soglio. The views are spectacular and the opportunity exists for some marvelous walks. Superbly situated on its own terrace overlooking the valley and mountains sits one of our favorite places to stay, the **Hotel Meisser**—a modest hotel, reasonably priced, with a most attractive dining room and exceptional panoramas.

The main recreation in Guarda is enjoying the stunning views or hiking along one of the many easy trails. However, if you want to sightsee, **Tarasp Castle**, picturesquely perched on a nearby hillside, has guided tours available in summer months. From this beautiful valley, it is an easy half day's drive either to Zürich or Lucerne.

Tarasp Castle

Best on a Budget

Hotel Descriptions

On my first visit to the Star and Post Hotel my heart was won by Faro, an enormous Bernese mountain dog napping in the middle of the lobby. Faro was such a fixture that postcards of this gentle, affectionate overgrown "puppy" were sent to his many admirers. Unfortunately Faro has died, but Haro, an equally gentle, lovable Bernese mountain dog is now winning the hearts of guests of all ages. The Star and Post has been in the Tresch family for several hundred years. Herr Tresch, once president of the Swiss Hoteliers Association, oversees his hotel with an unparalleled professionalism. He welcomes guests from all over the world with a gracious and genuine warmth and always a twinkle in his eye. His family heirlooms adorn the public rooms and a wonderful story can be told about each—ask about the veterinary cabinet or the lock-up cabinet for the hotel silver, necessary in days of old when the employees were not to be trusted. Right on the main thoroughfare of Amsteg, the oldest part of the house dates back to 1789, when the inn was built to provide shelter to weary travelers. Today the Star and Post, or "Stern and Post," is the only remaining coaching station along the St Gotthard Pass road. About one-third of the rooms have an antique decor, but the majority are modern, so be sure to specify your preference at the time you make your reservation. The public areas abound with antiques and are very cozy.

HOTEL STAR AND POST
Hotelier: Herr Tresch-Gwerder
CH-6474 Amsteg, Switzerland
*tel: (044) 64 440, fax: (044) 63 261 **
*New 03/96: tel: (041) 883 14 40, fax:(041) 883 02 61
35 bedrooms, 20 with private bathrooms
Double: Sfr 160 to Sfr 240
Closed Tuesdays and Wednesdays in winter
Credit cards: all major; Restaurant open daily
Train 3 km from hotel, free pick up
Canton: URI, 14 km S of Altdorf

New to this edition, we include the Hotel Appenzell to compliment the highly recommended Hotel Säntis. The attractive town of Appenzell with its cobbled streets and bounty of shops is at the heart of the region that bears the same name. At the edge of the pedestrian district, opposite the Hotel Säntis on the historic Landsgemeindeplatz, the Hotel Appenzell benefits from the expertise and warmth of the Sutter family that owns it. Margrit is often present to greet guests at the front desk, and Leo is responsible for the fine offerings of the restaurant. The hotel has sixteen lovely guest rooms all with private bathroom and either tub or shower. The hallways leading to the guest rooms are uncluttered and attractive with a few well-placed antiques. Guest room doors are trimmed and adorned with lovely stenciling. The rooms are all similar in their decor and differ only in their color scheme, a soft yellow for the first floor rooms, and a soft rose for the second floor accommodations. The guest rooms are new, tastefully and comfortably appointed. The restaurant is always bustling either with lunch or dinner guests, or between meals, with those who are tempted by pastries from the adjacent bakery. A standard dinner menu offers traditional Swiss fare at a reasonable price. A breakfast buffet for hotel guests is offered in the intimate Dr Hildebrand Suite.

HOTEL APPENZELL
Hoteliers: Margrit and Leo Sutter
CH-9050 Appenzell, Switzerland
tel: (071) 87 42 11, fax: (071) 87 42 84*
*New 03/96, unavailable-but old will be good through 1996
16 rooms with private bathrooms
Double: Sfr 180 to Sfr 200
Open: December 1 to November 15
Credit cards: all major
Restaurant and bakery open daily
Train 400 meters from hotel
Canton: Appenzell, Interior Rhodes, 20 km S of St. Gallen

The facade of the Hotel Säntis, located on the central square in the picturesque village of Appenzell, has been gaily painted a rust red with yellow and black scrolling. The terrace in front is a favorite place for a cool drink on a warm day. Recently renovated, guest rooms are decorated either in reproduction country-style wooden furniture or attractive modern. The price for the room depends mostly upon its size. My favorite guest rooms are in the original part of the main house, although those in the newer wing are also very pleasant. The decor of each bedroom in the new wing is the same except for the color scheme. The public rooms seem geared to the influx of tourists who drop in for a midday meal. However, the lobby offers a country welcome, and the hotel has wisely insulated a quiet, peaceful lounge just for guests. Joseph Heeb has turned most of the management of this hotel over to his gracious son, Stefan, and his delightful new bride from Scotland. It is the family's pride and dedication as owners that are apparent from the friendliness of the front desk receptionist to the smile of the chambermaid. The Säntis has been in Mr Heeb's family for several generations—it was owned by his grandfather and his father before him, and will hopefully continue to pass down within the family for many generations to come.

ROMANTIK HOTEL SÄNTIS
Hotelier: Stefan Heeb Family
CH-9050 Appenzell, Switzerland
tel: (071) 87 87 22, fax: (071) 87 48 42*
*New 03/96, unavailable-but old will be good through 1996
30 rooms with private bathrooms
Double: Sfr 160 to Sfr 240
Open: February to December
Credit cards: all major; Restaurant open daily
Train 400 meters from hotel
U.S. Rep: Euro-Connection 800 645-3876
Canton: Appenzell, Interior Rhodes, 20 km S of St Gallen

The Castello del Sole, situated within sprawling private park-like grounds, has earned a five star rating and the acknowledgment of the Swiss government tourist office as being amongst the most deluxe hotels in Switzerland. Located east beyond Ascona in the direction of Locarno, the Castello del Sole is a bit difficult to find, but it is well worth the effort. The Castello del Sole is graced with elegance and a subdued formality. The atmosphere is evident from the moment you enter the lobby and view the beautiful lounge areas accented with antiques and lovely paintings hung on pale colored walls. From the public rooms to the comfortable spacious bedrooms, the decorating is delightful. The Barbarossa restaurant maintains an exceptional reputation, specializing in fresh products from the hotel's farm and wines from its own vineyard. The gardens of the Castello del Sole stretch down to Lake Maggiore where the hotel has a beach with small boats and windsurf boards. The hotel also has an indoor-outdoor swimming pool, sauna, steam bath, five outdoor tennis courts and two tennis courts in a magnificent tennis hall that would fulfill any tennis buff's dreams. A beautiful new pavilion, fully air-conditioned, with 15 deluxe rooms and two suites has been added.

CASTELLO DEL SOLE
Hotelier: Bruno Kilchenmann
Via Muraccio 142
CH-6612 Ascona, Switzerland
tel: (093) 35 02 02, fax: (093) 36 11 18*
*New 10/95: tel: (091) 791 02 02, fax: (091) 792 11 18
85 rooms with private bathrooms
Double: Sfr 450 to Sfr 580, Suites from Sfr 680
Open: April 1 to November 4
Credit cards: all major
Restaurant open daily
Train to Locarno, 6 km from hotel
Canton: Ticino, 3 km SW of Locarno

The Hotel Castello Seeschloss enjoys an imposing presence at one end of the lakeside promenade of Ascona. Completely renovated in 1989, the Castello Seeschloss now offers modern comfort and attractive accommodation within the walls of an impressive fortress. Guest rooms with handsome wood doors are decorated with a mix of modern and traditional furnishings, and all have private bathrooms. One can specify a preference in decor when making a reservation. Guests who elect to stay on a demi-pension basis are offered an enticing menu served in a special dining room just for hotel guests. An à la carte restaurant, the Locanda de'Ghiriglioni, is also available for guests opting not to stay *en pension* and for non-resident guests. Tucked in the cellar, an attractive wine bar is also a cozy place to settle either before or after dinner. At the back of the castle an inviting pool is shadowed by two newly constructed wings of rooms. Guests of the hotel can also enjoy the lovely lake-side garden. The hotel also has an underground garage. The luxury of ample parking spaces is a welcome amenity in a town where parking can be extremely difficult.

HOTEL CASTELLO SEESCHLOSS
Hotelier: Werner Ris
Lakeside Promenade
CH-6612 Ascona, Switzerland
tel: (093) 35 01 61, fax: (093) 35 18 04*
*New 10/95: tel:(091) 791 01 61, fax:(091) 791 18 04
45 rooms with private bathrooms
Double: Sfr 260 to Sfr 500
Open: March 15 to November 5
Credit cards: all major
Restaurant open daily
Train to Locarno, 6 km from hotel
U.S. Rep: Euro-Connection 800 645-3876
Canton: Ticino, 3 km SW of Locarno

In an oasis buffered by gardens of pink roses, pink rhododendrons, pink azaleas, and lush greenery, the Hotel Giardino offers the ultimate in luxury. Draped in ivy, only two of the soft pink stucco buildings offer overnight accommodation, the others house condominiums. From the reception area of the hotel, gorgeous fabrics drape off intimate sitting areas set either before a crackling fire, or exposed to the lush outdoor gardens. Tiled stairways and hallways hung with a changing exhibition of art, wind up to the bedrooms. The upstairs hallways are accented by painted murals. Guest rooms vary in color schemes from rose to green to blue and are priced according to size and whether they enjoy morning or afternoon sun. The atmosphere is one of privilege and prices are high to match the level of comfort. Pension guests enjoy an à la carte offering of sixteen dishes in either the romantic restaurant, Aphrodite, whose tables are set on a lovely terrace overlooking the waterlily pond, or in the intimate Italian restaurant, Osteria Giardino. Lighter meals are available at the more casual poolside cafe. A multitude of activities: wine tastings, hikes, bike trips and picnics are orchestrated by Hans C. Leu. On Sunday evenings the water garden becomes an enchanting open air theater for ballet, musicals, and operas.

HOTEL GIARDINO
Hotelier: Hans C. Leu
Via Segnale, CH-6612 Ascona, Switzerland
tel: (093) 35 01 01, fax: (093) 36 10 64*
New 10/95: tel: (091) 791 01 01, fax: (091) 792 10 64
54 double rooms, 18 suites, all with private bathrooms
Double: Sfr 630 to Sfr 930*
*includes breakfast and dinner
Open: March 18 to mid-November
Credit cards: all major
Restaurants open daily
Train to Locarno, 15 minutes from hotel
Canton: Ticino, 3 km SW of Locarno

The Hotel Tamaro, ideally situated across the street from Lake Maggiore, has cheerful little tables set out in front of the hotel. Strollers settle here and enjoy a cup of coffee or an ice cream while leisurely watching boats glide in and out of the harbor. As you enter the hotel, the reception lounge has an inviting array of comfortable antiques. One of the most charming features of this small hotel is an interior courtyard crowned by a glass ceiling for protection against the weather. This small inside patio has tables set gaily amongst many plants, giving the feeling that you are dining in a garden. The guest rooms are situated on various levels, and it's almost a game to find your room. Each guest room varies greatly in style of decor, views and size. The rooms are attractively decorated, but not luxurious in their decor, and understand that even the most expensive rooms are a bit snug. I prefer the rooms in the front with a view of the lake, and some even have a small balcony overlooking the traffic-free plaza. Annetta and Paolo Witzig are the owners of the Tamaro, and they are very involved in the management of this delightful old Ticino-style patrician house. Charming and attractive Annetta is frequently at the reception desk greeting guests as they arrive.

ROMANTIK HOTEL TAMARO
Hoteliers: Annetta and Paolo Witzig
Piazza G. Motta 35
CH-6612 Ascona, Switzerland
tel: (093) 35 02 82, fax: (093) 35 29 28*
*New 10/95: tel:(091) 791 02 82, fax:(091) 791 29 28
51 rooms, 41 with private bathrooms
Double: Sfr 170 to Sfr 260
Open: March to November
Credit cards: all major; Restaurant open daily
Train to Locarno, 15 minutes from hotel
U.S. Rep: Euro-Connection 800 645-3876
Canton: Ticino, 3 km SW of Locarno

The Hotel Drei Konige (Three Kings Hotel), the oldest hotel in Europe (1026), was originally called *Zur Blume* (At the Sign of the Flower). But soon after the inn was founded, a historic meeting took place among three kings: Conrad II (Emperor of the Holy Roman Empire), his son (who became Henry III), and Rudolf III (King of Burgundy). At the meeting a treaty was drawn up for the transference of the territories that are now western Switzerland and southern France. The hotel's name was then changed, understandably, from Zur Blume to the Drei Konige. The Drei Konige is decorated with exquisite taste—formal antiques and lovely reproductions are found in the public and guest rooms. Many family oil paintings adorn the walls, creating a homey ambiance throughout the hotel. A sweeping staircase leads to the bedrooms and each floor that opens to a central atrium. All of the bedrooms (even those in the standard category) are tastefully furnished. The guest rooms on the second or fourth floor that have a balcony overlooking the Rhein are truly superb. The suites also are spectacular, especially the Napoleon Suite, in regal shades of blue with an ornate ceiling—fit for a king.

HOTEL DREI KONIGE
Hotelier: Jacques Pernet
Blumenrain 8
CH-4001 Basel, Switzerland
tel: (061) 26 15 252, fax: (061) 26 12 153
88 rooms with private bathrooms
Double: Sfr 400 to Sfr 560
Open: all year
Credit cards: all major
Restaurant open daily
Train 1 km from hotel
U.S. Rep: LHW 800 223-6800
U.S. Rep: Utell 800 448-8355
Canton: Basel Stadt, 100 km N of Bern

At the heart of the medieval city of Bern, on Bahnhof Platz, is a beautiful city hotel whose name reflects the caring family behind its operations. The decor of the hotel benefits greatly from the fact that the Gauer family love antiques–they are found in abundance throughout. The hallways are lined with priceless antiques—the contents of the hotel constitute the largest private art and furniture collection in Bern. Although a new wing of twelve rooms has been added, the majority of rooms are housed in a building that dates back 135 years. A traditional decor has been selected for most of the guest rooms, so be sure to state a preference for traditional or modern when making a reservation. Also, even though the rooms at the front overlooking Bahnhof Platz are amazingly quiet behind double paned windows, rooms at back are assured of quiet even with the windows ajar. For dining, the hotel has two restaurants on the first floor. Both restaurants are intimate. The Yamoto has Japanese decor the other, the Schultheisen Stube, is Swiss cozy with a beamed ceiling and walls hung with tapestries. For more casual fare, just off the reception are an inviting pub and bar, and a bustling Brasserie, Jacks. The hotel is renowned for its traditional ambiance, elegant comfort and gracious amenities.

GAUER HOTEL SCHWEIZERHOF
Hotelier: Jean Jacques Gauer
Manager: Ueli Münger
Bahnhofplatz 11, CH-3001 Bern, Switzerland
tel: (031) 311 45 01, fax: (031) 312 21 79
90 rooms with private bathrooms
Double: Sfr 390 to Sfr 2,000
Open all year
Credit cards: all major
Restaurants open daily
Train walking distance from hotel
U.S. Rep: LHW 800 223-6800
Canton: Bern, at the heart of old Bern

If you are a fan of Art Nouveau, the Hotel Belle Époque is tailor-made for you. The owners, Dr Philippe Ledermann, a dentist, and his wife, Marina, are avid art collectors. Over the years they have acquired paintings by Toulouse-Lautrec, Sandier, Gaudí, Masriera and 100 other artists. The Belle Époque has become a virtual gallery where the Ledermann's display their collection. Art Nouveau (Belle Époque) furnishings and art from the early 1900s set the theme for the hotel—from the large paintings and murals in the cozy breakfast room and intimate bar, to the paintings hung in each of the bedrooms. The bedrooms, though not large, are attractive. Each has a pastel color scheme that compliments the original art displayed. Many up-to-date amenities are offered such as a mini bar, direct dial telephone, color television, radio, and even a fax outlet. The windows are insulated to protect those rooms facing the street from noise. There is no restaurant, but this is not a problem: Bern abounds with places to dine, and light refreshments can always be ordered from the bar. Even if your interest does not lie with art of this period, the Belle Époque has much to offer as a small and intimate hotel.

HOTEL BELLE ÉPOQUE
Hoteliers: Marina and Philippe Ledermann
Manager: Cordelia Kunz
Gerechtigkeitsgasse 18
CH-3011 Bern, Switzerland
tel: (031) 22 43 36, fax: (031) 22 39 36
14 rooms, 2 jr. suites, all with private bathrooms
Double: Sfr 286 to Sfr 316
Open all year
Credit cards: all major
No restaurant, breakfast and snacks only
Train 2 km from hotel
Located in old section of Bern
Canton: Bern, 111 km W of Lucerne

The Hospiz zur Heimat is housed in an historical building at the heart of old Bern, opposite one of the colorful statues of lovely Gerechtigkeitgasse. The hotel is near the clock tower, cathedral, town hall, and bear pit. The Hospiz zur Heimat is a good value if all you want is clean and convenient accommodation. Very basic in decor, the hotel lobby is simple and the doors and hallways, painted in shades of gray are appropriately reminiscent of a hospital. Guest rooms are basic, but clean, and color is introduced in the coverings that encase the down comforters that deck each of the beds. Back guest rooms enjoy the quiet of a small street, as opposed to front rooms that open onto the sounds of one of the city's most popular boulevards. Only seventeen of the rooms enjoy a private bathroom and are set at the luxury price of Sfr 124. Of the other rooms, the majority do have a sink in the room, while community bath and toilets are found down the hall–but rates are a bargain at below Sfr 100. Breakfast is included in the price and served in a neighboring building, accessed by a first floor corridor. Although the dining room is equipped with a full service kitchen, breakfast is currently the only meal served. Note: the only true objection I found to this hotel was the lingering smell of cigarettes. Over 80% of Europeans still smoke and ventilation in this older building is difficult.

HOTEL HOSPIZ ZUR HEIMAT
Hotelier: K.J. Westphal
Gerechtigkeitsgasse 50
CH-3001 Bern, Switzerland
tel: (031) 311 04 36, fax: (031) 312 33 86
40 bedrooms, 17 with private bathrooms
Double: Sfr 96 to Sfr 124
Open all year
Credit cards: all major
No restaurant, breakfast only
Train 1 km from hotel
Canton: Bern, at the heart of old Bern

Located in a residential district on the outskirts of Bern, the Innere Enge affords travelers a very peaceful setting close to the heart of this capital city. This is a lovely two-storey hotel whose windows are dressed with green shutters, on soft peach stucco, criss-crossed by burgundy timbers and topped by dormer windows. Nestled amongst greenery and a multitude of parks, the Innere Enge is an ideal selection for someone who likes to jog as there are endless miles of neighboring park terrain. The exterior color scheme of greens and burgundies is also used in the interior decor and warms the public rooms. A cozy fireplace in the entrance hall is an enticing place to settle, or you may be lured further to the historic Park Pavilion restaurant whose windows overlook the park. Here guests enjoy a morning breakfast buffet, lunch, dinner or afternoon tea. With just twenty six guest rooms, service is very personalized and attentive. The rooms, even the "standard" are quite comfortable in size and look out on the quiet of the surrounding greenery. The Innere Enge, although a new recommendation for us, has been an excursion destination since the early 18th Century. Eminent visitors include the Empress Josephine (the wife of Napoleon). On a clear day you can enjoy views from the garden across the city skyline to the distant Alps.

INNERE ENGE
Hoteliers: Hans Zurbrügg and Marianne Gauer
Manager: Marianne E. Bon
Engestrasse 45, CH-3012 Bern, Switzerland
tel: (031) 309 61 11, fax: (031) 309 61 12
26 bedrooms with private bathrooms
Double: Sfr 205 to Sfr 285, Suites Sfr 380 to Sfr 520
Open all year
Credit cards: all major
Restaurant open daily
Train 5 minutes by Bus No. 21 from railway station
Canton: Bern, on the outskirts of Bern

This lovely inn with its candy-striped, shuttered facade enjoys a tranquil setting on the banks of Lake Constance. We visited as mist settled on the water. The only sounds were lines flapping against the masts of harbored sailboats, and the squawking of ducks and swans in flight. It was misty when we arrived, but within an hour the sun had pierced the fog, making the lawn of the hotel that stretches down to the river's edge a most inviting spot. On summer days, guests lounge at tables set in the shade of trees and swim in the lake. Just inside the entry of the hotel is the reception, often serviced by someone from the coffee shop or restaurant. Opening onto the back garden is the Schifferstube, an informal but cozy restaurant offering luncheon and breakfast. A gourmet restaurant is found up another flight of steps whose tables are elegantly set with pastel colored linens and fine china. The Schlössli Bottighofen has eleven guest rooms. Four of the rooms enjoy the spaciousness of a sitting area, the others are smaller, but comfortable. Most rooms have views looking out through thick set windows directly onto, or across the boats and harbor to the lake. The guest room decor is exceptionally pretty with the use of lovely country prints. Converted to an inn in the last century, Schlössli Bottighofen had a number of owners, one of its most famous, the French liquor king, Pernot.

SCHLÖSSLI BOTTIGHOFEN
Hotelier: Bruno Lüthy
Seestrasse, CH-8598 Bottighofen, Switzerland
tel: (072) 75 12 75, fax: (072) 75 15 40*
*New 03/96, unknown, old good through 1996
11 rooms with private bathrooms
Double: Sfr 195 Sfr to 260 Sfr
Open all year
Credit cards: all major
Restaurant open daily
Train 2 minutes walk from railway station
Canton: Thurgau, 5 km SE of Constance

Window boxes hung heavy with geraniums color the wonderful weathered facade of the Chalet Schönegg. With views looking out over Brienz and across the lake to the majestic peaks beyond, this charming country hotel enjoys a lovely, peaceful setting. Guest rooms are housed in three buildings, the Schönegg, Chalet and Spycher. A wonderful free standing chalet-cottage, the Schönegg, a chalet that dates back to 1602, houses three rooms that are gems, rooms 61, 62 and 63. Rooms 62 and 63 are found on the second floor of the chalet, tucked under beamed ceilings, with wood-paneled walls, sitting areas and views out through low windows to the lake. Room 62, a personal favorite, has Swiss, farm style painted furnishings and cozy fabrics selected for the drapes and comforter duvets. Each room has a private bath. Room 61, a garden level room in the same petite chalet, is also charming, but not quite as cozy without the angled ceilings. In both the main house, the Spycher, and the neighboring Chalet, guest rooms are more motel-like in style and furnishings. They are, however, quiet and enjoy wonderful views. Breakfast is offered in the main house, and a sitting area off the breakfast area is a friendly spot to gather, particularly when the fire is lit. A grassy terrace off the dining area and salon is a peaceful spot to enjoy a lazy afternoon or enjoy a game of ping-pong.

CHALET HOTELS SCHÖNEGG & SPYCHER GARNI
Hotelier: Christine Mathyer
Talstrasse 8, CH-3855 Brienz, Switzerland
tel: (036) 51 11 13
16 rooms, 10 with private bathrooms
Double: Sfr 100 to Sfr 140
Open: April to end of October
Credit cards: EC, MC, VS
No restaurant breakfast only
Train 0.5 km from hotel
Canton: Bern, 18 km W of Interlaken

Champex-Lac is a resort town nestled by a jewel-like, tree-rimmed lake high in a mountain valley above Montreux. The Relais du Belvédère is a short distance away from the lake, where instead of a view of the lake, there is a sweeping view of the Entremont Valley bound by the Combin Massif and the foothills of Mont Blanc. The Relais du Belvédère reminds me very much of a bed and breakfast you might find in the United States: the rooms are filled with little homey touches such as a spray of dried flowers hanging by the mirror, lacy pillows, crocheted doilies, knick-knacks on the dresser. The pine-paneled bedrooms (each with a balcony) are simple but attractive. Almost all have antique beds (with good mattresses) and practical niceties such as good reading lights. In some of the bedrooms the showers are tucked into a corner of the room, as are the wash basins. Request room number four, it is really choice—a corner room with lovely views from two balconies. Irene and Gabriel Favre prepare the meals that are hearty and delicious with many vegetables and fresh greens straight from the garden. In addition to good cooking the dining room offers a panoramic view through large windows to the valley and mountains. The Relais du Belvédère is a simple, inviting hotel where your hostess, Irene Favre, extends an old-fashioned welcome.

RELAIS DU BELVÉDÈRE
Hoteliers: Irene and Gabriel Favre
CH-1938 Champex-Lac, Switzerland
tel: (026) 83 11 14, fax: (026) 83 25 76
9 rooms, 8 with private bathrooms
Double: Sfr 130 Sfr to 150 Sfr
Closed: Dec 1 to Christmas, May 15 to May 20
Credit cards: EC, MC, VS
Restaurant closed Wednesdays
25 minutes by postal bus from Orsières
Canton: Valais, 15 km south of Martigny

Chur, one of the oldest cities in Switzerland, retains a large, attractive medieval section with hidden squares, colorful fountains, remains of ancient walls and an enticing network of cobbled streets. The Romantik Hotel Stern is situated in the heart of the charming, old part of the city. Pink with green shuttered windows, the building sits right on the street, but has a small garden terrace to the side. Inside, the public areas have many antique accents, but the bedrooms are standard in decor, with light knotty pine furniture typical of the Grison region. Each bedroom is individual in decor and size. The building is 300 years old and has many nooks and crannies reached through a maze of hallways. This well-managed hotel's most attractive room is the charming restaurant with mellowed-with-age pine paneling and rustic, country style chairs with carved hearts. The food is excellent. Because Chur is on the main rail line, it makes a convenient hub for exploring Switzerland. Although most people think of St Moritz as the terminal for the Glacier Express (for more information see Zermatt in the Sightseeing Section), Chur is an alternate choice.

ROMANTIK HOTEL STERN
Hotelier: Walter Brunner
Reichgasse 11, CH-7000 Chur, Switzerland
tel: (081) 22 35 55, fax: (081) 22 19 15*
*New 04/96: tel: (081) 252 35 55, fax: (081) 252 19 15
57 rooms with private bathrooms
Double: Sfr 195 to Sfr 245
Open: all year
Credit cards: all major
Restaurant open daily
Train 500 meters from hotel, free pick up
U.S. Rep: Euro-Connection 800 645-3876
Canton: Graubünden, 120 km SE of Zürich

The Hotel du Lac is located on the lake only about 12 km east of Geneva. Although the hotel is on a busy road, behind the hotel is a delightful garden on Lake Geneva. The lawn stretches down to a private pier. The Hotel du Lac carries the air of an elegant home rather than that of a hotel. It does not appear very old, but it is. In fact, in 1626 the Hotel du Lac was granted the exclusive right to receive and lodge people arriving by coach or horseback. At that time travelers by foot were excluded as guests of the inn because as a memorandum dated 1768 decreed: "The titled man of wealth riding in his own coach and four must not be housed with the peasant, the knife-sharpener, the chimney-sweep—the latter would feel too ill at ease." The Hotel du Lac has been carefully restored, and now you too, can dream you are one of the guests arriving by "coach and four." The hotel has retained many of its old beams, stone walls and lovely antique furniture and artifacts. All the bedrooms are attractive. Some have kitchenettes, seven suites have balconies with lake views, and some have a small terrace squeezed into the jumble of tile roof tops. For those who want to be away from the city, the Hotel du Lac makes an attractive choice for visitors to Geneva. The hotel belongs to Relais & Chateaux.

HOTEL DU LAC
Hotelier: O. Schnyder
CH-1296 Coppet, Switzerland
tel: (022) 77 61 521, fax: (022) 77 65 346
19 rooms with private bathrooms
Double: Sfr 230 to Sfr 300
Open: all year
Credit cards: all major
Restaurant open daily
Train 1 km from hotel, Boat 2 blocks from hotel
Canton: Vaud, 12 km E of Geneva

Le Vieux Chalet is located on the Jaunbach Pass as it winds east from Gruyères. Although not an old building, the inn exudes an old world charm and is built in the typical chalet style with dark timbered beams, white stucco, deep overhanging eaves and balconies heavily laden with flowers. Although the architecture is most attractive, what really makes Le Vieux Chalet so very special is the superb setting. Built on a small knoll, the inn has a spectacular view looking out to Lake Montsalvens and beyond to green pastures and forests that extend to a horizon of rugged mountain peaks. Behind the hotel, a spacious terrace wraps around two sides of the building. The terrace restaurant is a favorite place to dine and soak in the panoramic view while enjoying excellent food. There is also another dining room for cool weather dining. Throughout the interior there is a country ambiance, created by many rustic antique accents, including an enchanting set of enormous cow bells. The emphasis of this inn is definitely on dining, as there are only five bedrooms, and two of these are singles. Although not large, each bedroom is pleasantly decorated, and all have splendid views. Crèsuz-en Gruyère is a convenient base from which to explore by day the nearby, charming hilltown of Gruyères, or the beautiful city of Fribourg to the north.

LE VIEUX CHALET
Hotelier: Sudan Family
CH-1653 Crèsuz-en Gruyère
Switzerland
tel: (029) 7 12 86
5 rooms with private bathrooms
Double: Sfr 130
Closed January
Credit cards: all major
Restaurant closed Tuesdays
20 minute by postal bus from Bulle
Canton: Fribourg, 29 km S of Fribourg

The Auberge du Raisin is located in Cully, a sleepy little wine growing village. About a block from the hotel is a small park stretching along the shore of Lake Geneva—a perfect place to stroll while waiting for one of the lake steamers that pull into the dock. The fame of the Auberge du Raisin is based on its reputation for serving exceptional food accompanied by the finest wines. There are two dining rooms, each is lovely. My favorite though, is the enchanting dining room just off the foyer. Here you will find an oasis of gentle decor with cream colored walls, soft white draperies, and white linen tablecloths draped across round tables spaciously set about on slate floors. Even the chairs, each stripped to a mellow light wood, maintain the pastel look. Although the exterior of the hotel looks quite stern—a square box of gray relieved only by cheery red and white striped shutters, the interior of the hotel is delightful. Individual in their decor, size and arrangement, each of the guest rooms is beautifully furnished in color-coordinated fabrics and maintained to perfection. Antiques are lavished throughout and are complimented by lovely, bountiful flower arrangements. This small hotel, dating back to the 16th Century, is a delightful choice while enjoying one of Switzerland's most charming wine regions.

AUBERGE DU RAISIN
Hotelier: Blokbergen Family
1, place de l'Hotel de Ville
CH-1096 Cully, Switzerland
tel: (021) 799 21 31, fax: (021) 799 25 01
10 rooms with private bathrooms
Double: Sfr 205 to Sfr 410
Open all year
Credit cards: all major
Restaurant
Boat dock 1 block from hotel
Canton: Vaud, 70 km E of Geneva

At the heart of one of Switzerland's finest wine producing regions, the picturesque village of Cully is wrapped by terraced fields of grapes on three sides and fronted by Lake Geneva. Not only are the vineyards beautiful, but Cully is also one of the most picturesque of the charming villages that dot the shores of Lake Geneva. Many ferry boats stop at Cully's small pier across from a grassy park lined with shade trees. Facing the park and the lake is the superbly positioned Hotel Major Davel, a pink stuccoed building with gray-green shutters and a mansard roof. Many come by boat and stop in Cully to enjoy lunch in the hotel's glass-enclosed terrace restaurant with a view of the lake. Rolf Messmer, the hotelier, is also the chef and the food is excellent. But in addition to the restaurant, those looking for a reasonably priced place to spend the night will find that the Hotel Major Davel offers good accommodation. Upstairs (there is no elevator), the guest rooms are not deluxe, but certainly adequate, and each has a private bathroom. Especially inviting is room 12, whose balcony is tucked into a small alcove of the roof. With just twelve rooms, the owners pride themselves on the personalized service that they are able to offer their guests—and guests show their appreciation by repeated visits. Rolf and Bernadette are a young couple and they bring a new enthusiasm and warmth to this wonderful country hotel.

HOTEL MAJOR DAVEL
Hoteliers: Bernadette and Rolf Messmer
CH-1096 Cully, Switzerland
tel: (021) 799 11 37, fax: (021) 799 37 82
12 rooms with private bathrooms
Double: Sfr 150 to Sfr 160
Open: mid-January to mid-December
Credit cards: EC, MC, VS
Restaurant open daily
Steps from the boat dock
Canton: Vaud, 70 km E of Geneva

Dielsdorf is a small town north of Zürich, only about twenty minutes by car from the Zürich airport, or about twenty-five minutes from Zürich by train. The hotel is owned by Christa and Eugene Schäfer who also own the Rote Rose, a wonderful little inn only a few minutes away by car in the town of Regensberg. The Rote Rose is small, with only five rooms, so it's nice to have this as a second choice. The Hotel Löwen, built in the 13th Century, has been completely renovated. The outside is painted white with small gables and shuttered windows enhancing the country appeal. Floral paintings by Lotte Günthardt, Christa's mother, the world renowned rose artist, decorate the walls throughout this small inn. The bedrooms are pleasantly decorated. The suite is an especially large, light and airy room. If you are on a budget, the guest room without a private bath is a good value, but the most attractive aspect of the hotel is the very cozy dining room. Beamed ceilings, pretty linens, antique accents and fresh flower arrangements combine to create an inviting mood. The food is excellent. There are two choices for dining—either in the comfortable restaurant or the sophisticated tavern.

HOTEL LÖWEN
Hoteliers: Christa and Eugene Schäfer
Directeurs: Erich and Yvonne Hornung
Hinterdorfstrasse 21
CH-8157 Dielsdorf, Switzerland
tel: (01) 853 11 32, fax (01) 853 17 24
18 rooms, 7 with private bathrooms
Double: Sfr 120 to Sfr 180
Closed: 1st week in January and mid to end of July
Credit cards: all major
Restaurant closed Saturdays and Sundays
Train 1 km from hotel
Canton: Zürich, 20 km N of Zürich airport

A challenge to find, this auberge is on a country lane whose signs reference well trod foot paths as opposed to any town. With a gorgeous landscape of quiet rolling hills and a forested backdrop, this is a region to walk, bike, or cross-country ski. Bells hung from cattle or sheep echo in the valleys and beckon you over yet another hilltop. We stumbled on this auberge one week after it opened under the direction of Heinz Rub and the Münger family. Gracious in his attentive service and versed in five languages, Heinz's background is luxury hotels, and it is his dream realized to settle in this region, have cattle and horses to graze his pastures and run a country auberge. Frau Münger is an architect from Bern and her family commutes on weekends. There is nothing luxurious about this ancient auberge, but details of comfort were not overlooked during its renovation. Bathrooms are new, modern, tiled, and equipped with towel warmers. Guest rooms are fresh, painted white, have lovely pine doors, and built in pine beds. The curtains and fabrics that top the wonderful, plump down comforters are the only color introduced. The entry of the inn is through the auberge's country restaurant, whose decor is fresh and simple with chairs set at sturdy pine tables. In the restaurant, I enjoyed a delicious fresh trout baked in parchment, while other guests lingered over a large crock of fondue, and chicken that had been roasted on an open grill.

AUBERGE "LA PUCE"
Hoteliers: C and P Münger and Heinz Rub
CH-2333 La Ferrière, near St. Imier, Switzerland
tel: (039) 63 11 44
6 rooms with private bathrooms
Double: Sfr 140
Closed: two weeks every November and April
Credit cards: none accepted
Restaurant open daily when the Auberge is open
Train at Renan, 1 km on foot, 3 km by car
Canton: Bern, 7 km NE of La Chaux de Fonds

Geneva is known for its lovely lakeside hotels, but my heart gravitates toward the old quarter. Luckily an appealing hotel exists in Geneva for those who prefer to be in the quaint, old section of the city. I was immediately taken with the Hotel les Armures from the first moment I walked into the intimate lobby. The hotel was converted from a private residence dating from the 17th Century. There were no signs of tour groups, only guests sitting in a small lounge, talking quietly or reading—using the hotel as they would their homes. All the guest rooms have handsome wood doors and are decorated with traditional pieces and antiques. I reserved a standard room on my visit. It had a queen-sized bed, a small round table, antique style high-backed armchairs, bedside tables with lamps, a small refrigerator, and a very nice bathroom with a hair dryer. The room was quite small, but cozy, with a beamed ceiling and wood-paned windows looking over a quiet, shaded square and old fountain. Other types of guest rooms are termed either a suite—more spacious with a separate sitting room, or junior suite—larger than a standard room. When making a reservation, request detailed directions as the hotel is a bit difficult to find, and if possible, request a room overlooking the square. The hotel also has a restaurant, staggered over three levels, that offers well priced fare in contrast to the high room rates.

HOTEL LES ARMURES
Hotelier: Amedee Granges
1, rue du Puits St. Pierre
CH-1204 Geneva, Switzerland
tel: (022) 310 91 72, fax: (022) 310 98 46
28 rooms with private bathrooms
Double: Sfr 380 to Sfr 460
Open: all year
Credit cards: all major
Restaurant open daily
Train 2 km from hotel
Canton: Geneva, in heart of old part of town

Well located just off the Quai General Guisan and just a block or so from the heart of the old pedestrian quarter of Geneva, the Hotel de la Cigogne offers the ultimate in personalized service and luxurious accommodation. The atmosphere reminds me of an exclusive club or membership hotel. Furnishings throughout the hotel are elegant and ornate. The sitting room off the lobby has painted murals and the beautifully paneled restaurant has a stain-glassed ceiling. Guest rooms are individual in their decor, from the one modern room whose walls have been created to effect a grotto, to the other fifty-one rooms, all beautifully appointed, decorated with fine antiques from a varying assortment of periods and styles. Even the so-called standard rooms are comfortable in size, but the junior suites afford the spaciousness of an additional sitting area. The majority of the master suites are on two levels and enjoy the added luxury of two bathrooms, one off the bedroom and one off the living room or salon. All guest rooms have private bathrooms, all with bathtub–there are no showers at this hotel. La Cigogne was first recommended to us by a reader from Aspen. The hotel is a member of the prestigious Relais & Chateaux group.

HOTEL DE LA CIGOGNE
Directeur: Richard Bischoff
17, place Longemalle
CH-1204 Geneva, Switzerland
tel: (022) 311 42 42, fax: (022) 311 40 65
52 rooms with private bathrooms
Double: Sfr 395 to Sfr 830
Open: all year
Credit cards: all major
Restaurant open daily
Train 2 km from hotel
Canton: Geneva, in heart of the old town area

Le Richemond, facing Lake Geneva from across the Brunswick Garden, enjoys fabulous views of the Alps and the lake. Le Richemond, founded in 1875, has been owned and personally managed by four generations of the Armleder family. The very personalized service gives a warm inviting air to this luxury hotel. You enter into a spacious, elegant lobby enhanced by a superb collection of seven painted sedan chairs dating back to the 17th and 18th Centuries. These fancy enclosed chairs were carried by two footman who hauled the aristocracy from place to place within their large estates. Just off the reception area is an attractive art-deco restaurant, *Le Jardin*, with a lovely flowered terrace, and on the right, an inviting bar with dark wood paneling. For gourmet meals the enchanting *Le Gentilhomme* with richly brocaded walls and crystal chandeliers, sets the mood for intimate dining on tables beautifully dressed with the finest china and linens. Each guest room is individually decorated in a lovely traditional style. Future plans of the Armleder family for the hotel include a major expansion that will add an 18th-century English-garden, complete with antique fountains and statues.

LE RICHEMOND
Hotelier: Victor Armleder
Jardin Brunswick
CH-1201 Geneva, Switzerland
tel: (022) 731 14 00, fax: (022) 731 67 09
98 rooms with private bathrooms
Double: Sfr 588 to Sfr 688
Open: all year
Credit cards: all major
Restaurant open daily
Train 500 meters from hotel
U.S. Rep: LHW 800 223-6800
U.S. Rep: Utell 800 448-8355.
Canton: Geneva, in heart of Geneva

Perched high in the hills above Montreux, the Hotel Victoria (a member of Relais & Chateaux) is a handsome hotel with a mansard roof. From the hotel, the pool, and the perfectly manicured gardens terraced below, there is a truly breathtaking panorama of Lake Geneva backed by jagged mountain peaks. From the moment you walk inside this beautiful inn, there is an old world ambiance enhanced by handsome antique furniture. There are many niches in the various lounges where guests can relax. One of my favorites is the cheerful, bright, garden "sun room," a delightful spot to enjoy a good book or afternoon tea. The bar area is inviting, with dark paneling enhanced by old paintings. There are two elegantly decorated dining rooms that serve superb meals. The owner, Mr Mittermair, mingles throughout the dining room at dinner to make sure that his guests are well cared for. The guest rooms have been completely renovated and glamorous new suites added, with views so spectacular that you will never want to leave your room. Although this is a grand hotel, it is run with such warmth and fine management, you will feel like a guest in a private home. Compared to what you would pay to stay at a hotel in Geneva, the Victoria is a great value.

ROMANTIK HOTEL VICTORIA
Hotelier: Toni Mittermair
CH-1823 Glion, Switzerland
tel: (021) 963 31 31, fax: (021) 963 13 51
40 rooms, 9 suites, all with private bathrooms
Double: Sfr 200 to Sfr 320
Open: all year
Credit cards: all major
Restaurant open daily
Train 200 meters from hotel, free pick up
U.S. Rep: Euro-Connection 800 645-3876
Canton: Vaud, 80 km E of Geneva

The setting of the Hotel Krone is idyllic. Just across the street from the hotel, the Rhein River flows by and narrows on its course from Lake Constance. The Krone has an outdoor terrace on the banks of the river, with a cluster of small tables where meals are served in warm weather. When first I stayed at the Hotel Krone, I fell in love with this beautiful small inn, so well managed by the gracious Schräner-Michaeli family, who personally pamper each guest. At the time of my original visit, the dining rooms were spectacular, but the guest rooms were simple in decor. On my recent visit, I was delighted to discover that all of the bedrooms have been totally redone, each individual in decor, and each lovely. My favorites were those decorated in a French style with beautiful rose-patterned fabrics. The dining room remains as always, an elegant, paneled room with tables exquisitely set with crisp linens and fresh flowers. Best yet, the food is exceptional. The Hotel Krone makes an excellent base for exploring the northern region of Switzerland. Just steps from the door you can board the ferry that will take you along the Rhein. On a day's boat excursion you can visit the delightful village of Stein am Rhein with its wonderfully painted buildings or the medieval town of Schaffhausen.

ROMANTIK HOTEL KRONE
Hotelier: George Schräner-Michaeli
CH-8274 Gottlieben, Switzerland
tel: (072) 69 23 23, fax: (072) 69 24 56
24 rooms with private bathrooms
Double: Sfr 180 to Sfr 260
Open: March to December
Credit cards: all major
Restaurant
Rhein ferry across from hotel
U.S. Rep: Euro-Connection 800 645-3876
Canton: Thurgau, 7 km W of Constance

Sometimes I include a town because of an inn's location, but in this case, I've included an inn because I fell in love with the town. The mountain village of Grimentz is a cluster of old, storybook, darkened wood-timbered chalets, brilliantly accented with colorful flowers. This village deserves to be explored, and its appeal demands that you linger. Tucked at the entrance to the village is a whitewashed inn with handsome wood shutters. When I originally visited the Hotel de Moiry, the bedrooms were quite simple, and only a few had the luxury of a private bathroom. But now all have been renovated in a wood-paneled style, and each has a private bath. The dining room is warmed by a lovely fireplace. We had a hearty lunch of fondue, salad, crusty dark bread and beer. The tables are set with fresh tablecloths and flowers. Be sure to notice a mural on one of the walls that portrays an annual, regional, cattle competition. (I am happy to report that the cows belonging to the Hotel de Moiry are consistently the winners.) On an upper floor, there is a guest dining room decorated in wood carvings by the owner, Aurel Salamin, who recently took over the management from his parents.

HOTEL DE MOIRY
Hoteliers: Andrea and Aurel Salamin-Walker
CH-3961 Grimentz, Switzerland
tel: (027) 65 11 44, fax: (027) 65 28 96
16 rooms with private bathrooms
Double: Sfr 108 to Sfr 118
Open: December 20 to April 20
and June to November 5
Credit cards: all major
Restaurant open daily
Train to Sierre, 1 hr by postal bus to Grimentz
Canton: Valais, 55 km SW of Brig

Overlooking the lovely little Grindelwald church, is the small, shuttered, chalet-style Hotel Fiescherblick. The hotel is not fancy, but does possess a most inviting atmosphere. As you enter the lobby the mood is set by a great old Swiss clock, a painted Swiss wall cupboard, a little table paired with a regional alpine chair and a few very old milking stools. The dining room is decorated with modern furniture, but the flowers on the tables and the pewter mugs and antiques that adorn the walls add warmth to this area. The food is quite well known locally. In addition to the main room, there is an outdoor restaurant at street level. I was intrigued with the many little niches throughout the hotel artistically displaying antique farm implements. Mr. Brawand explained that the inn was originally his family's home and the collection of various farm tools were used on his father's farm. In one area are a number of cheese-making utensils, churns, a milking stool, sieves and wooden frames. All of the guest rooms have been renovated and are very fresh and charming. All of the bedrooms have small balconies, many with a spectacular mountain view. There are two restaurants. One is quite elegant, the other, that specializes in regional specialties, has a more rustic ambiance.

HOTEL FIESCHERBLICK
Hotelier: Johannes Brawand
CH-3818 Grindelwald, Switzerland
tel: (036) 53 44 53, fax: (036) 53 44 57
25 rooms with private bathrooms
Double: Sfr 170 to Sfr 250
Open: June to November and
  Christmas to Easter
Credit cards: all major
Restaurant closed Thursdays
Train 1 km from hotel, free pick up
U.S. Rep: Euro-Connection 800 645-3876
Canton: Bern, 20 km SE of Interlaken

The Gletschergarten, built in 1899, sits in a meadow of wildflowers, overlooking a glacier—an idyllic setting that inspired Elsbeth Breitenstein's grandparents to name their home *Gletscher* (glacier) *Garten* (garden). Originally a large family home (Elsbeth's mother was one of twelve children—eleven daughters and 1 son), the home gradually evolved into a small hotel. While helping her parents, Elsbeth met Finn Breitenstein, a member of the Danish ski team housed at the Gletschergarten. On the last day of the competition, Finn had an accident that delayed his departure. The rest is history. Elsbeth and Finn fell in love and today they are the third generation to operate the Chalet Gletschergarten, continuing the tradition of outstanding hospitality. The hotel is filled with old world charm: pine paneled walls, antique accents, original oil paintings by Elsbeth's father, and Oriental carpets. The cozily paneled dining room serves excellent food (be sure to take demi-pension). The bedrooms are attractive, and each opens onto flower-laden balconies that wrap completely around each floor of the hotel. The rooms in front overlook the mountains, but I fell in love with our accommodation (room 21), a quiet room in the back with a pretty view of green hills. There is a saying on the front of the hotel that translates: "Gladness to the ones that arrive. Freedom to the ones that stay here. Blessing to the ones that move on"—truly reflecting the spirit and hospitality of this delightful inn.

CHALET-HOTEL GLETSCHERGARTEN
Hoteliers: Elsbeth and Finn Breitenstein
CH-3818 Grindelwald, Switzerland
tel: (036) 53 17 21, fax: (036) 53 29 57
26 rooms with private bathrooms
Double: Sfr 190 to Sfr 240
Open: Christmas to Easter and June to October
Credit cards: none accepted
Restaurant open daily
Train 1 km from hotel
Canton: Bern, 20 km SE of Interlaken

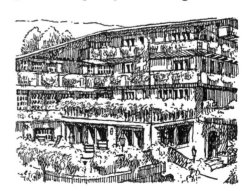

The Hostellerie des Chevaliers is located just outside the walls of the medieval village of Gruyères—up from the central parking area number 3. Guest rooms are found in the main building, each individually decorated with simple furnishings, country prints, and modern bathrooms. If possible request one of the rooms that overlooks the valley with a balcony. These rooms at back have stunning unobstructed views of the walled village of Gruyères and across the rolling hills grazed by sheep and cows, to high mountains. An underground gallery connects the guest rooms to a second building that contains a series of intimate dining rooms. Decorated with country antiques, copper pots, lovely hand painted tiles and masses of beautiful flower arrangements, the atmosphere in the dining rooms is one of elegance and romance. The kitchen under the direction of Monsieur Bouchery is renowned for its excellence. Monsieur Bouchery who is from Renaisson, France, studied with masters of French cuisine. Madame Bouchery told me that when she met her husband it was love at first sight! They married, Renaisson and Gruyères became sister cities, and the match of his wonderful culinary talent and her gracious warmth make the Hostellerie des Chevaliers a very special place.

HOSTELLERIE DES CHEVALIERS
Hotelier: Mr and Mrs Bouchery-Rime
CH-1663 Gruyères, Switzerland
tel: (029) 6 19 33, fax: (029) 6 25 52
34 rooms with private bathrooms
Double: Sfr 160 to Sfr 240
Closed: January 10 to February 10
Credit cards: all major
Restaurant closed Wednesdays
Train 1 km from hotel (in Gruyères/Pringy)
Canton: Fribourg, 35 km S of Fribourg

The Hotel Fleur de Lys is a beautiful old mansion located in the heart of the spectacular hilltop, walled medieval village of Gruyères. The hotel is family run, and Madame Doutaz's personal touch is ever present, from the supervision of the day's menu to the plumping of the comforters atop the guest room beds. The hotel caters to the number of tourists that understandably flock to Gruyères each day and offers them regional specialties. One dining room is reserved for groups, but there are two others for individual guests. One of these is located in the basement and is called the Cave. The Cave is a charming room, interesting in its display and use of artifacts involved in making cheese: hanging in the open fireplace is a large copper pot where cheese is still made, a marvelous, large whisk stands behind the pot, and hung over the fireplace is a wooden shoulder pack that balances on the shoulders of the cows for carrying cheese to village markets. The menu naturally features local specialties made from Gruyères cheese, famous the world over. In the evening as quiet settles over the town, it is nice to retire to one of the inn's eleven rooms. Simple in their decor and furnishings, the rooms are pretty with country print curtains, and down comforters topping the beds. Rooms at back enjoy views of the countryside and those at front overlook the square.

HOTEL FLEUR DE LYS
Hotelier: C. Doutaz-Bussard Family
CH-1663 Gruyères, Switzerland
tel: (029) 6 21 08, fax: (029) 6 36 05
11 rooms with private bathrooms
Double: Sfr 155
Closed: February
Credit cards: all major
Restaurant closed Tuesdays in spring
Train 1 km from hotel
Canton: Fribourg, 92 km E of Geneva

The Hostellerie de St Georges is a simple hotel in the heart of the beautiful hilltop, walled medieval village of Gruyères. The hotel is named for old St George himself, and you will see our mighty hero slaying the dragon on the brightly colored emblem proudly displayed over the front door, and again on a carving hung over an antique chest in the main hallway. Each bedroom door is specially numbered with a motif from the era of St George. On the door of one room there is a whimsical knight with a sword raised high, on another a musician playing an instrument similar to a bagpipe, while yet another has a witch-like character riding a broom. The bedrooms are currently being redecorated and are greatly improved since the first edition of our guide. Rooms 2 and 3 are especially attractive. The dining room is very popular and has a large, enclosed terrace with a stunning view of the valley. The food is good, and the menu naturally features local specialties made from Gruyères cheese. The quiche is so incomparably light, with such a delicate pastry, that it is tempting to order it at every meal. Our visit coincided with strawberry season, so dinner concluded with a large bowl of fruit smothered in the thickest cream I had ever seen—another product of these clever Gruyères cows.

HOSTELLERIE DE ST GEORGES
Hotelier: Francois Olivet
CH-1663 Gruyères, Switzerland
tel: (029) 62 246, fax: (029) 63 313
14 rooms with private bathrooms
Double: Sfr 150 to Sfr 200
Closed: January 10 to February 20
Credit cards: all major
Restaurant closed Mondays
Center of medieval Gruyères
Train 1 km from hotel
Canton: Fribourg, 40 km NE of Montreux

The Hotel Olden, a tradition for those in-the-know who visit Gstaad, is a chalet-style, cream-colored inn, embellished with flowers, cheerful green shutters and boxes of red geraniums. This charming inn is a favorite of all, not only the local farmers who come to the pub, Pinte, for refreshment, but also the jet-set of the world. They come to dine and dance in the Olden's chic restaurants where the food is superb and includes many regional favorites such as fondues and scrumptious desserts. Each of the individually decorated bedrooms has an attractive, traditional ambiance. Some have stylized paintings on the cupboards and doors, painted by Heidi Donizetti, whom I should add, is truly the heart and soul of this very special little hotel. I am quite sure that although the rooms are inviting and the food outstanding, it is Heidi (who was born at the Olden and, as a little girl, entertained guests by yodeling) that brings the guests back year after year. She seems to be a friend of every one in town—the local farmers as well as kings and movie stars, and treats them with the same genuine, warm hospitality. She is also an accomplished singer, so don't be surprised some night if she gets up to join Lisa Minelli as they belt out *New York, New York* together. Even if you do not stay at the Hotel Olden when in Gstaad, stop by and enjoy a superb meal, and look around. Who knows, at the next table you might see Julie Andrews, Elizabeth Taylor, or Roger Moore.

HOTEL OLDEN
Hotelier: Heidi Donizetti
CH-3780 Gstaad, Switzerland
tel: (030) 4 34 44, fax: (030) 4 61 64
18 rooms with private bathrooms
Double: Sfr 150 to Sfr 345
Closed: May
Credit cards: all major
Restaurant open daily
Train 3 minute walk from hotel
Canton: Bern, 64 km NE of Montreux

The Post Rössli is an appealing small hotel in the pretty town of Gstaad. Little touches show a special personal warmth. There are plants in the entry and a few well-placed antiques to give an inviting welcome, and off the hall are two marvelous dining rooms. One dining room tends to be used for casual lunch. The other is truly charming, with wood paneling, alpine-style chairs (carved with heart designs and tied merrily with rose-colored cushions), green plants, some old prints, and copper pieces displayed on the walls. Like the decor, the cuisine is exceptional. The bedrooms have recently all been renovated (some of them in beautiful old wood) and equipped with every comfort including TV, mini bars and direct-dial phones in every room. Room 112 is especially nice with dark wood paneling, and a door opening onto a rooftop terrace. Gstaad is a busy tourist town, but the country village aspect has not gone away, as we discovered upon awakening to the sound of melodic cow bells instead of the noise of traffic. Out of the window we saw a herd of cows whose pace was governed by the singsong chant of a young boy. Mr Widmer, the owner, not only acts as the gracious host, but also as a trail guide in the summer, and a ski guide in the winter.

POST HOTEL RÖSSLI
Hotelier: Mr Ruedi Widmer
CH-3780 Gstaad, Switzerland
tel: (030) 4 34 12, fax: (030) 4 61 90
18 rooms with private bathrooms
Double: Sfr 220 to Sfr 260
Open: all year
Credit cards: all major
Restaurant closed Wed. and Thurs. off season
Train 3-minute walk from hotel
Canton: Bern, 88 km E of Geneva

We were exploring the valley beyond Gstaad, heading south toward the soaring mountains, when we discovered the picture-book-perfect hamlet of Gsteig. In the middle of the village near the church is the Hotel Baren, with what must be one of the prettiest facades in Switzerland. The Hotel Baren is a typical Saanen-style house and this original 17th-century wooden inn is such an outstanding example that it is protected under special Swiss law. The heavy, sculptured beams and intricately carved exterior walls are exquisite. In summer, the cheerful geraniums at each window, red checked curtains peeking through the small window panes, plus the jaunty Swiss flags hanging from the upper windows enhance the image of the perfect Swiss inn. The decor in the dining room continues with the regional flavor. This room is richly paneled and furnished with country-style wooden chairs and tables. Red checked tablecloths and fresh flowers on the tables add further charm. The inn is largely famous for its cuisine and a wonderful Raclette is a favorite each evening. There are several small, but neat and clean, moderately priced guest rooms with beds decked with traditional soft, down comforters. When requesting a room, please note that only one, room 7, has a private bath, and that rooms 5 and 6, although, without private bath, are more spacious.

HOTEL BAREN
Hotelier: B. Ambort Family
Manager: Sonja Ambort
CH-3785 Gsteig, Switzerland
tel: (030) 5 10 33, fax: (030) 5 19 37
7 rooms, 1 with private bathroom
Double: Sfr 100 to Sfr 140
Closed: November
Restaurant closed Mondays
Credit cards: all major
Train to Gstaad, then postal bus to Gsteig
Canton: Bern, 10 km S of Gstaad

The Alpenrose was closed between seasons when I visited the Gstaad area, but when I called ahead, the owner, Monika Von Siebenthal, graciously offered to meet me at the inn and give me a personal tour. It was snowing as I arrived, and Monika appeared at the same time, walking briskly up the road, warmly dressed in boots and cap with her enormous, lovable dog Sammy in tow. Although the inn was in the midst of spring cleaning, I saw all of the guest rooms and had the opportunity to become friends with Monika, a very special person, filled with a gracious warmth. With the support of her five children, she runs the Alpenrose and personally assists in the decorations of each of the rooms. Her loving touches are everywhere. Her son, Michael, having graduated from his apprenticeship at the prestigious Real in Vaduz, plus famous restaurants in France, assists in maintaining the excellence of the kitchen. (The restaurant at the Alpenrose is renowned for outstanding cuisine.) One of her lovely daughters is in charge of the front desk. When this book was first published, there were only five guest rooms. Now after extensive renovations, there are twenty, yet none of the personal family warmth has been lost with the increased size. Each of the bedrooms is stunningly decorated with a happy, country flair, and each has a balcony with a gorgeous view of the mountains. The Alpenrose is a member of Relais & Chateaux.

HOTEL ALPENROSE
Hotelier: Von Siebenthal Family
CH-3778 Gstaad-Schönried, Switzerland
tel: (030) 46 767, fax: (030) 46 712
20 rooms with private bathrooms
Double: Sfr 260 to Suite Sfr 460
Closed: November 20 to mid-December
Credit cards: EC, MC, VS
Restaurant closed November and December
Train 1 km from hotel
Canton: Bern, 7 km N of Gstaad

Guarda, a cluster of very old, intricately painted farmhouses with flowers at every window, nestles on a mountain shelf high above the Engadine valley. Without a doubt, this is one of the most picturesque hideaways in Switzerland. Happily, there is a gem of a hotel to match the perfection of the village. The Hotel Meisser is beautifully situated on a promontory overlooking the expanse of green valley below, with a terrace where guests can enjoy refreshments served by waitresses in local costume—truly a blissful scene. The hotel, a typical Engadine farmhouse, dates back to the 17th Century. It was Mr Meisser's great grandfather who, in 1893, first converted a few rooms for paying guests. Do not expect fancy, decorator-perfect sophistication. This is a simple hotel, but one of our favorites. And it really has everything: the town is charming, the setting breathtaking, the food delicious, the warmth of the owners outstanding and the ambiance cozy. If you want an especially memorable stay, room 16 has a balcony with a view you will always remember. Two new suites are promised in the wonderful old annex for 1995. Throughout the hotel there is an old world ambiance achieved through the use of antique chests, pieces of old copper, oil paintings, and baskets of fresh flowers everywhere. We often recommend that you should not rush from hotel to hotel—it is especially true here, settle in to appreciate one of Switzerland's most beautiful valleys.

HOTEL MEISSER
Hoteliers: Kathrin and Ralf Meisser
CH-7549 Guarda, Switzerland
tel: (081) 862 21 32, fax: (081) 862 24 80
25 rooms with private bathrooms
Double: Sfr 170 to Sfr 230
Open: June to November
Credit cards: all major
Restaurant open daily
Postal Bus from Scuol
Canton: Graubünden, 81 km NE of St. Moritz

Several readers have written to us recommending the Hotel Krebs as their favorite place to stay in Interlaken. Whereas many places to stay in this bustling tourist center seem quite impersonal, the Hotel Krebs has real heart. This is not a tiny inn (it even caters to small groups), but somehow the owners, Marian and Peter Koschak, extend such a genuine warmth of welcome that guests feel very special. The hotel has been handed down through four generations of the Krebs Family. On the first floor are several small lounges, comfortable and homey with an old-fashioned ambiance. To the right of the reception are three dining rooms that open onto each other; in addition, meals are served outside on the terrace on sunny days. The bedrooms are all individually decorated in a somewhat standard hotel look. Each has television, comfortable beds, mini bar, and good reading lights. The rooms in the back are quieter, but those in front have a view of the Jungfrau. I was surprised that the mountains could be seen (since the hotel is in the center of town), but Mrs Koschak told me that her great grandfather, setting trends far before his time, negotiated with the city fathers that no tall buildings could be built to obstruct the view.

HOTEL KREBS
Hoteliers: Marian and Peter Koschak-Krebs
Bahnhofstrasse 4
CH-3800 Interlaken, Switzerland
tel: (036) 22 71 61, fax: (036) 23 24 65
51 rooms with private bathrooms
Double: Sfr 195 to Sfr 245
Open: May to October
Credit cards: all major
Restaurant open daily
Train 2 minute walk from hotel
U.S. Rep: Euro-Connection 800 645-3876
Canton: Bern, 68 km SW of Lucerne

The Hotel du Lac, owned by the Hofmann family for over one hundred years, is more French than Swiss in appearance with gray mansard roof and pink facade. The hotel is located directly on the banks of the Aare River as it flows between the two lakes of Brienz and Thun. Many of the bedrooms overlook the river—a peaceful scene of boats and swans gliding below. There are two dining rooms, and one, the Restaurant Rivière, is especially appealing with large windows opening onto lovely river views. In recent years, all forty guest rooms have been refurbished and all now offer modern comfort and stylish decor. Although too large to be considered a country inn, the Hotel du Lac does discourage conference and group bookings at the height of season, and if you want a convenient base for excursions, it cannot be surpassed. The Hotel du Lac's location is superb, just steps from where the trains depart for the Jungfraujoch excursion and minutes from the dock where the boats leave for exploring Lake Brienz.

HOTEL DU LAC
Hotelier: Hofmann Family
Hoheweg 225
CH-3800 Interlaken, Switzerland
tel: (036) 22 29 22, fax: (036) 22 29 15
Closed: mid-January to mid-February
40 rooms with private bathrooms
Double: Sfr 160 to Sfr 240
Credit cards: all major
Restaurant closed Wednesdays
Train and boat, both 100 m from hotel
Adjacent to train for Jungfraujoch trip
U.S. Rep: Best Western 800 528-1234
U.S. Rep: Euro-Connection 800 645-3876
Canton: Bern, 59 km SE of Bern

The Gasthof Hirschen, dating back to 1660, is located in Matten, just a ten-minute walk from the center of Interlaken. If you would like to stay in a picture-perfect chalet just oozing with charm, the Gasthof Hirschen is an ideal choice. In the not too distant past, the Gasthof Hirschen was surrounded by pastures, but today it is on the main road to the Jungfraujoch. Although located on a busy corner, in back of the inn is a tranquil, shaded garden. The facade is picture-perfect—darkened-with-age wood is set off to perfection by the brilliant red of cascading geraniums and intricately carved balconies. The Gasthof Hirschen is as charming inside as out. Marian and Peter Graf (the 9th generation owners of the Gasthof Hirschen) have created an appealing country ambiance using antique furniture, century-old cow bells, spinning wheels, and old clocks. The bedrooms are very attractively decorated in light pine furniture. On the ground level is a *stubli* where both local and international dishes are a specialty. Peter Graf is the chef, who when not tending the kitchen, is out working in the fields. All the eggs, butter, cheeses, chickens, and even beef, come straight off their farm—no wonder the food is so delicious.

GASTHOF HIRSCHEN
Hoteliers: Marian and Peter Graf-Sterchi
Hauptstrasse 11
CH-3800 Interlaken, Matten, Switzerland
tel: (036) 22 15 45, fax: (036) 23 37 45
24 rooms with private bathrooms
Double: Sfr 150 to Sfr 230
Closed: November
Credit cards: all major
Restaurant closed Tuesdays
Train 2 km from hotel
Canton: Bern, 180 km S of Zürich

The Landgasthof Ruedihus is the perfect Swiss inn, exactly what I'd always hoped to discover, but had almost decided did not exist except in my dreams: a cozy, flower-laden chalet, nestled in a lush meadow, backed by mountains and brimming inside and out with antique charm. This tiny chalet, dating back to 1753, is fashioned entirely of wood, darkened through the years and decorated with both carved and painted peasant designs. Two rows of small bottle-glass windows stretch across the front of the house, highlighted by boxes of red geraniums. Inside the romance continues—every room is a dream. Appropriate country antiques are used throughout. Most of the bedrooms have genuine antiques, and those that do not, have beautifully crafted reproductions. Some of the bedrooms have a view of the mountains, but because of the authentic nature of the building, some of the rooms have small windows peeking out from under the deep eaves. But no matter what bedroom you choose, if you enjoy an old world ambiance, you will be happy—each one is enchanting. Although there are only nine bedrooms, the inn has its own well-equipped kitchen, and excellent meals are served in the intimate dining room. Note: reservations are handled by the Waldhotel Doldenhorn—see page 177.

LANDGASTHOF RUEDIHUS
Hoteliers: Anne and René Maeder
CH-3718 Kandersteg, Switzerland
tel: (033) 75 15 80, fax: (033) 75 18 28
9 rooms with private bathrooms
Double: Sfr 170 to Sfr 200
Open: all year
Credit cards: none accepted
Restaurant closed Tuesdays
Train 2 km from hotel
U.S. Rep: Euro-Connection 800 645-3876
Canton: Bern, 45 km SW of Interlaken

The Royal Hotel Bellevue enjoys a very special position in the middle of the Bernese Oberland, between Gstaad and Interlaken—easily reached in three hours by direct train from the Zürich airport. Kandersteg offers a hiker's paradise through protected valleys to woods, mountains, lakes, and glaciers. The rear of the Royal Hotel Bellevue affords splendid views across gorgeous meadows to the soaring mountain peaks. The wide lawns of the hotel in summer are a velvet carpet of grass. In the garden is an outdoor pool; inside another pool, sauna and solarium. The Royal Hotel Bellevue, although recently constructed, reflects an old-world elegance with cavernous fireplaces, comfy leather sofas, 17th-century tapestries and a scattering of antiques to accentuate the ambiance. The dining room is especially elegant: tables set with crisp white tablecloths, upholstered armchairs, and giant chandeliers. (Jacket and tie required for dinner.) The bedrooms are elaborately decorated. Some of the furnishings are a bit too ornate for my taste, but very luxurious. In addition to the swimming pools, the hotel has its own riding stables, a tennis court, plus motor and sail boats (on nearby Lake Thun). Like so many of the excellent inns within Switzerland, the gracious owner, Albert Rikli, is the fourth generation Hotelier.

ROYAL HOTEL BELLEVUE
Hotelier: Albert Rikli
CH-3718 Kandersteg, Switzerland
tel: (033) 75 12 12, fax: (033) 75 13 33
35 rooms with private bathrooms
Double: Sfr 400 to Sfr 760*
*includes breakfast and dinner
Open: mid-December to March and June to September
Credit cards: all major
Restaurant open daily
Train 1 km from hotel
U.S. Rep: LHW 800 223-6800
Canton: Bern, 66 km SE of Bern

The Waldhotel Doldenhorn is beautifully positioned at the end of the Kandersteg Valley. Behind the hotel the wooded mountains rise precipitously. Alongside, a creek winds through the trees then gently loops through the meadow in front of the hotel. There are two sections to the hotel, the main building and an adjacent chalet (where the guest rooms are less expensive). Registration is in the main hotel. Steps lead up to a reception area that opens onto an attractively decorated lounge with dark paneling, handsome striped fabric on high-backed chairs and intimate groupings of leather chairs. Beyond the lounge is the Grüner Saal, an elegant, rather formal, dining room with green striped draperies framing large windows, silver chandeliers, and tables properly set with pretty linens and fresh flowers. There is also the Restaurant Burestube, a wood paneled dining room with rustic country wooden chairs and milk-glass lamps hanging from decoratively paneled wood ceiling. Each of the bedrooms is individually decorated, many with lovely antiques. One of the more expensive, but especially lovely rooms is 109, a spacious bedroom with lovely antique furniture and a pretty view. Anne and René Maeder also own the Landgasthof Ruedihus situated in a meadow across the road. The Waldhotel sets a more formal charm, while the Landgasthof Ruedihus exudes a rustic, ambiance.

WALDHOTEL DOLDENHORN
Hoteliers: Anne and René Maeder
CH-3718 Kandersteg, Switzerland
tel: (033) 75 18 18, fax: (033) 75 18 28
24 rooms with private bathrooms
Double: Sfr 180 to Sfr 290
Closed: November to mid-December
Credit cards: all major
Restaurant closed Tuesdays
Train 2 km from hotel
U.S. Rep: Euro-Connection 800 645-3876
Canton: Bern, 156 km E of Montreux

Almost considered a landmark of Switzerland, the Kleine Scheidegg Hotel sits on a barren, windswept landscape that challenges all but the giant Eiger. It is recognized by many for its part in the staging of the adventure movie *The Eiger Sanction*. The public rooms are attractive with a turn-of-the-century mountain hotel ambiance. The overall name is the Kleine Scheidegg, but the hotel is actually in two parts: the Bellevue and the Des Alpes. The guest rooms (located in both buildings) vary tremendously in size and decor. Some are very dated, others have been recently rejuvenated, but all have character. You may not have a choice of accommodation, but if you do, I suggest you ask for one of the best rooms that have been recently refurbished in the Des Alpes section. The hotel has been in the same family for many years and is now owned by Heidi von Almen, who continues to take a very active part in the management. The town of Kleine Scheidegg consists of just a few sparsely scattered buildings serving as the junction for trains from Grindelwald and Lauterbrunnen bound for the Jungfraujoch. But even though quite isolated, in summer Kleine Scheidegg is bustling with activity. Many hikers can be seen having a snack before heading off on their adventures, and tourists bask in the sun while waiting for their train up to the Jungfraujoch.

KLEINE SCHEIDEGG HOTEL
Hotelier: Heidi von Almen
CH-3801 Kleine Scheidegg, Switzerland
tel: (036) 55 12 12, fax: (036) 55 12 94
63 rooms, 33 with private bathrooms
Double: Sfr 240 to Sfr 280*
*includes breakfast and dinner
Open: December to April and June to October
Credit cards: EC, MC, VS
Restaurant open daily
Train 2 minute walk from hotel
Canton: Bern, 28 km S of Interlaken

When preparing for the first edition of our guide to Switzerland, Klosters was on our itinerary. It had been twelve years since I had stayed at the Chesa Grischuna, but the vivid memories of that visit lingered with such pleasure that I knew if the hotel still existed I would want to include it. The season was different, winter's cozy blanket of snow having turned with spring into clusters of brightly colored flowers, but the interior was as I remembered—romantic and warm. Mellow, weathered paneling enriches most of the public rooms, while antique furnishings and accents of copper pieces and artistic flower arrangements blend beautifully. Without the benefit of antiques, the bedrooms achieve the country feeling utilizing charming provincial wallpapers and matching fabrics, copies of traditional Swiss furniture, exposed beams and gently sloping floors. Some of the bedrooms are small, but all are nicely decorated. If you are on a budget, you might want to consider a room without bath. The dining room is exceptional in cuisine and service with a country-formal atmosphere. The personality of the staff matches the character and charm of the inn. With each edition of our Swiss guide, we visit the Hotel Chesa Grischuna. It never disappoints us. It always remains a favorite.

HOTEL CHESA GRISCHUNA
Hotelier: Guler Family
Bahnhofstrasse 12, CH-7250 Klosters, Switzerland
tel: (081) 69 22 22, fax (081) 69 22 25*
*New 04/96: tel: (081) 422 22 22, fax: (081) 422 22 25
26 rooms, 17 with private bathrooms
Double: Sfr 160 to Sfr 340
Closed: Easter to mid-June and November
Credit cards: all major
Restaurant open daily
Train 300 meters from hotel
U.S. Rep: Euro-Connection 800 645-3876
Canton: Graubünden, 58 km E of Chur

The Hotel du Lac Seehof is in Küssnacht, a small town on Lake Lucerne. Many steamers that ply the lake stop here. The hotel is ideally situated directly on the waterfront where the boats dock, and serves as a popular luncheon spot. The town of Küssnacht is bustling with tourists, but there is a feeling of tranquillity in the oasis of the hotel's terrace restaurant. (The garden restaurant is a very popular attraction for tourists who have taken the boat for a day's adventure from Lucerne.) The Hotel du Lac Seehof has been in the Trutmann family for five generations and is now managed by Albert Trutmann and his attractive wife, Joan. Albert Trutmann lived in the United States for a number of years, speaks perfect English, and understands American tastes. Downstairs, the dining room to the left of the front hall is furnished with antiques and has an unpretentious touch of elegance. The food is excellent with fish featured on the menu. When we first visited the Hotel du Lac Seehof, it was very simple, but over the years the hard-working Trutmanns have been constantly upgrading and renovating their small inn. Now almost all of the bedrooms have a private bathroom.

HOTEL DU LAC SEEHOF
Hoteliers: Joan and Albert Trutmann
Seeplatz 6, CH-6403 Küssnacht am Rigi, Switzerland
tel: (041) 81 10 12, fax: (041) 81 56 96*
*New 11/95: tel: (041) 850 10 12, fax: (041) 850 10 22
15 rooms, 12 with private bathrooms
Double: Sfr 160 to Sfr 210
Closed: November
Credit cards: all major
Restaurant open daily
Lakeside setting–next to pier
Train 1 km from hotel
U.S. Rep: Euro-Connection 800 645-3876
Canton: Schwyz, 13 km NE of Lucerne

Meandering through the serenely beautiful Emmental Valley when researching the first edition of our Swiss guide, I happened upon the Hotel Hirschen. I remember being captivated by the small inn's wonderful facade of little shuttered windows sheltered by a deeply overhanging roof—a typical Emmental chalet. But on my first visit I thought the guest rooms needed a touch-up. Happily the hotel has been refurbished, and now it is attractive outside and inside. There are several dining rooms, all extremely popular, especially on Sundays when the rooms bustle with families sharing the noonday meal. The food is excellent. The kitchen has earned many honors, including *Officier Maître Chaîne des Rotisseur* and *Commandeur des Cordons Bleus de France*. To accompany your meal you can choose from 24,000 bottles of wine stored in a 15th-century wine cellar. There are only a few guest rooms. These are simply decorated, but pleasant, with light wooden built-in furniture, good reading lights, and modern bathrooms. The town of Langnau is one of the most charming in the Emmental Valley.

HOTEL HIRSCHEN
Hoteliers: U Weyermann Family and U Messerli
Dorfstrasse 17
CH-3550 Langnau im Emmental, Switzerland
tel: (035) 2 15 17, fax: (035) 2 56 23
19 rooms with private bathrooms
Double: Sfr 120 to Sfr 150
Closed: December and January
Credit cards: all major
Restaurant closed Mondays and Tuesdays
Train 700 meters from hotel
Canton: Bern, 31 km E of Bern

As you drive through the village of Lenzerheide, you are surrounded by the commercialism of a major ski resort—too modern, too new. But follow the signs to Sporz, into the hills, and suddenly you are in a high mountain hamlet. The area consists of mountain meadows enhanced by a backdrop of mighty mountain peaks. Nothing mars the landscape dotted by only a few weathered farmhouses. This is the location of the Hotel Guarda Val. At first glance you would never guess that a deluxe hotel is nestled into this tiny village, but closer inspection reveals a gourmet restaurant in one building, a Swiss regional restaurant in another, and guest rooms cleverly incorporated into a selection of smaller farmhouses. In winter the fields are blanketed with snow—a mecca for the skier. In summer the meadows are sprinkled with wildflowers and laced with paths—a delight for the hiker. The guest rooms, that vary from quite small rooms to suites, are all being redecorated in a modern decor. There are two choices for dining: one is an elegant, well-known French restaurant, the other a cozy, stubli-style restaurant that specializes in regional dishes.

HOTEL GUARDA VAL
Hoteliers: Beatrice and Heinz Wehrle
CH-7078 Lenzerheide, Sporz, Switzerland
tel: (081) 34 22 14, fax: (081) 34 46 45*
*New 04/96: tel: (081) 384 22 14, fax: (081) 384 46 45
34 rooms with private bathrooms
Double: Sfr 270 to Sfr 600
Open June to October and December to April
Credit cards: all major
Restaurant open daily
Postal bus from Chur to Lenzerheide, free pickup
U.S. Rep: Utell 800 448-8355
Canton: Graubünden, 150 km SW of Zürich

Fronted by a pretty fountain on a lovely little piazza, the Garni Cà Vegia is a beautiful Ticino patrician home dressed in the warmth of family antiques. The facade is painted in a warm wash of cream, the windows hung with green shutters, and the door is of heavy wood, framed in stone and topped by three lovely painted murals. The entry with its stone floors and walls hung with copper pieces and lined with handsome, antiques is most welcoming. Off the entry, there is a charming breakfast room with tables set before an open fireplace whose mantel boasts a display of pewter plates and with windows dressed in red and white checked curtains. Opposite the breakfast room is a room for guest use with television and game tables. Behind the home is a private garden, where in warmer weather, you can enjoy breakfast in the quiet of the country garden. Guest rooms are found upstairs, off hallways that are beautifully decorated with family antiques. The guest rooms are fresh and simple in their decor, sparing of antiques, but comfortable with basic, modern bathrooms. Located just six kilometers from Locarno and Ascona, you can escape to this rustic Ticino village with less than two hundred and fifty inhabitants and enjoy a quiet setting and reasonably priced accommodation. It also serves as an ideal starting point for some beautiful woodland and river valley walking trails.

GARNI CÀ VEGIA
Hotelier: Rodolfo Fusetti Family
CH-6656 Golino, Switzerland
tel: (093) 81 12 67, fax: (093) 81 24 07*
*New 10/95: tel: (091) 796 12 67, fax: (091) 796 24 07
12 rooms with private bathrooms
Double: Sfr 118 to Sfr 160
Open: March 15 to October 31
Credit cards: none accepted
No restaurant
Train Intragna station, 2 km from Golino
Canton: Ticino, 6 km NW of Locarno

The Hotel des Balances, located on the banks of the Reuss River has undergone an extensive renovation, transforming this potentially good, but previously somewhat dreary hotel, into a real winner. The characterful exterior remains unchanged. The riverside view of the building is white, highlighted with window boxes brimming with blue, yellow and pink petunias; the side of the hotel that faces a small square is totally covered with intricate paintings of angels, columns, warriors, costumed peasants, and flowers. From the hotel entrance, steps lead up to the lobby that opens into a cheerful lounge with an Oriental carpet and clusters of chairs, sofas, and writing tables. To the right of the lobby is the breakfast room, very attractive with large oil paintings on the walls. French doors from the lounge lead to a balcony that overlooks the river. As you enter the hotel, if instead of going up to the lobby, you take the steps to the lower level, you will find a choice of either a casual bistro with a delightful terrace looking out over the river, or a gourmet restaurant decorated in trendy modern colors. The guest rooms have also received a face lift and are now attractively decorated in pastel hues. The choice rooms, of course, are those with a balcony overlooking the river.

HOTEL DES BALANCES
Hotelier: Peter E. Busser
Weinmarkt, CH-6000 Lucerne 5, Switzerland
tel: (041) 51 18 51, fax: (041) 51 64 51*
*New 11/95: tel:(041) 410 30 10, fax:(041) 410 64 51
60 rooms with private bathrooms
Double: Sfr 310 to Sfr 350
Open all year
Credit cards: all major
Restaurant
Train 700 meters from hotel
U.S. Rep: Best Western 800 528-1234
Canton: Lucerne, 68 km NE of Interlaken

High on the hill, commanding spectacular views of the wonderful city of Lucerne is the dramatic Château Gütsch. Reached by a road that winds up behind the château, or by a wonderful private train that departs from the base of the hillside, this château was previously in our guide when it was personally owned. It then closed for a number of years and has since reopened with a flourish after an input of 10 million Swiss Francs. Rooms have all been redecorated with handsome fabrics and lovely furnishings. They appear all to be the equivalent of suites in style, size, and comfort. Many rooms enjoy spectacular views. A stone stairway leads down to a restaurant that is lovely, light, and open, with lots of windows. The views of Lucerne, both from the tables set indoors and the lovely outdoor terrace, are spectacular. Also downstairs is an intimate wine cellar, cozy and intimate. Upstairs, guests can enjoy another bar, again with great views and piano music. There are also a number of other large rooms used for private functions—please note, that although the château is intimate in number of rooms, 31, it can accommodate hundreds of people on a given weekend for special functions.

CHÂTEAU GÜTSCH
Directeur: Ivo Scala
Kanonenstrasse
CH-6000 Lucerne 7, Switzerland
tel: (041) 22 02 72, fax: (041) 22 02 52*
*New 11/95: tel:(041) 240 02 72, fax:(041) 240 02 52
31 rooms with private bathrooms
Double: Sfr 320 to Sfr 450
Open all year
Credit cards: all major; Restaurant
Train 1,5 km from hotel
U.S. Rep: Euro-Connection 800 645-3876
U.S. Rep: Utell 800 448-8355
Canton: Lucerne, on the hillside above Lucerne

Located at the heart of the pedestrian district of old Lucerne, just two blocks from the river and its multitude of bridges, it is hard not to notice the Hotel Krone with its soft yellow facade trimmed in gray and the striking black and gold signs. Well located, this is a reasonably priced hotel that offers clean and comfortable rooms. Just off the entrance the windows of the attractive lobby restaurant overlook the plaza. In the morning there is a buffet breakfast and light meals are offered during the day. Guest rooms are reached by an elevator or a spiraling stairway to the four upstairs levels. The rooms on each floor overlook the plaza at front or a quiet street in the back. I was a bit disappointed that the decor of the rooms did not match the quaint exterior, but they were spotlessly clean, comfortable, and are offered at a good price. The furnishings are identical throughout— chrome and leather, and fabrics of gray trimmed with a few soft pastels. Lighting appeared adequate, and bathrooms functional and modern. Rooms varied a bit in size and orientation, but otherwise seemed uniform in their style and decor.

HOTEL KRONE
Hotelier: Ursula Otto
Manager: Dominik Jost
Weinmarkt 12
CH-6004 Lucerne, Switzerland
tel: (041) 51 62 51, fax: (041) 51.53.15*
*New 11/95: tel: (041) 914 44 99, fax: (041) 914 44 90
24 rooms with private bathrooms
Double: Sfr 140 to Sfr 205
Open all year
Credit cards: all major
No restaurant, cafe
Train 700 meters from hotel
U.S. Rep: Utell 800 448-8355
Canton: Lucerne, 111 km E of Bern

The Wilden Mann is unique—an oasis of charm and hospitality located in the heart of the medieval city of Lucerne. The hotel has been in the Furler family for many years. Their love and caring are very evident. The hotel has a "genuine" feel of quality. Lovely antiques are used everywhere, not only in the lobby and lounges, but also scattered artistically throughout the hotel. There are three dining rooms, each delightful in its own way. The Gourmet is a French-style restaurant with pink tablecloths, candlelight, and in cold weather, a cozy fire. This dining room has a special feature: on one of the walls there are three framed scenes depicting the Wilden Mann as it appeared in the mid-1800s. Upstairs there is another dining area—an outdoor garden terrace where tables are set for dining on warm summer days. But my favorite place to dine is the Burgerstube, a charming, very Swiss country-style dining room with an ambiance of informality and warmth. Around the tables are wonderful wooden chairs—many of them antiques. The room's atmosphere is accentuated with wrought iron artifacts and colorful crests bordering the wall. Should you want to have a drink before your meal, there is an exceptionally cozy bar on the second floor.

Since the Wilden Mann is such an old building, the bedrooms vary considerably. If you are traveling with friends, you might each have a room entirely different in size and style of decor, even though the price may be similar. However, this is really one of the charms of this hotel. It is not a large commercial operation where everything has a stamp of sameness. Instead, each bedroom varies as it would if you were a guest in a friend's home. Many are decorated in coordinating colors with attractive bedspreads matching the wall paper and draperies. All of the rooms I saw were delightful, even the singles had charm. On one of my research trips I fell in love with my room, quite small but appealingly furnished with a single bed, dresser and desk—a perfect oasis to sit writing hotel descriptions while overlooking the weathered, red-tiled rooftops of Lucerne. It is no wonder that each detail of decor throughout the hotel is perfect—Mrs Furler personally supervises the decorating down to the selection of the fabrics used and the placement of the antiques. It is her caring touch that helps to make the Wilden Mann so warm and home-like. Recently she has completely renovated the entire hotel and even added several penthouse suites. Everything is fresh, new and exquisite. The antiques remain, but there is now a new, more up-to-date look to the hotel. The Wilden Mann has been in the family since the 19th century and the Furlers carry on the tradition that "every guest be pampered in this house." The staff is especially caring and attentive.

On their first visit to Lucerne, some tourists opt for one of the hotels along the lake. However, my choice is to be in the heart of historical old Lucerne and immersed in the romance of days gone by. Lucerne is such a convenient, walkable city, that no matter where you stay, all the sights are available by foot. My choice will remain the Wilden Mann, one of Switzerland's most personal small hotels, and always one of my very favorites.

WILDEN MANN HOTEL
Hotelier: Furler Family
Bahnhofstrasse 23
CH-6000 Lucerne 7, Switzerland
tel: (041) 23 16 66, fax: (041) 23 16 29*
*New 11/95: tel (041) 210 16 66, fax:(041) 210 16 29
43 rooms with private bathrooms
Double: Sfr 210 to Sfr 400
Open all year
Credit cards: all major
Restaurant open daily
Train 500 meters from hotel
Located in the heart of old Lucerne
U.S. Rep: Euro-Connection 800 645-3876
U.S. Rep: Utell 800 448-8355
Canton: Lucerne, 56 km SW of Zürich

The medieval section of Lugano is a marvelous maze of twisting alleys, stairways, pedestrian streets, a delightful confusion of little squares, restaurants and boutiques. The Hotel Ticino is located right at the heart of the old city on one of its most charming little plazas. It is an easy walk from the Hotel Ticino to the waterfront for a romantic evening stroll, or to where you can board steamers that leave every few minutes for lake adventures. Although the hotel is in an area closed to traffic, you can drive along designated pedestrian streets directly to the hotel to unload your suitcases, and then the staff will assist in parking your car in their private garage. Actually as parking is almost impossible in Lugano, I would recommend proceeding directly to the hotel and seek their assistance. Tucked just off the cobbled street, the entry of the Hotel Ticino is cozy and there is almost always someone at the front desk to greet you and welcome you to Lugano. Just beyond the entry, the inn opens up to a wonderful inner courtyard (reflecting the hotel's past history as a convent) that adds a feeling of spaciousness and an appealing garden atmosphere. The bedrooms and lounge areas are found on the upper floors off the hallway. Our bedroom window opened onto the central courtyard and the evening of our visit we were lulled to sleep by the heavy patter of rainfall that fell on the sheltering roof. Intimate lounge areas and guest rooms have a lovely selection of fabrics and furnishings and dramatic flower arrangements. Guest rooms tend to be small and unsuitable for large suitcases, and are without the benefit of air conditioning in the warmer summer months, but they are equipped with every modern convenience and comfort: hair dryers, soft, plush towels, bathrobes, luxury soaps, cotton balls, q-tips, notepads, pencils, papers—anything you could possibly want. Each level is bright with flowers and greenery and graced with some lovely paintings and handsome antiques.

On the first floor of the hotel, tucked off the lobby is the restaurant of the Hotel Ticino, one of Lugano's most intimate and popular restaurants. As it is a favorite with local residents as well it is wise to make restaurant reservations when booking your room. Mr

Buchmann is responsible for the kitchen and oversees the superb menu based on what he finds fresh each day at the market. Mrs Buchmann, multi-lingual, is a most attractive and gracious hostess who attends to guests and assists them with their selection of courses and complimenting wines. The Hotel Ticino, is a lovely, very old Tessin house that flourishes under the personal management and care of the Buchmanns. The Buchmanns effectively practice their motto "to serve is our duty—to serve well our pleasure." This is a very special inn.

The Buchmanns profess a great love and interest in art and the walls of their inn are hung with a diverse and wonderful collection of paintings. The city of Lugano attracts a number of international exhibits, and should you be interested, the Buchmanns knowledge is vast and they can well advise you on museums. (Not to be missed are the lovely gardens and museum of the Villa Favorita—perched on the hillsides above Lake Lugano.)

ROMANTIK HOTEL TICINO
Hoteliers: Claire and Samuel Buchmann
Piazza Cioccaro 1
CH-6901 Lugano Switzerland
tel: (091) 22 77 72, fax: (091) 23 62 78*
*New 10/95: tel:(091) 922 77 72, fax:(091) 923 62 78
20 rooms with private bathrooms
Double: Sfr 340 to Sfr 400, Apartment: Sfr 540
Open: February to December
Restaurant open daily
Credit cards: all major
Train 2 minutes from hotel
Located in the heart of old Lugano
U.S. Rep: Euro-Connection 800 645-3876
Canton: Ticino, 30 km N of Como

　　　　　　　　　Hotel Descriptions

The Villa Principe Leopoldo, a member of Relais & Chateaux, is located in the hills to the southwest of Lugano—about a 10-minute drive away. The hotel is very impressive from the first encounter—a stately, two-storied, ochre-colored building, softened by vines that lace the front and enhanced by a heavy red-tiled roof accented by many small chimneys of all shapes and sizes. This isn't just any villa—the Villa Principe Leopoldo was, as the name implies, at one time the residence of princes. There is not a warm, homey ambiance such as one receives in an owner-managed hotel, the feeling is more of a commercial operation. But for those who love opulence—this is the hotel for you. The air of sleek sophistication is set as you enter the long reception hall with its creamy-white marble floors, stately marble columns and potted palms. The living room, bar and dining room maintain the same air of elegance with abundant use of rich fabrics integrated with modern decor. Each of the bedrooms is a suite with a spacious sleeping area divided by tie-back draperies from the sitting area that has a sofa, desk and chairs. A hint of the clientele of this fancy hotel is that each room not only has the bedside phone, but also a portable phone so that the guests can keep in touch at all times. For the health enthusiast, there is a pool, tennis, gymnasium, sauna and solarium.

VILLA PRINCIPE LEOPOLDO
Hotelier: Peter Gantenbein
Via Montalbano 5, CH-6900 Lugano, Switzerland
tel: (091) 55 88 55, fax: (091) 55 88 25*
*New 10/95: tel:(091) 985 88 55, fax:(091) 985 88 25
24 suites with private bathrooms
Double: Sfr 540 to Sfr 600
Open all year; Restaurant open daily
Credit cards: all major
Train 7 km from hotel
U.S. Rep: Utell 800 448-8355
Canton: Ticino, 10 minutes SW of Lugano

La Elvezia al Lago is an attractive small hotel peacefully located along the lakeside footpath joining the towns of Castagnola and Gandria. There are seven guest rooms, each with its own bathroom and a balcony overlooking the lake. There is a small, attractive restaurant on the first floor of the hotel, but the favorite place to eat is the terrace restaurant on the edge of the water. La Elvezia al Lago is pretty, with a white facade cheerfully enhanced by blue and white awnings—a color scheme repeated in the blue striped awning over the waterside terrace and the blue checked tablecloths. Because the hotel is small, the Luckes do not accept reservations for less than five days, but if you call them upon your arrival in Switzerland, they will be delighted to arrange a room for a shorter stay if space is available. La Elvezia al Lago is a bit tricky to find. If you are driving from Lugano, head east toward Castagnola. Just beyond the Villa Favorita, take Via Cortivo, a small road ending at parking area called San Domenico. Call from the phone booth in the parking area—the Luckes will send a boat to pick you up at the adjacent dock. (If you prefer to walk, you can take the footpath from the parking area along the Sentiero di Gandria continuing east along the lake–about a 7 minute walk.) You can also take the ferry from Lugano to Grotto Elvezia.

LA ELVEZIA AL LAGO
Hoteliers: Mr and Mrs Lucke
Santiero di Gandria, 21
CH-6976 Lugano-Castagnola, Switzerland
tel: (091) 51 44 51*
*New 10/95: tel: (091) 971 44 51
7 rooms with private bathrooms
Double: Sfr 160 to Sfr 180
Open: April to November
Credit cards: all major
Restaurant; Train 4 km from hotel
Canton: Ticino, 1.2 km E of Lugano

Overlooking the greens of the neighboring 18-hole Lugano golf course, the Villa Magliasina is also referred to as a "golf hotel." This lovely terra cotta two-storey villa with a tile roof is set on lush acreage, and has a beautiful swimming pool. The feeling is one of a private club. Public rooms are decorated with comfortable, traditional furnishings and a few well-placed antiques. The restaurant is elegant and on summer nights the tables are set on the garden terrace–dining by candlelight under the stars. Breakfast is enjoyed in a salon overlooking the side garden, or on the patio by the pond, in the warmth of the morning sun. The guest rooms overlook the pool and golf course. Most guest rooms are located in the Villa and they are referred to and priced in two categories–the Flower and Villa Rooms. The Flower Rooms are the most expensive, elegant in their decor and vary in that they might be a bit more spacious, have a fireplace, or perhaps a large balcony. The less expensive Villa Rooms are a bit dated in their bathroom appointments and their furnishings. In a modern wing off the front drive, the Villetta offers the most reasonably priced accommodation. The Villa Magliasina, opened in 1956 and while we found the decor to be tired we appreciated the quiet, the attentive service, and the comfortable rooms.

VILLA MAGLIASINA
Hoteliers: M.L. Abbühl-Borter
Managers: Anne-Françoise and Claude Buchs-Favre
Via Vedeggi, CH-6983 Lugano-Magliaso, Switzerland
tel: (091) 71 34 71, fax: (091) 71 68 29*
*New 10/95: tel: (091) 606 34 71, fax: (091) 606 68 29
25 rooms with private bathrooms
Double: Sfr 260 to Sfr 340
Open: mid-March to mid-November
Credit cards: AX, VS; Restaurant open daily
Train 50 meters from hotel
Canton: Ticino, 7 km SW of Lugano

The Carina-Carlton is situated on the road facing Lake Lugano in the picturesque small village of Morcote, just a 15-minute drive south of Lugano. Across the street from the hotel is an outdoor cafe perched on stilts out over the lake. Flowers and a brightly striped awning add even further enchantment to this dining haven. An inside dining room has a wood-beamed ceiling, white walls accented by green plants, and a few well-placed antiques and Oriental rugs—a very inviting room decorated with style and good taste. The hotel is built into the hillside and there are multiple levels as the rooms climb the hill. The bedrooms in front can be a bit noisy with the traffic on the street below, but they are still my favorites. Quieter rooms are found in the back, many of those look out to the small pool snuggled in the upper terrace above the hotel. If you really want to splurge, room 45 is very special—a large bright corner room with two balconies, one looking out over the tiled rooftops to the lake and the other overlooking the pool with a vista to the church. If you want to make your base in Morcote while in Switzerland's beautiful southern lake district, the Hotel Carina-Carlton is convenient. You do not need a car, just climb aboard one of the many ferries that ply the lake for excursions to the many quaint towns on the water's edge.

HOTEL CARINA-CARLTON
Hoteliers: Ingrid and Rudolf Tschannen
Via Cantonale
CH-6922 Lugano, Morcote, Switzerland
tel: (091) 69 11 31, fax: (091) 69 19 29*
*New 10/95: tel:(091) 996 11 31, fax:(091) 996 19 29
23 rooms with private bathrooms
Double: Sfr 170 to Sfr 305
Open: March to November
Credit cards: all major; Restaurant open daily
Train 6 km from hotel
Canton: Ticino, 6 km S of Lugano

The village of Malans enjoys a spectacular setting on a hillside of green with a backdrop of forests and majestic snow covered peaks. At the heart of the quaint village of cobbled streets, the Hotel Weiss Kreuz is a structure of two buildings joined together by a glassed in stairway. Its four story facade is painted white and its windows are adorned with geometric designs painted in gray, yellows and orange. With their architectural expertise and life savings, Maria Elizabeth Hitz and her son, have completely renovated the building. Marrying modern with old, they have achieved an unusual mix of styles and ambiance. Five intimate rooms paneled in gorgeous woods with soft lighting and beautiful antiques are offered as individual dining rooms—they are absolutely splendid. Michelin has awarded the restaurant three forks and the reasonably priced menus are worth a detour. For an afternoon refreshment, a cozy, informal stube is a fun spot to settle and its terrace extends out on the rooftop with vistas of the surrounding hillsides. In the evenings you can enjoy piano music performed by Mrs Hitz, and the sound echoes softly down the central stair. Oriental carpets and handsome old chests decorate the hallways that lead to the eleven guest rooms. In contrast to the charm of the public rooms and restaurants, the guest rooms are surprisingly modern, and very expensive for the amenities they offer.

HOTEL WEISS KREUZ
Hotelier: Maria Elizabeth Hitz
CH-7208 Malans, Switzerland
tel: (081) 51 81 61, fax: (081) 51 81 62
11 rooms with private bathrooms
Double: Sfr 110 to Sfr 220
Closed: February
Credit cards: all major
Restaurant open daily
Train 5 minutes from nearest station
Canton: Graubünden, 21 km N of Chur

Window boxes hung heavy with deep red geraniums tiered against a wonderful old wood shingle facade caught our attention as we drove through Merlischachen. The Swiss Chalet was once the family home of the owners, Joseph and Ernst Seeholzer. Inside this marvelous old farmhouse, their family rooms have been converted to an intimate melange of dining nooks. Tables are set in what used to be the living room; in front of the old stove that used to service the kitchen—all nestled under old beams and clustered in intimate numbers surrounded by antiques and cozy furnishings. Downstairs where they used to burn schnapps and distill apples and pears is another lovely restaurant. Guest rooms in the original farmhouse are found at the top of a steep flight of stairs. Tucked under low ceilings, the accommodations are small, simple in comfort and decor. Only a few have a private bath, but the tariff is quite reasonable. In a newer, connecting building, the Queen Astrid, (dedicated to the Belgium Queen who died nearby), a private dining room is found in what was once the house chapel, and upstairs a few rooms have been converted to guest rooms—one a honeymoon suite. Because the dining rooms of the Swiss Chalet were so exceptionally inviting, we ventured further to investigate two additional buildings that offer accommodation under the same ownership. The newly built Schloss Hotel across the street from the Swiss Chalet has a lakeside garden. Inside antiques, armor, heavy beams, and wonderful large wooden doors create an appealing, almost theatrical, atmosphere. Guest rooms are modern in comfort, richly decorated and many look out onto the lake. The Château Golden Gate, also newly constructed, is opposite on the hillside above the other two buildings. Again the use of armor, beams, and heavy doors give a feeling of an old castle, and the hotel has all the modern conveniences including a sauna, solarium (small charge for use), and whirlpool. The guest rooms are large, lovely, and many enjoy wonderful views of the lake. There is also a rooftop terrace with spectacular views of the lake and distant mountains. The walls of the Château Golden Gate are hung with portraits of his many close friends and frequent guests all dressed ready for the hunt, and exhibit many hunting trophies. The owner does enjoy a sense of the whimsical. Honeymoon suites feature swinging, rocking, or floating beds (in the hotel pool), even carriages have been adapted to accommodate mattresses. If you stick with the traditional or standard rooms, you should be pleased with both the decor, comfort, views, and value in either the Schloss Hotel or the Château Golden Gate. Lunch and dinner for all three properties are offered in the charming dining rooms or terrace cafe of the Swiss Chalet (recognized by Michelin with two forks). There is a breakfast room and a terrace cafe (drinks only) at the Château Golden Gate. Again, what attracted me to this hotel "complex" was the idyllic weathered facade of the Swiss Chalet. But please note, that rooms in the Chalet are very basic, and although, rooms in both the Schloss and Château are spacious and well appointed, there is a bit of theatrics in the decor.

SWISS CHALET
SCHLOSS HOTEL
CHÂTEAU GOLDEN GATE
Hoteliers: Joseph and Ernst Seeholzer
CH-6402 Merlischachen, Switzerland
tel: (041) 37 12 47, fax: (041) 37 12 50*
*New 11/95: tel: (041) 850 02 50, fax:(041) 850 02 52
Swiss Chalet: 20 rooms, 7 with private bathrooms
Double from Sfr 89 to Sfr 129
Schloss Hotel: 26 rooms all with private bathrooms
Double from Sfr 144 to Sfr 244
Chateau Golden Gate: 25 rooms with private bathrooms
Double from Sfr 144 to Sfr 244
Closed: January 2 to February 16
Credit cards: all major
Restaurant open daily
Train 5 min. walk from hotel
Canton: Schwyz, 12 km NE of Lucerne

Mürren is nestled on a high mountain shelf. Across the valley are the giant peaks of the Bernese Alps. From the village, massive granite walls drop straight down to the Lauterbrunnen Valley far below. There is no access by automobile. The only way to reach Mürren is by cable-car from Stechelberg or by funicular from the Lauterbrunnen station—or for the true athletes, there is also the awesome option of hiking up the mountain. The Hotel Alpenruh is conveniently located adjacent to the Schilthornbahn cable-car (that begins in the valley floor at Stechelberg, stops in Mürren and continues on to the Shilthorn). The hotel is not old, but it is built in an attractive, low-rise chalet style. Wrapping around the front corner of the hotel is a large balcony, a favorite place for guests to gather on a sunny day to relish the view while enjoying a cup of tea or perhaps lunch. Inside, the hotel is tastefully decorated in traditional style. Just to the left of the reception area is a cozy, pine paneled lounge where guests can relax with a good book on a chilly day. The large dining room has a more modern look, but is softened by peasant-style paintings on paneled walls and brass gas-lamp-style light fixtures. The bedrooms are fresh and attractive with typical Swiss pine furniture with a built-in headboard, table, and two chairs. Most of the bedrooms have balconies with glorious views of the mountains.

HOTEL ALPENRUH
Hotelier: Juerg Schuler
CH-3825 Mürren, Switzerland
tel: (036) 55 10 55, fax: (036) 55 42 77
26 rooms with private bathrooms
Double: Sfr 180 to Sfr 200
Open: all year
Credit cards: all major
Restaurant open daily
Funicular from Lauterbrunnen, 5-minute walk
Canton: Bern, 20 km S of Interlaken

Located on the outskirts of the walled town of Murten, directly on the banks of Lake Murten, the Hotel Schiff enjoys a lovely waterside setting. With a multitude of dining rooms, a bar and evening music, the Hotel Schiff caters to day travelers and large groups. The hotel can accommodate up to three hundred people in its Lord Nelson, Salon Bleu, Bistro and outdoor terrace dining. However, in terms of guest rooms the number is intimate—just fifteen. Guest rooms, in contrast to the more modern public rooms, are pleasingly and surprisingly traditional in their decor and many of the rooms overlook the lake. All the rooms have a private bathroom and are equipped with direct dial phone, television, and mini bar. The corner rooms at the back are especially lovely and spacious, with windows on two sides. You can easily walk up to the walled town of Murten from the Hotel Schiff, and walks along the water front are lovely. From a long line of Hoteliers, Pierre Lehmann has chosen to anchor where Lord Nelson docked his boat. He is a charming young man, who oversees the Hotel Schiff with a gracious warmth and astute professionalism.

HOTEL SCHIFF
Hotelier: Pierre Lehmann
Direkt am See
CH-3280 Murten, Switzerland
tel: (037) 71 27 01, fax: (037) 71 35 31
15 rooms with private bathrooms
Double: Sfr 170 to Sfr 240
Open: all year
Credit cards: all major
Restaurant
Train 10 min. walk from hotel
Next to the ship docks
Canton: Fribourg, 31 km W of Bern

Hotel Descriptions   199

The Weisses Kreuz, located within the medieval walls of Murten, has been in the Bischoff family for over seventy-five years. It demonstrates the warmth and special caring that comes only with owner-managed properties. The hotel consists of four very old buildings. One part of the hotel (that was originally the stables) is a modern, white reception area. Stairs lead up to a lovely dining room highlighted by a giant crystal chandelier. A wall is dominated by an oil painting of Swiss soldiers preparing to fight Charles the Bold, Duke of Burgundy. This historically important battle took place in Murten in 1476. If the Swiss army had lost, Switzerland might today belong to France. On warm days, meals are served outside on a magnificent balcony that has a panoramic view of Lake Murten. Not only is the view stunning, but the food is outstanding (the restaurant has the coveted "Fish Medallion"). The majority of the rooms are across the street in old characterful adjacent houses that have been lovingly refurbished with fine antiques, handsome fabrics, and color coordinated wallpaper. In the main part of the hotel, upstairs from the restaurant, there are some rooms with French doors opening to small balconies. These rooms with a view of the lake are more modern in their decor and recently renovated, but are prime in terms of their views.

HOTEL WEISSES KREUZ
Hoteliers: Dr and Mrs Daniel Bischoff
Rathausgasse 31
CH-3280 Murten, Switzerland
tel: (031) 71 26 41, fax: (031) 71 28 66
27 rooms with private bathrooms
Double: Sfr 140 to Sfr 200
Open: March to December
Credit cards: EC, MC, VS
Restaurant closed Mondays off season
Train 1 km from hotel
Canton: Fribourg, 28 km E of Neuchâtel

My anticipation was high the first time I drove up to Le Vieux Manoir (a member of Relais & Chateaux) as I had already fallen in love with the image projected by the brochure. I was not disappointed. The hotel is a wonderful combination of weathered wood, stucco, little gables, high pitched roofs, overhanging eaves and whimsical chimneys. A warm sunny day completed what seemed a perfect welcome. Our room, that looked out over the expanse of lawn and the peaceful lake, was small but nicely decorated with a provincial print that covered the walls and ceiling and extended into the dressing area and bathroom. All the other bedrooms seemed delightful as I peeked over the maids' shoulders while they were making them up the next morning—room 9 had a large canopy bed and room 24, a lake view. That night we ate à la carte—a delicious meal of fresh fish and green salad. There were several choices for complete dinners, though they seemed quite expensive. The atmosphere of the dining room was romantic, with lovely table settings and fresh flowers, a perfect end to a perfect day. Over the years that our guide has been out, Le Vieux Manoir au Lac has constantly expanded and refurbished. Each time we visit, it is prettier than ever.

LE VIEUX MANOIR AU LAC
Hotelier: Elisabeth and Erich Thomas
Route de Lausanne
CH-3280 Murten-Meyriez, Switzerland
tel: (037) 71 12 83, fax: (037) 71 31 88
22 rooms with private bathrooms
Double: from Sfr 280 to Sfr 380
Tower suites: Sfr 450
Open: mid-February to mid-December
Credit cards: all major
Restaurant open daily
Train 3 km from hotel
Canton: Fribourg, 120 km NE of Geneva

As you enter through the Gothic archway into the Chasa Chalavaina, you slip back in time—every piece of timber, every nook and cranny, breathes the history of yesteryear. In 1499, when the troops gathered in front of the inn prepared to battle the German Emperor, Maximilian, the Chasa Chalavaina was already at least two hundred years old. From the beginning it was designed as an inn, as confirmed by the large stable where the coachmen sheltered their horses after arduous journey over the passes. The old stone floor of the entrance hall is worn smooth by the passage of countless guests. The Chasa Chalavaina has been restored with great respect for its past: thick walls hung with farm instruments, doors with antique iron locks, old beams secured by wooden pegs, carved pine paneling wearing the patina of time, and rustic antiques galore. The inn has maintained the sturdy, simple, clean lines of the past while adding the conveniences of the present day. Delicious, home cooked meals are served in the pine paneled dining room. Each of the guest rooms has its own personality such as: La Palantshotta, a large room with antique pine furniture and a large terrace tucked in under the eaves; La Stuietta, on the first floor with its own private terrace; La Stuva del Preir, with a deck overlooking the square in front of the hotel. The Chasa Chalavaina is a marvelous value.

HOTEL CHASA CHALAVAINA
Hotelier: Jon Fasser
Plaza Grond, CH-7537 Müstair, Switzerland
tel: (082) 85 468*
*New 04/96: tel: (081) 858 54 68
15 rooms, 12 with private bathrooms
Double: Sfr 130 to Sfr 180
Open all year
Credit cards: none accepted
Restaurant open daily
Train to Zernez, 39 km by bus to Müstair
Canton: Graubünden, 73 km NE of St Moritz

The Rote Rose is *the perfect inn*. It has a superb setting on the knoll of a vineyard-laced hill, a meticulously restored, old-timbered home in a beautiful walled village, exquisite antiques, splendid views, and just next door, the Gasthaus Krone, a gourmet restaurant. Best of all though, the Rote Rose has as its owner, Christa Schäfer, with her special qualities of warmth and hospitality is one of the finest hostesses I have ever met. And if this is not enough to win your hearts, the walls of the inn are filled with the paintings of the renowned rose artist, Lotte Günthart, Christa's mother. Lotte Günthart's contribution to the world of roses has been so significant that a beautiful red rose is named for her. There is a gift store and gallery featuring her paintings in the Rote Rose below the two guest room suites. A short stroll away is Lotte Günthart's garden with over one thousand varieties of roses–the inspiration for her splendid paintings.

Regensberg is a tiny village founded by the Baron Lutold V in 1245. I don't know who Lutold was, but he certainly recognized a beautiful location. The town is so perfectly situated that there is a three hundred and sixty-degree view. You can spot Regensberg as you leave Dielsdorf. It is perched on a nearby hilltop with a fairy tale view out over the vineyards all the way to Zürich. On a clear day, magnificent mountains frame the horizon. The Rote Rose has no restaurant, but is adjacent to one of Switzerland's finest, the Gasthaus Krone (the Krone is closed on Mondays and Tuesdays, but there are other nearby restaurants). Since there is no dining room at the Rote Rose, at your door each morning a pretty little cloth draw string bag is discreetly left, filled with fresh breads to be enjoyed with tea or coffee that can be brewed in your room. Each room has a refrigerator with milk for your coffee, cheeses, butter and jellies to complete your morning meal.

As you can surmise from the above write up, the Rote Rose is one of our favorite places, but the problem in the past has been that with only two rooms, it was very difficult to secure space. Happily, we can now report that fewer travelers will be disappointed because more rooms have been added across the square. Now a total of three suites and two rooms are available. However, it is still very important to call well in advance for your reservation, and when confirmed, a deposit is required within two weeks. If you can extend your stay, there are lower rates for a three-night package. Note: also, Christa has asked me to let our readers know that check in is between 2:00 pm and 6:00 pm (and on Sundays, between 6:00 pm and 7:00 pm). Every one of the rooms is a prize, but I think my favorite room remains Rose Dream—a suite with a sitting room, bedroom with canopy bed, a dressing room, kitchenette and windows overlooking the vineyards.

ROTE ROSE
Hotelier: Christa Schäfer
CH-8158 Regensberg, Switzerland
tel: (01) 85 31 013, fax: (01) 85 31 559
3 suites, 2 rooms, all with private bathrooms
Double: Sfr 250 to Sfr 300
Closed: January and February
Credit cards: none accepted
Restaurant closed Mondays and Tuesdays
Train 2 km from hotel in Dielsdorf
20 minutes from Zürich airport
Canton: Zürich, 24 km N of Zürich

Hotel Descriptions

Were it not for the old woman, all knowing, who observed me on the doorstep from her window across the street, instructing me to knock harder, insisting someone was home— I might not have persisted, and missed this gem of a hotel. Rebuilt in 1685, Au Lieutenant Baillival is easy to spot with its charming yellow facade dressed with rust colored shutters. Inside, low beamed ceilings and paneled walls hung with tapestries and paintings offer a cozy, yet dusky ambiance. Antiques abound and it was therefore not surprising to learn that Mr and Mrs Surer are also antique dealers. Off the entry, furnished with one long trestle table paired with two upholstered chairs and a gorgeous grandfather clock, is an intimate room with a lovely old tiled stove, a gorgeous table set center stage for breakfast (or evening meals if pre-arranged), whose walls display a treasure of beautiful old plates. On summer mornings, tables are set on a back terrace that overlooks the immaculately groomed gardens. The six guest rooms are in a neighboring building, two on each of three floors. All six guest rooms are decorated with handsome antiques (the bed sizes are small as they have not been altered from days of old) and overlook the street in front through thick walls. Bathrooms are a recent addition (long since 1685) and are functional with sink, toilet, and either tub shower or just shower. On each level one of the two rooms has a separate sitting room furnished with an extra bed.

AU LIEUTENANT BAILLIVAL
Hoteliers: Theodore and Gabrielle Surer
CH-1323 Romainmôtier, Switzerland
tel: (024) 53 14 58, fax: (024) 53 18 30
6 rooms with private bathrooms
Double: Sfr 134
Closed February
Credit cards: EC, MC, VS
Dinner by arrangement, minimum of six guests
Train 1 km from hotel
Canton: Vaud, 33 km NW of Lausanne

The Hotel Kreuz is located in the historically interesting town of Sachseln where the famous religious philosopher, Niklaus von Flüe, lived. He is now buried in the local parish church. This stately white manor-style hotel has been in the same family since 1489. Family antiques are used throughout—old chests, wonderful clocks, cradles, armoires, paintings, antique tables, beautiful old chairs and other heirlooms highlight the tasteful decor in all the public rooms. The guest rooms are each different in decor, but all are attractive with a sophisticated, traditional ambiance. Adjacent to the main building is my favorite part of the hotel, a fabulous small chalet that not only oozes with charm, but abounds with historical importance. Dating back to 1291, this chalet is supposedly the oldest wooden chalet in Switzerland. All the rooms are beautifully decorated with antiques, and share an intimate, antique filled parlor. This characterful little building is called the "colored house" because it used to be painted red, signifying that this was the home of the magistrate, the most important man in town. In the rear of the main residence is an old mill that has also been converted into guest rooms. Room 73 is an especially attractive suite with marvelous antique paneling. As an added bonus, the hotel has its own small garden area on the lake.

HOTEL KREUZ
Hoteliers: Susi and Wim Sprokkereef-Moser
Dorfstrasse 15
CH-6072 Sachseln, Switzerland
tel: (041) 66 14 66, fax: (041) 66 81 88*
*New 03/96, check with international operator
54 rooms with private bathrooms
Double: Sfr 150 to Sfr 170
Open all year
Credit cards: all major; Restaurant open daily
Train 300 meters from hotel, free pick up
Canton: Obwalden, 80 km S of Zürich

What a surprise it was after visiting Meierei Landgasthof on the edge of Lake St Moritz to walk into the Hotel Eden, and find it is owned by the same family. Their son, Maurizio, is busy managing the Meierei while his sister is busy at the Hotel Eden. Both seem to have the same cordial management style that is so frequently reflected when family is at the front desk. Although under the same ownership, there is no competition since each is entirely different. Whereas the Meierei Landgasthof is rustic in decor and well known for its restaurant, the Hotel Eden, which is well located in the heart of St Moritz, is elegant and serves only breakfast. As you enter the Eden, straight ahead is an atrium, a sunny place to relax. On your right, is an old-fashioned, intimate parlor, furnished with rather formal antiques. Breakfast is served in a spacious dining room. Each morning a bountiful buffet is artistically presented on an antique sleigh. The bedrooms are individual in decor, but those I saw were all furnished in light knotty pine—not nearly as formal a look as the downstair's parlor. Room 138, a corner room with a bay window overlooking the lake, is particularly attractive.

HOTEL EDEN
Hotelier: Jehle-Degiacomi Family
CH-7500 St Moritz, Switzerland
tel: (082) 3 61 61, fax: (082) 3 91 91*
*New 04/96: tel:(081) 833 61 61, fax:(081) 833 91 91
36 rooms with private bathrooms
Double: Sfr 190 to Sfr 220
Open: mid-June to mid-October and
  December to mid-April
Credit cards: none accepted
No restaurant, breakfast only
Train 1 km from hotel
U.S. Rep: Euro-Connection 800 645-3876
Canton: Graubünden, 88 km SE of Chur

From outside, the Hotel Languard looks like a typical patrician residence of wealthy Engadines with the lovely, regional, painted facade. Once within the front door, this small family owned and managed hotel, has a warm country ambiance. Beyond the reception desk is an especially bright and cheerful breakfast room with large sunlit windows, overlooking a panorama of Lake St Moritz. Here the theme is rustic country, with wooden pine tables and quaint carved wooden chairs. The bountiful breakfast buffet is laid out each morning on a fabulous, 17th-century carved wedding chest. There are only twenty-two guest rooms. Each is individually decorated, but all maintain the same country feel with pine paneling and pine furniture. The corner rooms are the most expensive, large and very attractive. Especially outstanding is room 9, that not only has handsomely carved antique wood paneling, but also a beautifully painted ceiling. There are splendid views of the lake and mountains from many of the rooms, a few even have a small balcony. The Hotel Languard is directly across a small square from the Hotel Eden. Both are small, personalized, family-run hotels. The Languard has a country ambiance, while the Eden is more formal.

HOTEL LANGUARD
Hotelier: Giovanni Trivella Family
CH-7500, St Moritz, Switzerland
tel: (082) 3 31 37, fax: (082) 3 45 46*
*New 04/96: tel:(081) 833 31 37, fax: (081) 833 45 46
22 rooms with private bathrooms
Double: Sfr 180 to Sfr 320 (summer rates)
Open: June to October; December to April
Credit cards: all major
No restaurant, breakfast only
Train 1 km from hotel
U.S. Rep: Euro-Connection 800 645-3876
Canton: Graubünden, 63 km SW of Scuol

Although the address is St Moritz, the Meierei Landgasthof is across the lake, with a pretty view back over the water to town. Though many renovations have been made over the years, the hotel is actually an old farm whose origins date back to the 17th Century when it was owned by a bishop. It was here that produce for the bishop's table was grown, tithes collected from the surrounding peasants and beds kept ready for visiting dignitaries of the church. When the Degiacomi family bought the property, it had fallen into sad disrepair. They converted one wing into a very popular restaurant—a favorite place for those hiking around the lake to stop for lunch. The original part of the hotel is a white stucco, two storied building with brown shutters. The old restaurant wing, wrapped in weathered brown shingles, blends in very well. As you approach the main entrance, there is a children's play-yard to the right and also an enticing corral with ponies. On sunny days, the most popular spot to dine is on the outdoor terrace that is protected from the wind by a wall of glass. It appeared to me that the main activity of the Meierei Landgasthof was its restaurant, but there are also ten bedrooms that are furnished in a rustic pine decor. If you want to go into St Moritz for shopping, it is a very pleasant 20 minute walk. St Moritz-Bad is also a twenty-minute walk by a different path that loops around the lake.

MEIEREI LANDGASTHOF
Hoteliers: Sabina and Maurizio Degiacomi
CH-7500 St Moritz, Switzerland
tel: (082) 32 060, fax: (082) 38 838*
*New 04/96: tel: (081) 833 20 60, fax: (081) 833 88 38
10 rooms with private bathrooms
Double: Sfr 160 to Sfr 220
Open: June to October and December to April
Credit cards: none accepted
Restaurant closed Mondays
Train to St Moritz, postal bus to hotel
Canton: Graubünden, Across the lake from St Moritz

The Hotel Chasa Capol, located in the characterful village of Santa Maria in the lovely Müstair Valley, has a history going back to the 8th Century. In fact, the Capol's genealogical tree has been traced to the Venetian, Marco Polo! Although, in a remote corner of Switzerland where little English is spoken, you will have no language problem at the Chasa Capol: Karen, the extremely gracious young hostess, who along with her husband and son manage the inn, speaks fluent English and can offer a wealth of sightseeing suggestions. This cozy inn has a museum-like quality: there is a small chapel in the basement with precious icons, a little theater in the attic where special concerts are still given, artifacts throughout such as antique costumes and old sleds. The lovely small dining room, furnished in light wood antiques, serves excellent meals. Specialties of the house are dishes from the local region that are complimented by the inn's own wines. Each of the guest rooms is named for a famous guest and has its own personality, such as: the Guerg Jenatsch, overlooking the back garden, dressed in a pretty red and green provincial print fabric, the Benedikt Fontana room has a large arched window overlooking the village and out to the mountains, and the newly renovated Petrus Sebastianus Suite is lovely with its local period style decor, separate parlor and antique wood-burning stove.

THEATER-HOTEL CHASA CAPOL
Hoteliers: Karen, Ernest and Ramün Schweizer
CH-7536 Santa Maria, Switzerland
tel: (082) 8 57 28*
*New 04/96: check with international operator
14 rooms all with private bathrooms
Double: Sfr 170 to Sfr 220
Open: all year
Credit cards: none accepted
Restaurant open daily
Train in Zernez, 36 km from hotel
Canton: Graubünden, 10 km SW of St Moritz

The Domaine de Châteauvieux is located just a fifteen-minute drive from the Geneva airport, a convenient hotel choice for a first night in Switzerland. It is difficult to comprehend that you are only a few miles west of a large city as you approach this 15th-century stone manor situated on the knoll of a hill laced with vineyards. You enter through the front gates into a courtyard with an antique wine press surrounded by an abundance of bright flowers. Inside the Domaine de Châteauvieux, there is a tasteful array of antiques gracefully intermingled with new furnishings to give a feeling of coziness and warmth. The emphasis is on dining that is truly gourmet. In the summer, meals are served out on the terrace overlooking the vineyards. On chilly days, meals are served in a very attractive dining room with old world ambiance. The hotel is owned by the Chevrier family, and Philippe Chevrier is a superb chef who has justifiably earned two stars from Michelin for his fine restaurant. His wife, Bettina, is an extremely gracious hostess whose charm adds to the friendly atmosphere of the hotel. Since the Chevriers have purchased the hotel, they have been constantly refurbishing the comfortable guest rooms.

ROMANTIK HOTEL DOMAINE DE CHATEAUVIEUX
Hoteliers: Bettina and Philippe Chevrier
Peney-Dessus
CH-1242 Satigny, Geneva, Switzerland
tel: (022) 75 31 511, fax: (022) 75 31 924
20 rooms with private bathrooms
Double: Sfr 155 to Sfr 225
Closed: December 20 to January 10 and
  August 1 to August 14
Credit cards: EC, MC, VS
Restaurant closed Sundays and Mondays
Train 1 km from hotel, free pick up
U.S. Rep.: Euro-Connection 800 645-3876
Canton: Geneva, 4 km W of Geneva airport

The Rheinhotel Fischerzunft is beautifully situated along the banks of the Rhein. The ferry leaves only a few steps from the hotel—making it a most convenient choice if you want to explore the river or just to watch the boats go by. As you enter the hotel, an elegantly furnished dining room is to the left, and a sophisticated lounge furnished in muted colors to the right. There is a small staircase just off the hallway leading to a few bedrooms, each is spacious and individually decorated with impeccable taste. The rooms in front are more expensive and have views of the river. There are three suites that are particularly lovely. Until a century ago, the building used to house a fishermen's guild. It was converted to a restaurant, and then about fifty years ago it was expanded into a simple hotel. In recent years the hotel was purchased by the very talented Jaegers, who renovated the entire building; and their exquisite taste is responsible for making the hotel so remarkably attractive. Doreen is Chinese, and there is a subtle Oriental flavor both to the decor and the cuisine. The food is outstanding and attracts many guests from Zürich. The hotel is a member of Relais & Chateaux.

RHEINHOTEL FISCHERZUNFT
Hoteliers: Doreen and André Jaeger-Soong
Rheinquai 8
CH-8200 Schaffhausen, Switzerland
tel: (053) 25 32 81, fax: (053) 24 32 85
10 rooms with private bathrooms
Double: Sfr 270 to Sfr 400
Closed: mid-January to mid-February
Credit cards: all major
Restaurant open daily
Train 2 km from hotel
U.S. Rep: Euro-Connection 800 645-3876
Canton: Schaffhausen, 50 km N of Zürich

Although the spa town of Bad Scuol is a hub of activity, the Hotel Guardaval is isolated from the action. Located on a road above the highway, the hotel maintains its own little world of tranquillity. The hotel is quite old, there are parts of it dating back to 1691. The main building is simple in design—painted white with bright geraniums adorning the window boxes. The reception area and lounges, filled with antiques, lead to the rear deck where tables are set for enjoying the sun and the spectacular vista. Stairs lead down to a lower level where there is a very large, especially attractive, dining room. It is airy and bright with light wooden furniture. Heavy beams with intricately carved supports, and enormous windows view the mountains. An adjoining house, now turned into part of the hotel, is oozing with antiques—cradles, old clocks, sleds, beautiful country peasant style chairs, tables and shiny copper set a perfect mood. Our room was in an annex located just half a block up the hill from the main hotel. Decorated simply, the rooms are very pleasant and the views dramatic. Our corner room, number 66, had a bay window that allowed us to have a delightful panorama of the valley below.

ROMANTIK HOTEL GUARDAVAL
Hoteliers: Mr. and Mrs. Peider Regi
CH-7550 Bad Scuol, Switzerland
tel: (081) 864 13 21, fax: (081) 864 97 67
45 rooms, 42 with private bathrooms
Double: Sfr 230 to Sfr 300
Closed: April and November
Credit cards: all major
Restaurant open daily
Train 1 km from hotel
U.S. Rep: Euro-Connection 800 645-3876
Canton: Graubünden, 60 km NE of St Moritz

Originally a large private residence, the Hotel Margna was built in 1817 by Johann Josty. Johann took advantage of a prime location, building his home on a small spit of land between two lakes. In the summertime there are countless paths along the lake front or leading up to imposing mountain peaks, while in the winter this is a cross-country skier's paradise. Johann Josty's manor is now a beautiful hotel with a gracious touch of sophistication. There are several lounges, a grill restaurant with an open fireplace, plus a second dining room—the Stuva. The hotel has game rooms, a television lounge and even a whirlpool and steam-bath. Each room is delightful, with warm, cream-colored walls, antique accents such as an old sleigh laden with flowers, Oriental rugs, a cozy lounge with fireplace, and a beautiful dining room with a beamed ceiling. The few guest rooms I saw were charming, with the same ambiance found throughout the hotel. Number 49 has an exceptional view across the meadows and lake.

HOTEL MARGNA
Hoteliers: Dorly and Sepp Müssgens
Manager: Christoph Müssgens
CH-7515 Sils-Baselgia (Engadine), Switzerland
tel: (082) 4 53 06, fax: (082) 4 54 70*
*New 04/96: tel: (081) 826 53 06, fax: (081) 826 54 70
72 rooms with private bathrooms
Double: Sfr 320 to Sfr 380
Open: June to October and December to April
Credit cards: none accepted
Restaurant open daily
Postal bus from St Moritz, 12 km from hotel
Canton: Graubünden, 12 km S of St Moritz

The Hotel Pensiun Privata and the Hotel Margna share the same lovely strip of land dividing two mountain bound lakes. Since the prices at the elegant Hotel Margna are over the budget of many readers, we were glad to find the Hotel Pensiun Privata, where the rates are more reasonable and include both breakfast and dinner. The pretty, four-storied, beige building with brown shutters is located on a small square in the village of Sils-Maria. Just to the left of the building, is the gathering place for the colorful horse-drawn-carriages which take guests on sightseeing jaunts. The hotel is strategically located for hiking. Just outside the door, trails lead off in every direction: up into the mountains, into the meadows, and around the lakes. Although not deluxe, there is a homey, comfortable ambiance. The flag-stoned entrance with a reception counter opens onto two cozy lounges. A hallway leads to an especially attractive, spacious dining room with windows overlooking the back garden. The dining room has a paneled ceiling, an antique armoire, pine chairs, and tables set with fresh flowers. The menu each night offers several courses and the food is excellent. The bedrooms are individually decorated, and like the rest of the house, have a country feel with light pine furniture.

HOTEL PENSIUN PRIVATA
Hoteliers: D. and U. Giovanoli
CH-7514 Sils-Maria, Switzerland
tel: (082) 4 52 47, fax: (082) 4 61 83*
*New 04/96: tel:(081) 826 52 47, fax:(081) 826 61 83
25 rooms with private bathrooms
Double: Sfr 220 to Sfr 280*
*includes breakfast and dinner
Open: December 18 to mid-April and
 June to mid-October
Credit cards: none accepted; Restaurant open daily
Postal bus from St Moritz
Canton: Graubünden, 13 km S of St Moritz

The ski resort of St Moritz attracts the wealthy, international jet set and is always a bustle of activity, but few of the hotels have the ambiance of a small inn. However, if you don't mind being six kilometers down the road, La Staila (an Engadine farm house built in 1710) abounds with an old world atmosphere. Although not adjacent to one of the several ski areas, there is a convenient shuttle bus every half hour to the various ski lifts. (The bus is free when you buy your ski pass, interchangeable throughout the St Moritz region.) The bus to the ski-areas stops just down the road. St Moritz is also justifiably popular in summer when there are many possibilities for walking and hiking. La Staila has a traditional ambiance with many carefully chosen antiques—trunks, armoires, oil paintings, tables and chairs—throughout the hotel. Mr. Strähle, a talented chef, is in charge of the kitchen and meals are served in any of the pretty dining rooms. Each of the guest rooms has its own personality, and all are well decorated. Some guest rooms in the original part of the house are richly paneled and especially appealing. If you stay a minimum of three days, half pension is available. With such an excellent kitchen, it is highly recommended that you choose this option.

LA STAILA
Hotelier: Strähle-Bezzola Family
CH-7513 Silvaplana, Switzerland
tel: (082) 4 81 47, fax: (082) 4 91 51*
*New 04/96: tel: (081) 828 81 47, fax: (081) 828 9151
17 rooms, 15 with private bathrooms
Double: Sfr 150 to Sfr 250
Open: June to October and December to April
Credit cards: EC, MC, VS
Restaurant closed Wednesdays
Train in St Moritz, 6 km from hotel
Canton: Graubünden, 6 km S of St Moritz

La Soglina is a gem of a hotel in an incredibly picturesque village, high on a shelf-like terrace overlooking the Bregaglia Valley. The hotel is owned by the Nass-Schumacher family. Mr. Nass, originally from Strasbourg, France, is the talented chef in charge of the kitchen. His gracious wife was born in Soglio. The hotel is found in three buildings of this small village. Two stand together at the top and outskirts of town and one is just at its entrance. The reception is located in the newer of the two buildings at the top, along with a recently built restaurant and ten guest rooms. Clean and simple in their decor, the guest rooms are spacious, with Burberry style carpets, whitewashed walls and sturdy, light pine furniture. The bathrooms are modern. The restaurant is beautiful with its Bavarian pine furnishings, walls and carved ceilings. Tables overflow onto an expanse of terrace and enjoy absolutely spectacular vistas. An underground passageway connects the two buildings, the second houses guest rooms and a fitness center with sauna and solarium. Although the rooms are nice and the meals hearty, the outstanding feature of La Soglina is its location. Request one of the most expensive rooms with a view balcony, then settle in for a long stay. You will come home with memories of walks through fields of flowers and mountain panoramas that are almost too perfect to be true.

LA SOGLINA
Hoteliers: E. and R. Nass-Schumacher
CH-7610 Soglio, Switzerland
tel: (082) 41 608, fax: (082) 41 594*
*New 04/96: tel: (081) 822 16 08, fax: (081) 822 15 94
33 rooms with private bathrooms
Double: Sfr 130 to Sfr 150*
*Sfr 190 to Sfr 210 with breakfast and dinner
Credit cards: all major
Closed: November; Restaurant open daily
Postal bus St Moritz to-Promontogno to Soglio
Canton: Graubünden, 60 km south of St Moritz

The Hotel Krone, a 13th-century residence, is in the fascinating, walled medieval town of Solothurn. The cozy exterior leaves nothing to be desired: a pale-pink stuccoed building, muted green shutters, and window boxes overflowing with red geraniums. The location too, is perfect—facing onto the colorful main square, just opposite Saint Ursen Cathedral. The reception area is more formal than the exterior would indicate, but the dining room has an inviting country inn atmosphere and fresh flowers are plentiful on the tables. At the top of the stairwell is a large room often used for private parties. There is also a relaxing bar, perfect for a welcome drink. Outside, tables are set in good weather for light meals. The bedrooms are all very similar in decor, with copies of Louis XV furniture that blend nicely with genuine antiques. The more deluxe rooms are especially large and have spacious bathrooms with tubs so big you can almost go swimming in them. Since our original stay at the Hotel Krone, all of the bedrooms have been renovated, and now all of the double rooms are spacious in the old section of the inn. The smaller rooms are in the new addition and are used as singles.

HOTEL KRONE
Hotelier: Joseph Kung-Roschi
Hauptgasse 64
CH-4500 Solothurn, Switzerland
tel: (065) 22 44 12, fax: (065) 22 37 24
42 rooms with private bathrooms
Double: Sfr 185 to Sfr 235
Open: all year
Credit cards: all major
Restaurant open daily
Train 700 meters from hotel
Middle of medieval walled city
U.S. Rep: Best Western 800 528-1234
Canton: Solothurn, 76 km S of Basel

The Strandhotel Belvédère enjoys an absolutely spectacular setting of mountain and lake. Set on the hillside in a residential area of Spiez, the hotel looks across to the scenic harbor and medieval ramparts of Spiez and out across Lake Thun to the surrounding alpine peaks. A member of the Silence Hotels for already more than a decade, the hotel does enjoy a quiet setting with its own expanse of lawn that tumbles to the lake edge. There is also a private beach for guests to enjoy. The Strandhotel has surprisingly just thirty-one rooms, as its public rooms are large and spacious and one would imagine a larger occupancy. The hotel has a very traditional feel, and the staff is extremely courteous as well as professional. A lovely formal restaurant, Le Français is considered one of the finest restaurants in the Bernese-Oberland region of Switzerland. Not only does it promise fine food, but tables set in front of an expanse of windows overlooking the lake afford wonderful views. Breakfast is served in a more casual dining room or in the privacy of one's room. I saw a sampling of rooms in every price category. They are light and airy in their decor, more modern than traditional in furnishings, and many boast views of the lake and Spiez. A few guest rooms enjoy a private balcony. A hotel for eighty years, the Strandhotel Belvédère is a quiet and relaxing spot from which to explore the more bustling towns of the region.

STRANDHOTEL BELVÉDÈRE
Hotelier: Hans-Jörg Seiler
CH-3700 Spiez am Thunersee, Switzerland
tel: (033) 54 33 33, fax: (033) 54 66 33
31 rooms with private bathrooms
Double: Sfr 220 to Sfr 320
Open: March to December
Credit cards: all major
Restaurant open daily
Train 1,000 meters from hotel
Canton: Bern, 35 km S of Bern

The Hotel Rheinfels, a beige building with brown shutters, sits directly on the banks of the Rhein as it flows through the storybook-perfect medieval village of Stein am Rhein. In fact, the hotel is so close to the Rhein that the geranium festooned dining terrace actually stretches out over the water. The restaurant, where you register, seems to be the focal point of the Hotel Rheinfels, but a wide staircase, lined with family portraits, leads up to an attractive lounge decorated with several antique armoires, tables, paintings, and best of all, several suits of armor. Most of the guest rooms overlook the river. Recently they have all been completely renovated, so for the first time, a fine hotel is available in Stein am Rhein. The guest rooms are all very similar both in decor and size. Although the built-in furniture has a modern, hotel-like look, a traditional mood is achieved through the use of floral carpeting in shades of rose, pretty wallpaper and color coordinated fabrics on the chairs and sofas (which make into a third bed—perfect for families traveling with children). Every room has a mini bar, radio, direct dial telephone and its own attractively tiled bathroom. The bedrooms are exceptionally spacious bright, and cheerful. Almost all have two windows overlooking the river, so be sure to request a view of the water when making reservations.

HOTEL RHEINFELS
Hotelier: Edi Schwegler-Wick
CH-8260 Stein am Rhein, Switzerland
tel: (054) 41 21 44, fax: (054) 41 25 22*
*New 03/96: tel: (052) 741 21 44, fax: (052) 741 25 22
16 rooms with private bathrooms
Double: Sfr 160
Closed: December 20 to March 5
Credit cards: MC
Restaurant closed Thursdays
Boat dock 100 meters from hotel
Canton: Schaffhausen, 16 km E of Schaffhausen

Once in a while a hotel seems too perfect to be true. We couldn't believe our luck to happen upon the Schloss Hotel Chastè. This deluxe hotel is in a tiny village (just a cluster of farm houses) in a gorgeous high meadow of the glorious Engadine Valley, bounded by the soaring peaks of the majestic Dolomites. Completing the idyllic scene is the picturesque Tarasp Castle crowning a nearby hill and a small lake in the flower-filled meadow. Until the turn of the century, the hotel was a farmhouse, and has incredibly been in the same family since it was built in 1480. When Tarasp Castle was being renovated in 1912, Anton Pazeller, the grandfather of the present owner, opened a small restaurant to accommodate tourists coming to see the castle. His grandson, your gracious host, Rudolf Pazeller, trained as a chef and returned home to expand the hotel and add a gourmet restaurant. The facade is in the traditional Engadine style, painted white and accented with intricate designs. Pink geraniums cascade from every window box. Within, there is beautiful carved wood paneling throughout and country-style furnishings that create a charming, rustic ambiance. The bedrooms are each individual in decor, but all have a cozy look with furniture made from various woods native to the Engadine. This is a lovely inn in an idyllic setting. Just steps from the hotel, paths lead off in every direction.

SCHLOSS HOTEL CHASTÈ
Hoteliers: Daniela and Rudolf Pazeller
CH-7553 Tarasp-Sparsels, Switzerland
tel: (081)86 41 775, fax: (081) 86 49 970
22 rooms with private bathrooms
Double: Sfr 190 to Sfr 250
Open: June to October, and December to April
Credit cards: none accepted
Restaurant closed Mondays and Thursday noon
Train to Scuol, postal bus to Tarasp
Canton: Graubünden, 70 km NW of Moritz

The town of Verbier, on a high meadow overlooking the Bagnes Valley, is known to long-distance cross country skiers as the starting point of the "High Road Run," of which Saas-Fee or Zermatt is the terminus. I had always heard that Verbier was a modern town built expressly to satisfy the whims of the ardent skier. I was therefore pleased and surprised to notice, as the car twisted up the road from the valley, the many traditional wooden farmhouses that remain and add character to the otherwise modern ski facilities. In the center of town, the Hotel Rosalp is a typical chalet-style hotel. There are two restaurants. The main dining room has beautiful wood paneling and tables set with crisp linens and fresh flowers—the overall effect is one of style and chic. A second restaurant La Pinte, specializes in grilled meat. The owner, Roland Pierroz, is a renowned chef with a reputation of serving some of the finest food in Switzerland, and has received many prestigious awards. When we first visited the Rosalp, it was an intimate gourmet restaurant with a few guest rooms. It has expanded so dramatically through the years, that on our last visit we hardly recognized it. The intimate inn (now a world class hotel and a member of Relais & Chateaux) has deluxe rooms, jet-set boutiques and sleek decor.

HOTEL ROSALP
Hotelier: Roland Pierroz
CH-1936 Verbier, Switzerland
tel: (026) 31 63 23, fax: (026) 31 10 59
20 rooms, 19 with private bathrooms
Double: Sfr 240 to Sfr 270
Open: December to April; and July to September
Credit cards: all major
Restaurant open daily
20 minutes by postal bus from Le Châble
Canton: Valais, 28 km E of Martigny

If you want to combine resort-style living on the lake and still be within an hour of Lucerne by boat or half an hour by car, then the Park Hotel Vitznau might be your cup of tea. It is ideally set in a beautiful park-like setting directly on the banks of Lake Lucerne. This is not a rustic hotel in any way. Rather, it is sophisticated, with all the amenities that you would expect from a deluxe establishment—a large heated indoor-outdoor swimming pool, golf, table tennis, a motor boat for water skiing or excursions, and even a children's playground and pool. The lakeside setting also allows water-skiing, sailing, swimming, and fishing. The building is like a castle, with turrets, towers, gables and many nooks and crannies. A beautiful lawn surrounded by gardens runs down from the hotel to the edge of the lake where a promenade follows the contours of the lake front. The setting is one of such bliss that it is hard to believe you are so close to the city of Lucerne. Inside, the lobby, lounge areas and dining room are beautifully decorated with combinations of wood beams, fireplaces, Oriental rugs on gleaming hardwood floors, green plants and antique accents.

PARK HOTEL VITZNAU
Hotelier: Peter Bally
Kantonsstrasse
CH-6354 Vitznau, Switzerland
tel: (041) 83 01 00, fax: (041) 83 13 97*
*New 11/95: tel: (041) 397 01 01, fax: (041) 397 01 10
100 rooms with private bathrooms
Double: Sfr 400 to Sfr 540
Open: April 20 to October 20
Credit cards: all major
Restaurant open daily
Boat from Lucerne (20 km)
U.S. Rep: Crown International 800 628-8929
Canton: Lucerne, 20 km E of Lucerne

The Hotel Villa Maria, above the Engadine Valley, is on the road from Bad Scuol as it winds up into the hills toward the picturesque Tarasp Castle. Although the road loops around the hotel, there is a beautifully tended, secluded garden terraced along the side. The one hundred-year-old inn, painted a pale yellow with intricately carved wooden balconies and brown shutters, has a Victorian flair that is given a Swiss touch by the traditional boxes overflowing with geraniums tucked at every window. Inside, the ambiance exudes a country flair—carved pine ceilings, intricate paneling, pine furniture, antiques and fresh flowers abound. The bedrooms are exceptionally attractive. All have light pine furniture offset by the same provincial print fabrics used in the window coverings. Everything is fresh and new and very pretty. For guests who stay three days, half-pension plan is available where breakfast and dinner are included in the room rate. For these guests, there is a bright, cheerful dining room overlooking the back garden. In addition, on the street level there is a gourmet restaurant with beamed ceilings, thick planked wood walls, many antiques and a fireplace. The Villa Maria is in a wooded area with walking trails feathering off in every direction. For golf enthusiasts, there is a course nearby.

HOTEL VILLA MARIA
Hotelier: E. Jaeger Family
CH-7552 Vulpera, Switzerland
tel: (081) 864 11 38, fax: (081) 864 91 61
15 rooms with private bathrooms
Double: Sfr 200 to Sfr 256
Open: June to October and Christmas to Easter
Credit cards: none accepted
Restaurant open daily
Train to Bad Scuol, postal bus to hotel
Canton: Graubünden, 63 km NE of St. Moritz

The Hotel Alte Post, an old coaching inn, is a charming country hotel on the road between the international resort of Gstaad and the magnificent mountain and lake district of Interlaken. The hotel backs onto the rushing torrents of the Simme River. You enter the hotel off the street into a small informal entry. Off the entry, to one side is a simple country restaurant decorated with pine tables and benches and lovely painted beams. On the other side, is a more formal restaurant, elegant in decor and table settings. At the back of the inn is a very informal dining area whose tables are set against windows with views of the rushing waters of the Simme River. When the weather cooperates tables are also set outside on a terrace. All but one of the hotel's ten guest rooms are located on the top floor (the other is located on the floor below) and are very rustic in their decor with wood paneled walls and ceilings and furnished with country antiques–very reminiscent of a country farm auberge. Being on the top floor, the sound of the road traffic is diminished and any sound that could possibly be heard from the guest rooms at back is drowned out by the rushing river. Only six of the guest rooms have a private bathroom with shower, two have a private bathroom with tub and two are equipped with a sink only. The rooms are comfortably furnished, very reasonable in price. First class cuisine is prepared by the owner and chef, Herr Brazerol.

HOTEL ALTE POST
Hotelier: Brazerol-Berthol Family
CH-3764 Weissenburg im Simmental, Switzerland
tel: (033) 83 15 15
10 rooms, 8 with private bathrooms
Double: Sfr 80 to Sfr 150
Open: December to April and May to October
Credit cards: EC, MC, VS
Restaurant closed Wednesdays and Thursdays
Train 10 min. walk from hotel
Canton: Bern, 30 km from Gstaad

When at the end of the 19th Century word spread of the incredible beauty of the Alps, sporty travelers began to find their way to Wengen. At that time Wengen was merely a cluster of wooden farmhouses clinging to a mountain shelf high above the Lauterbrunnen Valley. In 1881, Friedrich and Margaritha Feuz-Lauener, (great-grandparents of the present owner Paul von Allmen) gambled on tourism and built the Alpenrose, the first hotel. Through the years, the hotel has expanded, but the traditional warmth of hospitality remains. Paul and his gracious wife, Margret (a Scottish lass who fell in love with Paul while on holiday in Wengen), make all guests feel very special. This is not a fancy hotel, but has great heart. The lounges are cozily decorated with a homey ambiance. The dining room is large, and becomes a meeting place where everyone has their own table for dinner each night—a time when guests share their adventures of the day and often become friends. The set dinner menu features good home cooking. The chef has been with the hotel for over ten years. Most of the bedrooms have been completely renovated and are fresh and pretty with light pine furniture. Request a south-facing room with a balcony to capture the splendor of the Jungfrau.

HOTEL ALPENROSE
Hoteliers: Margaret and Paul von Allmen
CH-3823 Wengen, Switzerland
tel: (036) 55 32 16, fax: (036) 55 15 18
50 rooms with private bathrooms
Double: Sfr 200 to Sfr 300*
* includes breakfast and dinner
Open: Christmas to Easter and mid-May to October
Credit cards: all major
Restaurant, open daily
Train 7 minute walk from hotel
U.S. Rep: Euro-Connection 800 645-3876
Canton: Bern, 16 km S of Interlaken

As your train pulls into Wengen (coming by train is the only access), you will see the Hotel Regina perched on the knoll above the station. If you call ahead, the hotel porter will be there to meet you. I saw one cart pull away brimming with several children, an enormous dog, mother, father and all their luggage. When you enter the hotel you will probably be reminded of one of the British resorts so popular at the turn of the century. The downstairs has large, rambling lobbies punctuated with small seating areas that have chairs encircling game tables, and a huge fireplace surrounded by overstuffed chairs. It all looks very "Swiss-British." The Chez Meyer dining room is very special, intimate in size, its walls hung with family photos–generations of Meyers who have operated hotels in first Kandersteg and now Wengen—Switzerland's beautiful mountain towns. Notice the chairs that have brass tags of the eleven family members who are always welcome at the Regina. The decor is lovely, and the Meyer family is extremely gracious and happily welcomes guests who return year after year—a tradition for many. The view from the Regina is so stunning that everything else pales in significance. Ask for a room with a balcony—when you're outside you feel as if you can touch the mountain peaks.

HOTEL REGINA
Hoteliers: Ariane and Guido Meyer
CH-3823 Wengen, Switzerland
tel: (036) 55 15 12, fax: (036) 55 15 74
90 rooms with private bathrooms
Double: Sfr 328 to Sfr 345*
*includes breakfast and dinner
Closed: October and November
Credit cards: all major
Restaurant open daily
Train 3 minute walk from hotel
U.S. Rep: Euro-Connection 800 645-3876
Canton: Bern, 16 km S of Interlaken

In the small town of Worb, just a few miles east of Bern, is the Hotel Löwen. This pretty inn is positioned at the junction of two busy streets, but even so, a country charm radiates from its colorful, shuttered exterior. On the entry level there are a number of small, beautifully decorated dining rooms. They vary in decor, but all abound with antiques and exude a country flavor. Dining is famous at the Löwen, attracting dinner guests from all over Switzerland. (If you are overnighting in Bern, Worb makes a fun luncheon excursion, as it is just a quick tram ride away.) The bedrooms are tucked upstairs, away from the activity of the restaurants on the ground floor. As you walk toward the guest rooms, antiques adorn the walls and halls giving a cheerful, cozy, friendly ambiance. The guest rooms are all different. They are not fancy, yet very comfortable and nicely decorated. The Hotel Löwen was established over six hundred years ago and has been in the same family for over eleven generations, so it is not surprising that the service and quality of this small inn are so special—a perfect example of one of Switzerland's most highly regarded professions, the hotel business.

HOTEL LÖWEN
Hotelier: Bernhard Family
Enggisteinstrasse 3
CH-3076 Worb, Switzerland
tel: (031) 839 23 03, fax: (031) 839 58 77
14 rooms with private bathrooms
Double: Sfr 160 to Sfr 175
Open: all year
Credit cards: all major
Restaurant closed Saturdays and Sundays
Train 200 meters from hotel
U.S. Rep: Euro-Connection 800 645-3876
Canton: Bern, 8 km E of Bern

The Alex Schlosshotel Tenne, just a two-minute walk from the main Zermatt rail terminal, is one of the few hotels in Zermatt to incorporate into its structure a very old wooden chalet. Part of the hotel is of more modern construction: the old and the new have been blended well. Since our original visit, the hotel has been purchased and completely renovated by the Perren Family. Alex Perren was a mountain guide until an accident necessitated a change of profession. He now owns two hotels in Zermatt, and luckily has a large family to help run them. The Tenne is managed by his daughters, Christina and Sonja, and their gracious hospitality makes guests feel very welcome. With refurbishing, the hotel now has an art deco ambiance, except for five new junior suites in the original section that are more of an alpine style. These are my favorites because of their marvelous darkened-with-age paneling, that can never quite be duplicated, and pretty fabrics. The dining room, which is in the chalet section, offers some of the best food in Zermatt. The cooking is matched only by the rustic, old Zermatt ambiance. Request demi-pension. The dinner served to house guests is truly a gourmet's delight.

ALEX SCHLOSSHOTEL TENNE
Hotelier: Alex Perren Family
Managers: Sonja and Christina Perren
CH-3920 Zermatt, Switzerland
tel: (028) 67 18 01, fax: (028) 67 18 03
35 rooms with private bathrooms
Double: Sfr 280 to Sfr 500*
*includes breakfast and dinner
Open: May to September and December to April
Credit cards: EC, MC, VS
Restaurant open daily
Train 50 meters from hotel
U.S. Rep: Euro-Connection 800 645-3876
Canton: Wallis, in the heart of Zermatt

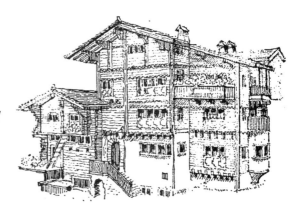

The Hotel Julen, an easy walk across the river from the center of Zermatt, is set away from the hustle and bustle of the tourist traffic. Renovated in 1981, the hotel is owned and operated by Daniela and Paul Julen who have kept the hotel's traditional atmosphere. It is definitely a wonderful exception to so many of the new hotels that are clean and attractive, but do not offer much old world charm. From the moment you enter the Julen's lobby and see the cozy fireplace and the comfortable leather sofas, you will feel the mood of relaxation and friendliness. You will be captivated by the extremely clever use of antiques, flowers and copper pieces. The bedrooms profit from the use of simple, clean-lined, light wood furniture so typical of traditional Swiss inns. Provincial fabrics and puffy comforters help create a charming ambiance in the pine-paneled guest rooms. If you have a choice, request a room in the back facing the Matterhorn. The most expensive, but also the best, are those on the upper floors with a balcony where you can sit and observe the every-changing moods of the Matterhorn. Behind the hotel there is a little garden, an oasis for luxuriating in the fresh mountain air while enjoying the magnificence of the mountains.

ROMANTIK HOTEL JULEN
Hoteliers: Daniela and Paul Julen
CH-3920 Zermatt, Switzerland
tel: (028) 67 24 81, fax: (028) 67 14 81
37 rooms with private bathrooms
Double: Sfr 172 to Sfr 339*
*includes breakfast and dinner
Open all year
Credit cards: all major
Restaurant open daily
Train to Zermatt, free pick up
U.S. Rep: Euro-Connection 800 645-3876
Canton: Wallis, 5 minute walk from center of Zermatt

The Seiler Family is an integral part of Zermatt. It was back in the mid 1800's when Alexander Seiler ventured into the hotel business with the first hotel in Zermatt—the Monte Rosa. The following generations have continued in the business of hospitality and expanded the family enterprise to include several of the finest hotels in Zermatt. Of these, the Hotel Mont Cervin is the most elegant. As you enter the elaborate front lobby it is hard to believe you could be in a tiny little village: the reception area is decorated with a sleek, sophisticated charm. The ceilings are high, with lovely paneling in some areas and wood beams in others; and there are flowers everywhere, Oriental carpets and fine antique furniture. The main dining room has a tranquil formality combined with a reputation for gourmet food and exquisite service (coat and tie are required for the evening meal). The Cervin Grill offers casual dining and piano music can be enjoyed in the Cervin Bar. The guest rooms are spacious and attractively furnished in a traditional style. The hotel has many amenities such as an indoor swimming pool, several saunas, a solarium, a fitness room, and in the Nicoletta Hotel (connected by an underground passage), a kindergarten in the winter for the supervision of children while their parents enjoy the mountain slopes.

SEILER HOTEL MONT CERVIN
Hoteliers: Claire and Wolfgang Pinkwart
CH-3920 Zermatt, Switzerland
tel: (028) 66 88 88, fax: (028) 67 28 78
148 rooms with private bathrooms
Double: Sfr 450 to Sfr 600
Closed: May and mid-October to end-November
Credit cards: all major
Restaurant open daily
Train 5-minute walk from hotel
U.S. Rep: LHW 800 223-6800
Canton: Wallis, In the center of Zermatt

The Hotel Monte Rosa, on the main street in the center of town, is a must when evaluating the hotels of Zermatt. How could you possibly not consider the original hotel in Zermatt, one that is so intricately interwoven with the history and romance of this wonderful old village? The members of the Seiler Family who own the Monte Rosa are descendants of Alexander Seiler who waved good-bye on July 13, 1865, to the famous Englishman, Edward Whymper, as he began his historic climb to become the first man to conquer the Matterhorn. Back in the 1800s, when Edward Whymper was asked about the best hotel in Zermatt, he always replied, "Go to the Monte Rosa—go to Seiler's." The answer really has not changed over the past century. There are now several Seiler hotels proudly dominating the hotel scene, but it is still the original Monte Rosa that best captures the nostalgia of the old Zermatt. It is not just the romance that makes this inn so special. The recently renovated lounges and guest rooms are all tastefully decorated in an old world style. Each is lovely in its own way with fine furnishings accented by pretty, color coordinated fabrics. Even more important is the personalized management. Mr. Bossart is the epitome of what a hotelier should be. His office is right by the reception area where he can keep an eye on the needs of his guests, most of whom he knows by name.

SEILER HOTEL MONTE ROSA
Hotelier: Jurg Bossart
CH-3920 Zermatt, Switzerland
tel: (028) 66 11 31, fax: (028) 67 11 60
45 rooms with private bathrooms
Double: Sfr 300 to Sfr 350, with breakfast and dinner
Open: mid-December to mid-April and June to October
Credit cards: all major
Restaurant open daily
Train 5 minute walk from hotel
U.S. Rep: LHW 800 223-6800
Canton: Wallis, in the center of Zermatt

We almost missed seeing the Seiler Hotel Riffelalp. Our time was short in Zermatt, but at the last minute, we decided to squeeze in the twenty-minute ride up the mountain on the cog-wheel tram to the Riffelalp station. Thank goodness we did. The Hotel Riffelalp instantly became one of our favorite places in Zermatt. The location on a sunny, high mountain meadow provides a straight-across, breathtaking view of the awesome Matterhorn. The Riffelalp sits on the site of one of Alexander Seiler's earliest hotels that was built in 1884. Unfortunately the original burned down, and in 1988, the new hotel was built. Happily, it has kept the traditional, rustic, country charm. Nothing is elegant or fancy, just fresh and pretty with light pine furniture, white walls accented by attractive country-print fabric curtains, abundant use of rustic pine paneling, bouquets of fresh flowers and wrought iron fixtures. The price (unbelievably low for the quality of hotel) includes breakfast and dinner. This is a real treat, as the manager, Thomas Moor, previously was the chef at the world class Seiler Hotel Mont Cervin. Splurge and request a room with a view balcony—the incredible panorama featuring the Matterhorn will surely be a highlight of your trip to Switzerland.

SEILER HOTEL RIFFELALP
Hoteliers: Cecile and Thomas Moor
CH-3920 Zermatt, Riffelalp, Switzerland
tel: (028) 67 53 33, fax: (028) 67 51 09
20 rooms with private bathrooms
Double: Sfr 246 to Sfr 320
*rates include breakfast and dinner
Open: Christmas to mid-April and July to September
Credit cards: EC, MC, VS
Restaurant open daily
Cog train from Zermatt (20-minute ride)
Canton: Wallis, On mountainside overlooking Zermatt

The Hotel Ochsen, owned by the Hegglin Family since 1921, is just across from the entrance into the colorful medieval heart of Zug. The Ochsen was built as an inn in 1480 and retains a characterful medieval facade with a steep roof stepping down on each side to twin bay windows with colorful tiled roofs. Completing the scene, directly across from the front door is a fountain with a jaunty, colorfully garbed warrior standing on a gold leaf pedestal. The old world ambiance does not extend to the interior decor. The entrance is modern with sleek furnishings in tones of blacks and grays with accents of maroon. Modern paintings highlight the walls. Although my personal taste runs to an antique decor, I would far prefer to have a fresh, tastefully executed modern interior than one that cries out for renovation. The restaurant (usually closed for a few weeks in July to August) beautifully reflects the heritage of the hotel. Here you will find mellow wood paneling, traditional wooden tables and chairs and colorful windows with insets of stained glass. The bedrooms are well furnished in muted colors with chairs in chrome and leather. Several of the rooms overlook the old town, but almost as much fun are the rooms looking over the characterful jumble of tiled roofs of the surrounding buildings. For a convenient, well-run hotel in medieval Zug, the Hotel Ochsen is choice.

HOTEL OCHSEN
Hotelier: Mathias Hegglin
Kolinplatz 11, CH-6301 Zug, Switzerland
tel: (042) 21 32 32, fax: (042) 21 30 32*
*New 03/96: check with the international operator
46 rooms with private bathrooms
Double: Sfr 260 to Sfr 280
Open: all year
Credit cards: all major
Restaurant closed 4 weeks in July and August
Train 1 km from hotel
Canton: Zug, 35 km S of Zürich

The Hotel Florhof has reopened, completely refurbished, and under new and enthusiastic management. Recommended in the very first edition of *Swiss Country Inns & Itineraries*, the Hotel Florhof was later deleted because of numerous complaints concerning the drab decor. Now elegant, yet comfortable and in keeping with the style of this lovely old patrician home, I am pleased to be able to recommend the Florhof once again, this time without qualification. A small hotel, more than four hundred years old, the Hotel Florhof is located on the north side of the Limmat River, on a small quiet street that twists up from the little squares and alleys of old Zürich. Removed from the bustle of activity, but close enough to walk to all attractions, the Florhof is more like a residence than a hotel. It is painted a pretty gray blue, and boasts an intimate patio at the rear—perfect for summer dining. Just off the lobby is a cozy dining room and the entry is warmed by a marvelous old blue and white rococo, tile stove. Perhaps, the greatest new asset of the Florhof is the graciousness of its new hosts, Brigitte and Beat Schiesser. Having traveled extensively they have now chosen to settle in Zürich and make this charming country inn their home.

HOTEL FLORHOF
Hotelier: Brigitte and Beat Schiesser
Florhofgasse 4
CH-8001 Zürich, Switzerland
tel: (01) 261 44 70, fax: (01) 26146 11
33 rooms with private bathrooms
Standard double: Sfr 290 to Sfr 320
Open all year
Credit cards: all major
Restaurant closed Saturdays and Sundays
Train 10 minutes walk, 2 tram stops
Canton: Zürich, near Lake Zürich

Hotel space in Zürich is sometimes almost impossible to find—so although the Seiler Hotel Neues Schloss (built in 1938) is not an old world hotel, it can certainly be recommended as an alternate choice for a place to stay in Zürich. From the outside the hotel is not outstanding—a rather boxy, modern gray building, improved somewhat by flower boxes on the corner windows. But after spending many hours walking from one end of Zürich to the other looking at dozens of drab, dark hotels, I was immediately captivated by the cheerful elegance of the Neues Schloss with its inviting lobby and lounges decorated with soft pastel carpets, cream colored walls, fresh flowers and traditional furniture accented by a few antiques. The recently refurbished bedrooms too, are extremely pleasant, again with traditional-style furniture. For dining there is an excellent restaurant, Le Jardin. Another plus: the hotel has a parking garage (there is a charge, but to have a spot to leave your car is a welcome convenience). The Hotel Neues Schloss is owned by the famous Seiler Family who, in the 1800's, opened the first hotel in Zermatt.

SEILER HOTEL NEUES SCHLOSS
Hotelier: Bernard Seiler
Stockerstrasse 17
CH-8022 Zürich, Switzerland
tel: (01) 20 16 550, fax: (01) 20 16 418
62 rooms with private bathrooms
Standard double: Sfr 300 to Sfr 380
Open all year
Credit cards: all major
Restaurant open daily
Canton: Zürich, near Lake Zürich

The Hotel Tiefenau is a real charmer, an appealing country inn away from the bustle of the city, yet within easy walking distance to the heart of Zürich. Lacy trees frame the yellow facade whose small paned windows are enhanced by off-white shutters. A gay yellow and white striped awning forms a cozy canopy over the front entry. From the moment you enter, you are surrounded by a homey ambiance—nothing slickly commercial, just comfortable chairs, antique chests, Oriental rugs, lovely paintings and sunlight streaming in through the many windows. A special surprise are the bedrooms. Each seems so large as to almost be a suite, with plenty of space to relax and read or write letters. There is a small a la carte restaurant, Au Gourmet. Fresh trout from the mountain streams is always included on the menu as are regional specialties. In warm weather, meals are served outside in a delightful little garden tucked against the side of the hotel. For guests who just want a snack, pastries, tea or a light meal, the Cafeteria Hottingen is just a minute's walk from the Tiefenau. A cozy bar serves drinks during the happy hour. Beat Blumer owns and personally manages this exquisite inn. His love and attention are evident in every small, perfect detail.

HOTEL TIEFENAU
Hotelier: Beat Blumer
Steinwiesstrasse 8-10
CH-8032 Zürich, Switzerland
tel: (01) 251 24 09, fax: (01) 251 24 76
30 rooms with private bathrooms
Double: Sfr 300
Open: January to Christmas
Restaurant open daily
Credit cards: all major
Located five minute walk from city center
U.S. Rep: Utell 800 448-8355
Canton: Zürich

The Hotel zum Storchen is so beautifully maintained as a luxury hotel, that at first glance it is difficult to conceive that it has been in operation for over six hundred and twenty years. Guests enjoy the most sophisticated luxuries in modern guest rooms, but the hotel still manages to retain a wealth of charm. The Hotel zum Storchen was strategically built at the narrowest section of the Limmat River as it flows out of Lake Zürich. At this narrow point a bridge was built that became the crossroads of the trade routes to Italy and Germany. Like many of the old inns that revel in tales of history, romance and intrigue, the Hotel zum Storchen is no exception. My favorite story is of Hanns Hennsler, owner of a rival hotel, the Sword Inn: Hanns brought suit against the owner of the Hotel zum Storchen in 1477 for stealing guests off the streets and enticing them away from his hotel. What a change has taken place over the many centuries—no enticing is needed. Now you are very lucky if the Hotel zum Storchen has a room for you.

HOTEL ZUM STORCHEN
Hotelier: J Philippe Jaussi
Am Weinplatz 2
CH-8001 Zürich, Switzerland
tel: (01) 211 55 10, fax: (01) 211 64 51
78 rooms with private bathrooms
Double: Sfr 350 to Sfr 500
Open: all year
Credit cards: all major
Restaurant open daily
Train 1.5 km from hotel
On bank of the Limmat River
U.S. Rep: Euro-Connection 800 645-3876
U.S. Rep: Utell 800 448-8355
Canton: Zürich, in the center of Canton: Zürich

The Hotel Sonnenberg is in a prestigious residential area in the hills overlooking Zürich. You can stay at the Sonnenberg for about half the cost of a luxury hotel in Zürich, but the real bonus is the fabulous view overlooking the city and the lake. Surrounding the hotel are forests, assuring peace and quiet. You can enjoy walks through the woods and the peaceful valleys, but for those who want to sightsee, there is a path leading down through a field of grapes to the tram stop. From there it is only a few minutes to the center of town. The public rooms are appealingly decorated with country antiques. The bedrooms are simply decorated without antiques, but quite pleasant. The dining room is in the main hotel and when the weather is nice, meals are served on the terrace where you can savor the panorama along with an excellent meal. There is a second dining room in a modern annex below the hotel. This dining room, open in the summer season, is blessed with a fantastic view of the lake and city of Zürich. Although in the suburbs, the Hotel Sonnenberg is an excellent choice for a place to stay if traveling with children. Not only can they romp in the adjacent forest, but there are animals to pet and a play-yard on the property.

HOTEL SONNENBERG
Hotelier: Rolf Wismer
Aurorastrasse 98
CH-8032 Zürich, Switzerland
tel: (01) 262 00 62, fax: (01) 262 06 33
34 rooms with private bathrooms
Double: Sfr 240 to Sfr 290
Closed: February 8 to 28
Credit cards: all major
Restaurant open daily
Train 2.5 km to hotel
U.S. Rep: Utell 800 448-8355
Canton: Zürich

Cantons of Switzerland

Schaffhausen

Thurgau

Jura

Basle

Aargau

Zürich

Solothurn

Appenzell

St Gallen

Neuchâtel

Lucerne

Zug

Schwyz

Glarus

Bern

Unterwalden

Uri

Grisons

Vaud

Fribourg

Geneva

Ticino

Valais

Key Map of Switzerland

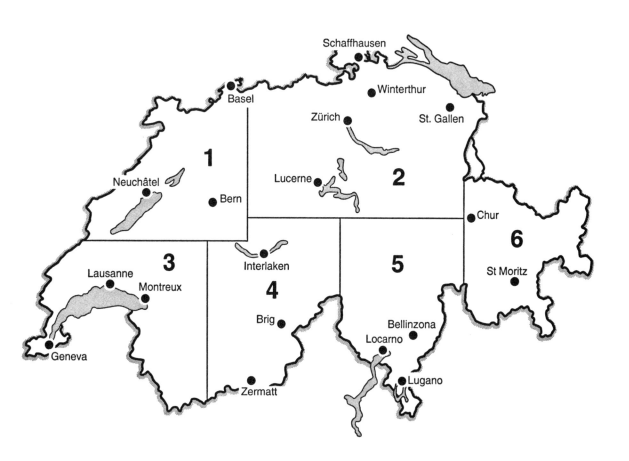

Map 1

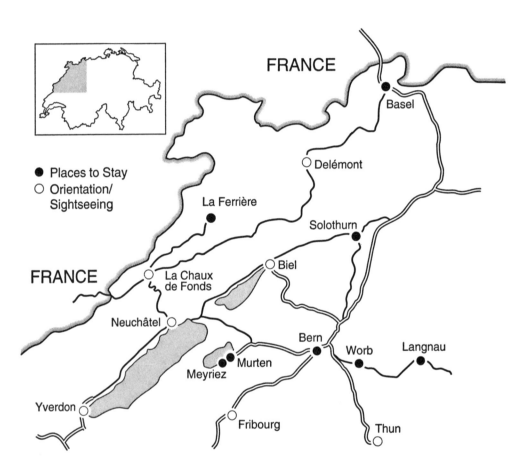

Legend:
● Places to Stay
○ Orientation/Sightseeing

FRANCE

Basel

Delémont

La Ferrière

Solothurn

Biel

La Chaux de Fonds

FRANCE

Neuchâtel

Bern

Worb

Langnau

Murten

Meyriez

Yverdon

Fribourg

Thun

244

Map 2

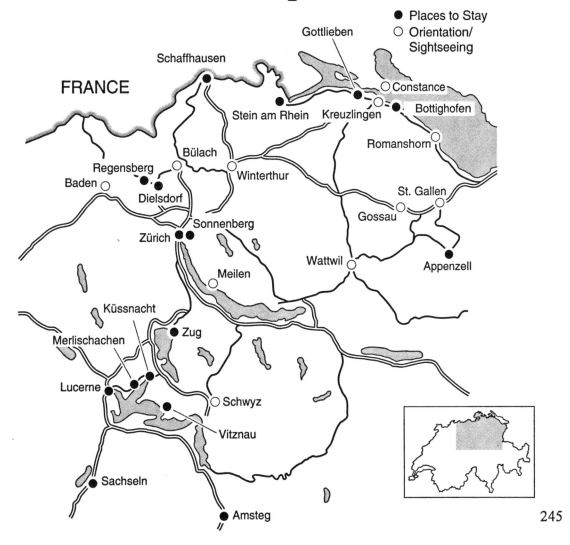

Places to Stay
Orientation/ Sightseeing

FRANCE

Schaffhausen

Gottlieben

Constance

Bottighofen

Stein am Rhein

Kreuzlingen

Romanshorn

Bülach

Regensberg

Baden

Dielsdorf

Winterthur

St. Gallen

Gossau

Sonnenberg

Zürich

Meilen

Wattwil

Appenzell

Küssnacht

Merlischachen

Zug

Lucerne

Schwyz

Vitznau

Sachseln

Amsteg

Map 3

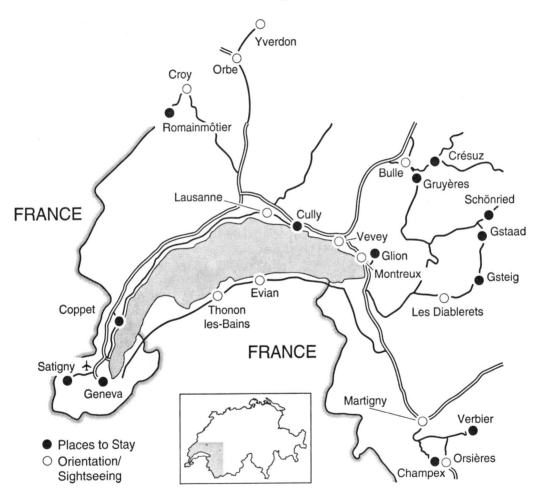

Yverdon

Orbe

Croy

Romainmôtier

Crésuz

Bulle

Gruyères

Schönried

Lausanne

Cully

Gstaad

FRANCE

Vevey

Glion

Montreux

Gsteig

Evian

Les Diablerets

Coppet

Thonon
les-Bains

FRANCE

Satigny

Martigny

Verbier

Geneva

Orsières

Champex

- ● Places to Stay
- ○ Orientation/
  Sightseeing

Map 4

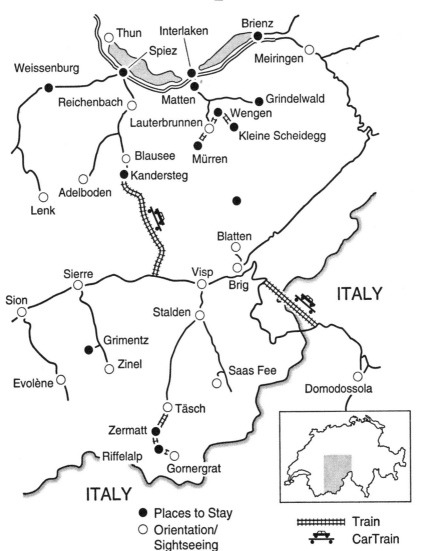

- Thun
- Spiez
- Interlaken
- Brienz
- Meiringen
- Weissenburg
- Matten
- Reichenbach
- Grindelwald
- Wengen
- Lauterbrunnen
- Kleine Scheidegg
- Blausee
- Mürren
- Kandersteg
- Adelboden
- Lenk
- Blatten
- Sierre
- Visp
- Sion
- Brig
- ITALY
- Stalden
- Grimentz
- Zinel
- Saas Fee
- Evolène
- Domodossola
- Täsch
- Zermatt
- Riffelalp
- Gornergrat
- ITALY

● Places to Stay
○ Orientation/
  Sightseeing

╫╫╫ Train
🚗 CarTrain

247

Map 5

● Amsteg

Disentis

Thusis

Andermatt

St Gotthard
Tunnel

San
Bernardino
Tunnel

● Places to Stay
○ Orientation/
Sightseeing

Biasca

Bignasco

Golino

Locarno

Bellinzona

Ascona

Lake Como

ITALY

Castagnola

Lugano

Bellagio

Magliaso

Lake Lugano

Verbania

ITALY

Morcote

Como

Lecco

Map 6

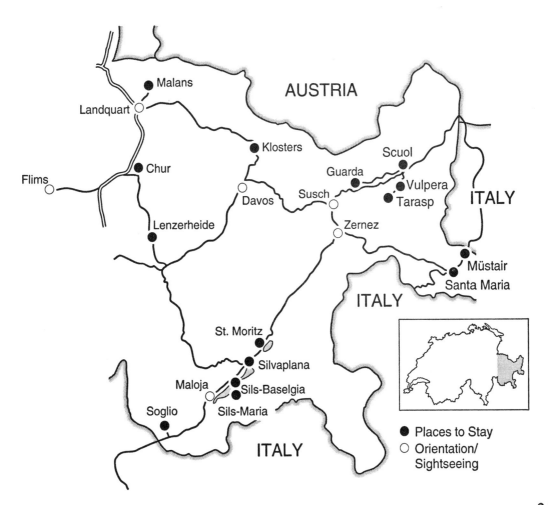

Flims

Malans

Landquart

Klosters

Chur

AUSTRIA

Scuol

Guarda

Vulpera

Davos

Susch

Tarasp

ITALY

Lenzerheide

Zernez

Müstair

Santa Maria

ITALY

St. Moritz

Silvaplana

Maloja

Sils-Baselgia

Soglio

Sils-Maria

ITALY

● Places to Stay
○ Orientation/
　Sightseeing

INDEX

We Love to Hear from Karen Brown's Readers

ACCOLADES: We'd love to hear which accommodations you have especially enjoyed—even the shortest of notes is greatly appreciated. It is reassuring to know that places we recommend meet with your approval.

COMPLAINTS: Please let us know when a place we recommend fails to live up to the standards you have come to expect from Karen Brown. Constructive criticism is greatly appreciated. We sometimes make a mistake, places change, or go downhill. Your letters influence us to re-evaluate a listing.

RECOMMENDATIONS: If you have a favorite hideaway that you would like to recommend, please write to us. Give us a feel for the place, if possible send us a brochure and photographs (which we regret we cannot return). Convince us that on our next research trip, your discovery deserves a visit. All accommodations included in our guides are ones we have seen and enjoyed. Many of our finest selections are those that readers have discovered—wonderful places we would never have found on our own.

Please send information to:

KAREN BROWN'S GUIDES
Post Office Box 70
San Mateo, California 94401, U.S.A.
Telephone (415) 342-9117   Fax (415) 342-9153

Be a Karen Brown's Preferred Reader

If you would like to be the first to know when new editions of Karen Brown's Guides go to press, and also to be included in any special promotions, simply send us your name and address. We encourage you to buy new editions and throw away the old ones. You'll be glad you did. Don't miss a wealth of wonderful new discoveries—or run the risk of staying in places that no longer meet our standards. We cover the miles searching for special places so that you don't have to spend your valuable vacation time doing so.

Name_____

Street_____

Town_____ State_____ Zip_____

Telephone:_____Fax:_____

Please send information to:

KAREN BROWN'S GUIDES
Post Office Box 70
San Mateo, California 94401, U.S.A.
telephone (415) 342-9117   fax (415) 342-9153

Karen Brown's Country Inn Guides
The Most Reliable & Informative Series on Country Inns

Detailed itineraries guide you through the countryside. Every recommendation, from the most deluxe hotel to a simple B&B, is personally inspected, approved and chosen for its romantic ambiance and warmth of welcome. Our charming accommodations reflect every price range, from budget hideaways to the most luxurious palaces.

U.S.A. Order Form

Please ask in your local bookstore for KAREN BROWN'S GUIDES. If the books you want are unavailable, you may order directly from the publisher.

California Country Inns & Itineraries $14.95

English Country Bed & Breakfasts $15.95

English, Welsh & Scottish Country Hotels & Itineraries $14.95

French Country Bed & Breakfasts $15.95

French Country Inns & Itineraries $14.95

German Country Inns & Itineraries $14.95

Irish Country Inns & Itineraries $16.95

Italian Country Bed & Breakfasts $14.95

Italian Country Inns & Itineraries $16.95

Portuguese Country Inns & Pousadas (1990 edition) $6.00

Spanish Country Inns & Paradors $14.95

Swiss Country Inns & Itineraries $16.95

Name _____ Street _____

Town _____ State _____ Zip _____ tel. _____

Credit (MasterCard or Visa) _____ Exp: _____

Add $4.00 for the first book and .50 cents for each additional book for postage & packing. California residents add 8.25% sales tax. Order form only for shipments within the U.S.A. Indicate number of copies of each title; send form with check or credit card information to:

KAREN BROWN'S GUIDES
Post Office Box 70, San Mateo, California, 94401, U.S.A.
tel: (415) 342-9117   fax: (415) 342-9153

KAREN BROWN wrote her first travel guide in 1979. Her personalized travel series has grown to eleven titles and Karen and her small staff work diligently to keep all the guides updated. Karen, her husband, Rick, and their children Alexandra and Richard, live on the coast south of San Francisco at their own country inn, Seal Cove Inn, in Moss Beach.

CLARE BROWN, CTC, has many years of experience in the field of travel and has earned the designation of Certified Travel Consultant. Since 1969 she has specialized in planning itineraries to Europe using charming small hotels in the countryside for her clients. The focus of her job remains unchanged, but now her expertise is available to a larger audience—the readers of her daughter's country inn guides. Clare lives in the San Francisco Bay area with her husband, Bill.

BARBARA TAPP, the talented artist responsible for all the delightful illustrations in this guide, was raised in Australia where she studied interior design. Barbara works freelance as a pen and ink illustrator for real estate companies. She specializes in exteriors, interiors and gardens. Barbara lives in the San Francisco East Bay with her husband, Richard, and children Jonathan, Alexander and Georgia.

JANN POLLARD, the artist responsible for the cover painting, has studied art since childhood, and is well-known for her outstanding impressionistic-style water colors which she has exhibited in numerous juried shows, winning many awards. Jann travels frequently to Europe (using Karen Brown's guides) where she loves to paint. Jann lives in the Burlingame with her husband, Gene, and their two daughters.

SEAL COVE INN—LOCATED IN THE SAN FRANCISCO AREA

Karen Brown Herbert (best known as author of the Karen Brown's Guides) and her husband, Rick, have put seventeen years of experience into reality and opened their own superb hideaway, Seal Cove Inn. Spectacularly set amongst wild flowers and bordered by towering cypress trees, Seal Cove Inn looks out to the ocean over acres of county park: an oasis where you can enjoy secluded beaches, explore tide-pools, watch frolicking seals, and follow the tree-lined path that traces the windswept ocean bluffs. Country antiques, original-watercolors, flower-laden cradles, rich fabrics, and the gentle ticking of grandfather clocks create the perfect ambiance for a foggy day in front of a crackling log fire. Each bedroom is its own haven with a cozy sitting area before a wood-burning fireplace and doors opening onto a private balcony or patio with views to the distant ocean. Moss Beach is a 35-minute drive south of San Francisco, 6 miles north of the picturesque town of Half Moon Bay, and a few minutes from Princeton harbor with its colorful fishing boats and restaurants. Seal Cove Inn makes a perfect base for whale-watching, salmon-fishing excursions, day trips to San Francisco, exploring the coast, or best of all, just a romantic interlude by the sea, time to relax and be pampered. Karen and Rick look forward to the pleasure of welcoming you to their hideaway by the sea.

Seal Cove Inn, 221 Cypress Avenue, Moss Beach, California, 94038, U.S.A.
telephone: (415) 728-7325   fax: (415) 728-4116